IMI *information service*
Sandyford, Dubl' 16

Managing Performance in Turbulent Times

Managing Performance in Turbulent Times

ANALYTICS AND INSIGHT

Ed Barrows
Andy Neely

WILEY

John Wiley & Sons, Inc.

Published by John Wiley & Sons, Inc., Hoboken, New Jersey.
Published simultaneously in Canada.

For general information on our other products and services or for technical support, please contact our Customer Care Department within the United States at
(800) 762-2974, outside the United States at (317) 572-3993 or fax (317) 572-4002.

Wiley also publishes its books in a variety of electronic formats. Some content that
appears in print may not be available in electronic books. For more information
about Wiley products, visit our web site at www.wiley.com.

Library of Congress Cataloging-in-Publication Data:

Barrows, Ed.
  Managing performance in turbulent times : analytics and insight /
Ed Barrows, Andy Neely.
    p. cm.
  Includes index.
  ISBN 978-1-118-05985-2 (hardback); ISBN 978-1-118-16159-3 (ebk);
  ISBN 978-1-118-16161-6 (ebk); ISBN 978-1-118-16168-5 (ebk)
    1. Organizational effectiveness.   2. Performance—Management.
  I. Neely, A. D. (Andy D.)   II. Title.
  HD58.9.B37 2012
  658.3'14—dc23
                                                    2011029139

Printed in the United States of America
10 9 8 7 6 5 4 3 2 1

To Shelley, Henry, Hannah, Hugh, and Howard
—E.B.

To Liese, Lizzie, Ben, Tom, and Emma
—A.N.

Contents

Foreword

The story of performance management for most organizations has not been a happy or successful one in the past. Organizations and their managers typically get excited about some specific aspect of the topic. Because of advances in information technology and the blandishments of IT vendors, the most common topic of enthusiasm is performance information—most frequently some form of scorecard. The vision is that better performance information will—more or less by itself—usher in a new level of performance management.

This vision is seldom achieved, of course. Performance information by itself cannot lead to better performance; it must be accompanied by effective decisions and actions, alignment with strategy and organization, and even other types of information. Better structuring of performance data, more colorful scorecard displays, or new analytics don't lead to higher revenues or profits. Better information alone is (at best) the engine of the performance management car; to get the car to transport us, however, we also need a body, transmission, wheels, and other important components.

What you have in your hands or on your screen is an entire performance management car. *Managing Performance in Turbulent Times* certainly focuses on the information side of performance management. But it also incorporates all the other necessary components to provide forward motion. Alignment to strategy, business or performance model, decision making, strategic intelligence, organizational alignment—all of that and more are here, ready to run.

Even better, this is not a particular model of car. It is really a framework for all the components you need to make a well-performing automobile—an open-source performance management approach, if you will. While it is clear in some cases that Barrows and Neely have their own preferred components—after all, they developed some themselves—their model of performance management allows for plugging in a variety of components. If, for example, you're a fan of the Balanced Scorecard or of strategy maps, they can fit right into this PM^{4}TE framework. The authors are even-handed about the strengths and weaknesses of various components. What's important is that you have each of the required components in place, not the subtle differences between them.

To take the car analogy a bit further (and I know I'm on dangerous ground here), this is a car built not for perfect weather and road conditions, but rather for turbulent, tough conditions. It can go off-road when there is no good map for the future of a business. And that, of course, is the environment in which most organizations find themselves these days. The authors are pretty convincing that unless your performance management approach is built with turbulent times in mind, you won't be successful with it in the contemporary world.

I am also a big fan of Chapter 7 of this book, "Strategic Intelligence." All too often, companies focus too much on the structured performance information that comes out of their financial systems and operational databases. This backward-looking detail doesn't tell you anything about whether you are looking at the right data and whether your business and markets are changing. The companies that succeed with performance management in turbulent times will keep one eye on the speedometer and instrument panel, and one on the road ahead.

There is a lot to like about other aspects of the book that have nothing to do with automobiles. Most performance management tomes don't even touch the subject of decision making. This is despite the fact that the primary purpose of performance management information is to inform decisions. This book has a nice chapter on the subject, and decision making is a core component of the PM^{4}TE process. And the authors correctly point out that too often decisions are based on art and gut feel rather than science and analytics.

One of the other highly desirable attributes of this book is the in-depth examples accompanying each chapter. There is little doubt that these approaches and components work in the real world, because you can read about their application in real organizations. This is hardly an abstract set of ideas.

Finally, it's all too common to read a management book and find no references to other management literature. In keeping with the open-source nature of their approach, the authors cite a wide variety of other thinking on the topic of performance management. They didn't necessarily intend it to be a review of the performance management literature, but in a way it performs that function.

If you are reading this book you are probably interested in the broad range of activities necessary to make performance management successful. You are probably not an advocate of particular and fleeting management fads, but rather you realize that many different management approaches can be useful if they are applied in the right context. You are in the market for a book that gives you the big picture, and trusts you and your organization to make your own choices about the detailed performance management tasks that you have to master. If you are this person, you have definitely come to the right place!

—Thomas H. Davenport
President's Distinguished Professor of Information
Technology and Management, Babson College
Co-Founder and Research Director, International Institute
for Analytics

Preface

This book sets out to answer a straightforward question: How should organizational performance be managed in turbulent times? When we first started looking into this issue, we were concerned with firms operating in highly turbulent environments. Some firms operate in markets where the technology moves so fast that they have to innovate constantly to survive. Other firms find they have new, low-cost competitors, which were not even players in their markets six months before. We were interested in the question of how existing ideas and technologies associated with performance measurement could be applied to these contexts. Measurement frameworks, such as the Balanced Scorecard and the performance prism, for example, are widely used to align measures to strategy. Yet experience with these frameworks shows that they can take upwards of 18 months to develop and implement. If your business exists in a market where three new generations of technology and four new competitors will emerge in that time period, you can't wait 18 months to embed your performance management framework.

Interestingly, as we explored the question of how firms that operate in highly turbulent environment manage their performance, we began to realize that the insights we developed applied more broadly. Indeed, one could argue that firms in many sectors face higher levels of turbulence than previously experienced. In the last couple of years, we have witnessed a major financial crisis, a period of massive business uncertainty when many executives complained that they had no way of getting market visibility. We have seen Sony suffer major setbacks with hackers accessing their security systems and the European travel industry descend into chaos because of volcanoes in Iceland. It is clear that in the twenty-first century, all organizations are operating in a turbulent environment. The pace of turbulence may vary for individual organizations, but turbulence exists all the same.

As we reflect on recent developments in performance measurement, we see great progress in some areas. Frameworks, such as the Balanced Scorecard and the performance prism, have helped executives clarify their strategies and align their performance measures accordingly. Technologies, including enterprise and corporate performance management solutions, have been developed to allow global consolidation and reporting, aligning operational measurement with budgeting and resource allocation, as well as external reporting. Yet all of these developments appear to take a long time to develop and embed. Experienced practitioners talk about measurement frameworks taking 18 months of more to develop and embed. Some of the larger technological solutions are part of five-year rollout programs. While these initiatives have their place, we can't wait for their full implementation in a turbulent world.

So what should we do? Drawing on our research and experience we have developed a new model approach to performance management for turbulent environments: PM^{4}TE. Drawing on the best ideas in the existing work on performance measurement—and coupling these to the reality of today's turbulent environments—we advocate the PM^{4}TE as a complement to existing performance measurement initiatives. Three elements are particularly important about the PM^{4}TE model. First, it explicitly separates three distinct cycles: the Performance Management cycle, the Execution Management cycle, and Model Enablers. These three cycles pay significant attention to the question of how we improve the practice of management itself, rather than simply focusing on improving the enabling technologies and organizing frameworks. Second, the PM^{4}TE model makes explicit the link between projects and performance. Increasingly, organizations are seeking to deliver high performance through specific projects conducted either in-house or in collaboration with outside organizations. We believe that incorporating a much stronger focus on projects is a valuable way of extending existing work on performance. Third, the PM^{4}TE model makes explicit the important of measurement as a learning cycle rather than simply a control cycle. When used properly, performance management systems should enable learning in organizations. In turbulent environments, the speed of learning is central to success. Hence our desire to propose a performance management process that explicitly seeks to enhance the learning cycle in organizations.

To explain how the PM^{4}TE model works, we have organized the book into four main parts. Each part is designed to build upon the previous one in a way that develops the reader's understanding of what turbulence is and why it is important, why traditional performance management falls short in today's rapidly changing environment, what exactly are the elements of a performance management system specifically designed for turbulent times, and how to use this system in an organization to good effect.

Part One builds the case for a new approach to managing performance in turbulent times. In Chapter 1, we present information and findings that support our claim that the world is indeed becoming more turbulent. The effects of turbulence are readily observable and many organizations today are feeling them—often painfully—regardless of whether the source of turbulence is considered. We also develop a working definition of turbulence that we use throughout the book and describe the effects turbulence has on organizations today. Chapter 2 is a performance management primer that discusses the characteristics of existing approaches to performance management. We share our viewpoints regarding shortcomings in commonly used approaches today and offer an explanation for why they don't work in turbulent environments. We then lay the foundation for a performance management approach that *does* work in turbulent settings by identifying key principles for effectiveness born from our earlier description of turbulence in Chapter 1. We also introduce the key elements of our performance management approach. By the end of Part One, we believe we will have effectively built the case for the system we are proposing.

Part Two is an in-depth discussion of the four key elements of a performance management system for turbulent environments. Chapter 3 highlights the process for modeling an organization's strategy and its performance drivers. Without a shared model, which depicts what an organization's objectives are and what drives its accomplishment, an organization will be hard pressed to sustain superior performance. Chapter 4 discusses how to organize and align key projects in an organization as a means to drive performance improvement. Without alignment of critical projects to the strategy, massive amounts of time and energy will be expended with little result. In Chapter 5, we draw upon our experience and show how to identify the right set of performance measures in an organization. Evidence shows that more and more measurement data is collected today, yet few organizations really manage to extract meaningful insights from the data. Chapter 6 investigates management problem solving and decision making. Here, we describe what is, perhaps, the key element of the model, vital to gaining insights regarding performance: a decision process driven by leading-edge analytics practices.

Part Three presents what we call Model Enablers. Enablers are not specific steps in the performance management process but rather key foundational components that must be present to ensure success. In Chapter 7, we discuss strategic intelligence—how to capture it, make sense of it, and use it to better maneuver in turbulent environments. Understanding where an organization is situated, specifically in its external environment, is a requisite to managing through it effectively. Chapter 8 highlights a new approach to organizational communication—what we refer to as *continuous conversation*. In a turbulent environment, information has to flow freely, in an almost constant stream throughout the organization, and this chapter describes how leaders facilitate this practice. Chapter 9 describes how organizations can cope with turbulence and improve performance by improving the speed at which learning occurs in the organization. We call this *accelerated learning*. Chapter 10 explains how to create *organizational alignment* using tools and techniques that align the major business and support units with the critical objectives, vital projects, and key measures described in Part One. Chapter 11 elaborates on what can be the most important enabler: *engaged leadership*. In most organizations, very little change happens without leadership of a major initiative such as this one.

In Part Four, we conclude with Chapter 12, "Making It Work." This part of the book is dedicated specifically to constructing the model in three separated stages within an organization. At the book's end, we refer readers to our companion web site, www.pm4te.com, which provides many of the tools we present in the book—along with thoughts regarding how to use them effectively—for free. We believe any organization can benefit from the principles and practices discussed here if managers take the time to learn how they work and organize their most important activities around them.

As with any writing of this kind, it is impossible to say where every idea expressed in this book comes from and to thank every person who has shaped our thinking and ideas over the years. Clearly our friends and colleagues at the U.K.'s Advanced Institute of Management Research as well as at Babson College, Cambridge University, and Cranfield School of Management, have been influential. So have the thousands of managers and executives—from both the public and private sectors—that we have worked with over the years. For both of us, organizations are our laboratories. Working with talented managers and executives, trying out new ideas and approaches in an attempt to solve real problems is how we learn and as you'll see when reading this book—increasing the rate at which learning takes place is a central theme to all of our endeavors. We hope you enjoy the book and would love to hear your thoughts and feedback—one of the key enablers in the PM^{4}TE *is* continuous conversation. We believe continuous conversations are central to the rate at which organizations learn and we hope we can engage with you in continuous conversations in the future to refine and enhance the PM^{4}TE model.

Ed Barrows, Boston
Andy Neely, Cambridge, U.K.

Acknowledgments

We would like to thank all of the people who in so many ways made this book possible.

First, we acknowledge the practical contributions of our clients, each of whom demonstrates on a daily basis the principles highlighted in this book. At Hubbell Lighting, Inc., we thank Scott Muse, Kevin Poyck, Anne Bailey, and the entire leadership team. We thank Major General Charles "Chuck" Hudson, former Commanding General of 1st Marine Logistics Group, not only for his great leadership, but also for his excellent writing. We also wish to acknowledge Tom Harrington, Dave Schlendorf, and Ryan Kennedy of the Federal Bureau of Investigation for their tireless dedication to improving the business of government as well as the safety of citizens around the globe. At Progress Software, we thank Rick Reidy and John Melo for their excellent examples of leadership and learning. Carl Christensen, Craig Schuele, and Anna Voronina of Altra Industrial Motion are also thanked for their commitment and creativity to the strategy process. As an example of leadership in action, we extend further gratitude to Art Coviello of RSA, the security division of EMC.

Second, we are grateful to our colleagues for their insight and perspectives on this process. They include Karen Dimartino of the Palladium Group for her behind-the-scenes support; Jan Koch for her excellent writing coaching, her tireless support, and for making one very important introduction; and, of course, Bob Kaplan and Dave Norton for their development of so many of the principles in this book. At Babson College, we thank Dwight Gertz for his leadership in executive education, as well as our colleagues at Cranfield and Cambridge, representing the Centre for Business Performance, the Centre for Strategy and Performance, and the Cambridge Service Alliance.

Finally, we appreciate all of the support of our friends and family. Writing a book is a time-consuming activity, and no group realizes that as much as those who sacrifice their time for the sake of the authors. Ed will be forever indebted to his family—Shelley and especially his personal "four-H club" for their tireless support during the research and writing of this book. And now Andy will come out of his study a little more frequently to spend time with Liese, Lizzie, Ben, Tom, and Emma.

Managing Performance
in Turbulent Times

PART 1

TURBULENCE AND PERFORMANCE MANAGEMENT TODAY

1

Understanding Turbulence

A time of turbulence is a dangerous time, but the greatest danger is a temptation to deny reality.

—Peter Drucker

Turbulence is growing in today's environment. As this chapter's opening quote ominously warns, the danger posed by turbulence stems not just from turbulence itself but from the temptation of managers to deny it. If the recent economic slowdown and related global financial crisis taught business leaders anything, it is that turbulence is very much here and it is not going away anytime soon. It is a condition that organizations must learn to cope with if they are to survive. This chapter explores the phenomenon of turbulence—difficult-to-predict environmental discontinuities—so as to help leaders gain a better understanding of what turbulence is as well as the debilitating effects it has on organizations today.

The World Is More Turbulent Today

Much information has been circulating today alleging that the business world is more turbulent today than ever before. Is this claim true? We believe it is and in the following sections we discuss findings—from corporate leaders, from the popular business press, and from academic sources—that reinforce this point of view.

3

Believing Is Seeing

As active researchers and advisors to organizations around the world, we can see that it is becoming a much more volatile place for organizations to operate in. Like most onlookers, we see the political instability in the Middle East reported daily, driven in part by the power of social media as a means of mass communication. We watch changes in capital flows and money as financial centers shift from the United States and Europe to the Far East. We also observe rapid growth and expansion of economies such as China's and India's. And we are not the only ones who view the world as becoming more turbulent.

When we talk to managers in the organizations we advise and in our executive education sessions, most feel that the world is getting increasingly unpredictable compared to just a few short years ago. Indeed, very few see it as less so. Capital markets contracted overnight as a result of the credit crisis, which made lending not just difficult, but impossible for some organizations. Demand for products and services, from automobiles to air travel, fell off precipitously. Companies were forced to scale back investments and quickly moved to trim workforces to face the new realities in front of them. Entire industries, such as publishing and film processing, are evaporating while new ones such as online retailing and digital audio grow explosively. Areas of business that were once stable or at least moderately reliable are now experiencing significant destabilization if not wholesale decline. Consider the following examples:

- A technology-based organization with a hundred-year history of successful process and product development in its core business finds its primary market reduced by over 50 percent in the span of five years due to the introduction of a competing technology.
- A company with a successful track record of offshore product manufacturing sees in the span of 18 months both a massive reduction and subsequent spike in demand it must contend with using a Far East–based source of supply that has a three- to four-month product shipment time.
- A regional construction firm, heavily reliant on government infrastructure projects, experiences a significant slowdown in

demand due to a reduction in spending that persists for four to five years, which forces it to shift into markets where it has never competed before.

- An international law enforcement organization undergoes a catastrophic external shock followed by a public mandate that requires altering its scope, shifting it from an entity focused largely on domestic crime fighting to one focused on both crime fighting *and* global intelligence dissemination.

- A branch of the military known for its rapid and ready ability to deploy has to reorient itself to engage in a decade of sustained ground combat in two theaters of conflict while still maintaining its rapid strike capabilities.

At first glance, these anecdotes may seem unrealistic or, at least, highly improbable given the magnitude of the challenge confronted by each organization. They may even seem fictitious, made up only to illustrate points in this book. Rest assured these are actual organizations and the challenges they face are very real examples taken from our own research and consulting. The plain fact is that organizations of all sizes, and at all levels, are being forced to change on an unprecedented scale due to turbulence. Organizations and their leaders have little choice but to respond or suffer the consequences associated with missed opportunities and challenges in performance.

Observations from Business Leaders

These are not only our observations. Senior managers from all types of organizations share these views. Business leaders are keenly aware of the pressures that confront them daily, and they, too, acknowledge that times have changed—perhaps permanently. Consider these observations from some leading executives:

> The question is: given the megatrends in the world and given the new economy, what changes do we have to make to continue to be successful? There is no playbook for what we are experiencing today.
>
> —*Ellen Kullman, CEO, DuPont, to attendees at a Wharton Leadership Conference*

On the business front, we face a growing global marketplace and far-flung organizations that span time zones and country borders. Information overload and the sheer pace of change have reached new heights.

> —*Ingar Skaug, Chairman of the Center for Creative Leadership,*
> *in a newsletter to members*

These are challenging markets, and the turbulence we've seen in recent months isn't likely to subside anytime soon.

> —*John Mack, CEO, Morgan Stanley, in a memo to employees*

The world your managers are dealing with is just more volatile than it used to be. You've got to find a way to buffer your investors and your employees from these wild swings.

> —*Jeff Immelt, CEO, General Electric, to MBA students at Stanford*
> *University's Graduate School of Business*

When you think about turbulent times, frankly, business is always in turbulent times—there are just degrees of turbulence.

> —*Hugh Grant, Chairman and CEO, Monsanto,*
> *at Towers Perrin HR Roundtable*

Hugh Grant (listed tenth among 2010's top CEOs by *Harvard Business Review*) is one leader who has been vocal on the topic. In a 2008 speech, he discussed the challenge of leading during turbulent times. When he was originally asked to discuss this topic, he planned a presentation geared to focus on explosive growth in the expanding agriculture markets in which his company participates, but between his acceptance of the invitation and the delivery of his speech came the 2008 financial meltdown. "In the last few weeks," he opined to his audience, "I think turbulence has taken on a whole different meaning. Now the challenge is, how do you lead when the economic and the financial environment that we live in is crumbling?"

This is the nature of turbulence—rapid and oftentimes unforeseen changes in environments that can dramatically alter the path and performance of organizations.

Thoughts from the Popular Press

The popular business press is quick to pick up on tastes and trends. In the main, they have spotted the underlying belief in increased levels of turbulence. The sense is that predictability has given way to the unpredictable in the business community now that the Information Age has swept across the organizational landscape.

The standard bearer for the new era of irrationality may be Alan Greenspan, former Chairman of the Federal Reserve, the central bank of the United States. Noted for coining the phrase, "irrational exuberance," a description of the stock market's stratospheric growth during the later stages of his tenure, Greenspan published the acclaimed book *The Age of Turbulence: Adventures in a New World,* in which he chronicles the massive transformation that took place during his time in office from 1987 to 2006.[1] The economy effectively globalized and became significantly more free flowing, self-governing, and rapidly changing. He sees a world of possibilities, but one full of challenges as well, by-products of turbulence associated with changing capital markets.

In 2008, acclaimed marketing professor Philip Kotler and his colleague John Caslione published *Chaotics: The Business of Managing and Marketing in the Age of Turbulence.*[2] This concise and well-reviewed text posits a variety of causes of turbulence. These authors, too, identified increasing globalization in the economy and the interlocked proliferation of technology. Turbulence, even chaos, is now the new normality. Organizations need to equip themselves and prepare for management in this new world. Kotler and Caslione provide a system they call the Chaotics Management System, intended to help organizations sense changes in the marketplace, develop scenarios from those signals, and then respond via one of their predetermined responses. They continue by explaining how to align business activities and functions with the Chaotics Management System and conclude by demonstrating how common responses to turbulence no longer work in the new globalized economy.

In 2009, London Business School professor and former McKinsey consultant Don Sull wrote a compelling book that explained and described how organizations can capitalize on volatility, *The Upside of Turbulence: Seizing Opportunity in an Uncertain World.*[3] The book is based upon his research of companies operating in turbulent industries, such as steel and technology, along with his personal observations. Interviewed by the *McKinsey Report,* Sull sees the current economic crisis "as just the latest symptom of underlying turbulence that's been on the rise for at least 20 or 30 years."[4] What is new is the severity and persistence, a fact that business leaders must learn to cope with.

The Economist Intelligence Unit published a research report in 2009 entitled "Organisational Agility: How Businesses Can Survive and Thrive in Turbulent Times."[5] The report, sponsored by EMC Corporation, is based on interviews of just under 350 executives from around the world and makes four key findings. The first, and perhaps most important, is that 90 percent of executives believe that organizational agility is critical to success in the today's business environment. *Agility*, according to business leaders, comprises rapid decision making and execution. The second finding, related to the first, is that leaders believe that their organizations are not flexible enough to respond to today's changes. Over one-quarter of the respondents felt their organizations were at a competitive disadvantage due to poor agility. The third finding reveals that more than 80 percent of the leaders polled claim their organizations have initiatives designed to improve agility, but one in three found these initiatives had failed to deliver results. Finally, technology was deemed to play a critical role in enabling organizational agility. Traits respondents identified as those of an agile organization are listed in Figure 1.1.

We could continue, but it is safe to note that among popular—and credible—publications, there is a sense that the world is moving faster and organizations need to develop systems and structures to keep pace. But popular business thinking alone is insufficient to build the case; we also need to explore the available research evidence.

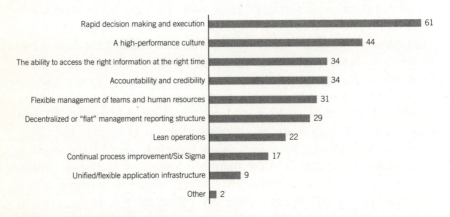

Figure 1.1   Traits of Agile Businesses
Source: Adapted from Economist Intelligence Survey 2009.

Evidence from Researchers

In 2006, two economics researchers, Diego Comin of Harvard Business School and Sunil Mulani, a senior analyst at Commonfund Capital, examined volatility at the individual company level using a sample of U.S. domestic firms. The sample, drawn from the COMPUSTAT database, examined publicly traded companies' net sales over rolling 10-year periods from 1950 until 2002. They ran several tests and found that the growth rates of sales at the firm level were becoming more volatile over time, effectively doubling over the time period examined. The same was true for profitability and employment. The trend of revenue is shown in Figure 1.2.

Two other Harvard Business School researchers, George Baker and Robert Kennedy, examined over 7,000 firms trading on the New York and American Stock Exchanges from 1963 to 1995.[6] They found the annual churn rate was high and there was a significant ongoing change in the market population. Only 6 out of 10 firms survive on average and the odds that a firm would disappear doubled from the start of the period to the end.

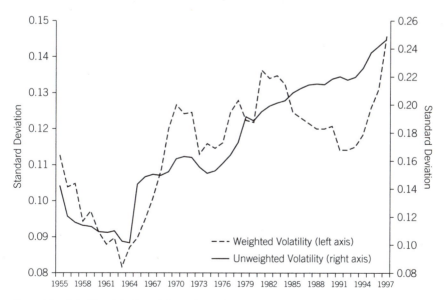

Figure 1.2   Volatility of the Growth Rate of Real Firm-Level Sales

Source: Reprinted from *Review of Economics and Statistics* 88, no. 2, Diego Comin and Sunil Mulani, "Diverging Trends in Aggregate and Firm Volatility," pp. 374–383. Copyright © 2006 by the President and Fellows of Harvard College and the Massachusetts Institute of Technology

Three researchers at Corporate Executive Board examined what they called company "stall points," where company growth falters and then falls off significantly. They looked at nearly 500 publicly traded firms from 1955 to 2000, examining 25,000 years of data.[7] They found that 87 percent of firms—almost 9 out of 10—stalled at least once during the period and those firms lost 74 percent of their market capitalization in the 10 years following the stall.

From our research, we found statistics that suggest increased rates of turbulence at the company-specific level. Of the 20 largest bankruptcies that occurred during the past 30 years in the United States, almost half occurred within the past three years, and four of those were among the largest of all time—Lehman Brothers, Washington Mutual, General Motors, and CIT Group.[8] Applications for patents in the United States grew 67 percent from 1999 to 2009 and the foreign share of U.S. patents grew from 45 percent to 51 percent during the same period, signaling that competition is intensifying not only from within the United States but from beyond as well.

The final, and most eye-opening, research came from well-known strategy researchers Andrew Henderson, Danny Miller, and Don Hambrick, who studied the speed at which CEOs become obsolete. Previous studies found that as new CEOs learned their job and applied their skills, they were effective when change in their industries took place over a longer period, before their knowledge and skill sets became stale. In their analysis of 288 high-technology CEOs, however, Henderson et al. found that CEOs could not adapt their mental models and paradigms of effectiveness to their new firms at a speed that kept up with a changing environment.[9] Their approaches and mind-sets tended to become obsolete very quickly in a highly dynamic and turbulent business landscape.

Based on our observations and various types of evidence from multiple sources, it is clear that turbulence levels are growing and the effect on organizations is significant, unavoidable, and must, in some way, be dealt with. But before we address how to cope with turbulence we need to first understand what it is.

Understanding Turbulence

Most people first encounter the word "turbulence" in relation to flying. Typically, aircraft fly free of turbulence. The air is void of any significant movement and the pilot guides the plane without much effort. Passengers enjoy a safe, comfortable takeoff, journey, and landing. Sooner or later, however, an aircraft flies into an area of turbulence, which the Federal Aviation Association (FAA) defines as "[a]ir movement that normally cannot be seen and often occurs unexpectedly. It can be created by many different conditions, including atmospheric pressure, jet streams, air around mountains, cold or warm weather fronts or thunderstorms."

Noteworthy is the fact that turbulence cannot be seen and occurs without warning. Yet the feeling of passing through turbulence—especially high levels of turbulence—is unmistakable. Much of the modern equipment used in aviation, such as conventional radar, is unable to detect turbulence, which is why it is so dangerous to passengers. Oftentimes turbulence occurs above 30,000 feet, about where the pilot turns off the fasten-seatbelt lights. According to other data from the FAA, in-flight turbulence is the leading cause of airline injuries to passengers and flight attendants.

Turbulence has other sources as well, including changes in weather, air temperature, and pressure, and sudden movements caused by changes in the jet stream. These characteristics of air turbulence have much in common with the turbulence that organizations experience and must navigate in their own environments.

Turbulence in Organizational Environments

Turbulence for organizations does sound like flying through the air. Management researchers refer to "high-velocity environments," "fast-moving industries," and "hypercompetitive settings." To be sure, each of these terms is related to our core concept of turbulence. When change is occurring quickly and from a number of different sources within an environment— from competitors and technology, for example—the resulting effect is an increased level of instability, or, in other words, *turbulence*. The following is the definition we will use throughout the book:

> *Turbulence* refers to volatility or difficult-to-predict discontinuities in an environment.

The level of turbulence in an environment is the result of three different underlying dimensions: dynamism, complexity, and munificence. *Dynamism* refers to the rate of change or the degree of change that is occurring in key elements of an underlying environment. *Complexity* refers to the number, the configuration, and interrelationship of environmental variables that the organization encounters in its operations. *Munificence* is the degree to which the environment can accommodate sustained growth.[10,11] The dimensions do not themselves cause turbulence; they are simply the lens through which turbulence can be seen. The actual factors that contribute to turbulence, while potentially many, can be reduced to five categories: technology, product, demand, regulatory, and competitive.

Technology Factors   Technology change refers to change in the rate and direction of production or process within an industry. For example, the advent of digital media represented a major technology shift for traditional media industry participants such as recorded music and motion picture production companies. The ability to create, modify, store, and transfer media digitally has affected the media business from the production of media all the way through the distribution and, ultimately, the consumption—which has its own technology advances that enable easy entertainment media storage, sharing, and management.

Product Factors   Changes in the rate and direction of new product introductions can be grouped under product factors. As mentioned earlier, the number of new patents introduced has grown steadily over the past 10 years. New products can cause significant turbulence, depending upon their success rates. While some represent modest advances, other patented products will ultimately revolutionize their industries. Take, for instance, this excerpt from the abstract of a new product patent issued in February 2011:

U.S. Patent 7,889,497

Description: Highly portable media device

Abstract: An improved portable media device and methods for operating a media device are disclosed. According to one aspect, the portable media device can also function as a solid-state drive for data storage. The form factor of the portable media device can be hand-held or smaller, such that it is highly portable. The portable media device has the capability to store media device status information in persistent memory before powering down. Thereafter, when the portable media device is again powered up, the stored media player status information can be retrieved and utilized. According to still another aspect, the portable media device can form and/or traverse a media asset playlist in an efficient manner.

Inventors: Jobs, Steve (Palo Alto, CA); Fadell, Anthony M. (Portola Valley, CA); Ive, Jonathan P. (San Francisco, CA)

Assignee: Apple, Inc. (Cupertino, CA)

Demand Factors   Many corporate leaders are painfully aware of changes in demand that have impacted their organizations over the past few years. Demand changes—both up and down—reflect the willingness or ability of market participants to pay for products or services. In the residential lighting market, demand for household fixtures sold through major retailers such as Home Depot and Lowe's was reduced by over half in the span of 24 months. In the auto industry, especially in the heavy equipment sector, data suggests that demand for new product fell by up to 80 percent at the peak of the recent economic downturn.

Regulatory Factors   The introduction of laws and regulations governing the actions of organizations in a particular industry can cause significant volatility and dramatic change in the way they operate. As the financial crisis was unfolding in 2008, Secretary of the Treasury Henry Paulson obligated the largest banks in the United States to accept what became known as *bailout money*. The purpose was to shore up bank balance sheets and boost investor confidence after the collapse of some of the biggest financial institutions in the United States. These government loans created a substantial burden for banks as well as their investors and the consumers of bank services.

Competitive Factors   Competitive factors represent change in the rate and composition of competition within an industry. The number of competitors, the intensity of their competition, and the activity level among them (mergers, alliances, and the like) contribute significantly to the level of dynamism with an industry. In the global brewing industry, for example, two recent mergers created global giants SABMiller and Anheuser-Busch/In-Bev, which produce 500 types of beer worldwide. This type of activity creates significant turbulence for firms—it forces them into potentially cost-disadvantaged positions within their industries.

Effects of Turbulence on Organizations

Like the turbulence that disrupts normal cabin activities for both the flight crew and passengers of an airliner in flight, turbulence in organizations has unfavorable effects on management teams when not recognized or managed properly. Many leadership teams will (in keeping with the airplane metaphor) simply take their seats, fasten their seatbelts, and hope the turbulence passes quickly. As we have pointed out, however, the likelihood that volatility in markets and organizations will somehow abate quickly is remote. Doing little more than hunkering down isn't a sensible response for leaders operating in organizations that need to be fast-moving today—especially those that have the willingness to capitalize on the *opportunity side* of turbulence. Those that remain in a defensive posture will feel harmful effects in both the short and long term on their organizations. The following unfavorable results are associated with the inability to manage turbulence.

Loss of Ability to Detect Market Changes

Much of today's increase in turbulence can be attributed to factors that are external to organizations. Increases in regulation, changes in capital availability, and changes in lifestyles or consumer attitudes have all occurred in the external operating environment. Thus, changes in market speed and composition are common features of heightened turbulence.

Unfortunately, heightened turbulence causes many management teams to focus inward—responding with well-worn tactics such as cutting costs and reorganizing in response to uncertain conditions. While improving operating efficiencies and enhancing internal alignment of an organization are important in any environment, during turbulence these changes tend to reinforce the belief that the best responses to turbulent times are internal ones. In reality, the best responses to turbulence are externally focused. Management teams need to reorient their attention—one of their scarcest resources—to the outside world, scanning the horizon for the sources of turbulence. Once identified, these sources can be understood, analyzed, and discussed among the executives with the express purpose of determining responses that make the best sense. As leaders consciously maintain their focus on the external environment, not only will they develop the ability to detect pending changes earlier, they can formulate proactive responses that capitalize on turbulence rather than simply enduring it.

Slower Decision Making

Rapidly changing conditions outside an organization and across multiple variables require management teams to interpret those changes more quickly and accurately and respond more decisively than in stable conditions. In turbulent environments, time is at a premium and those organizations that survive and thrive are the ones that have mastered the ability to make rapid, effective decisions in the absence of complete information and without the luxury of excess time.

Yet many management teams struggle to make effective decisions in this situation. They feel the increased pressure and anxiety associated with the uncertainty underlying changing conditions. They also realize that critical information is not available when needed and will likely not be available in time to facilitate a thoughtful decision. Consequently, managers will delay major decisions, such as resource reallocation, a major new product launch, or a technology upgrade, at a time when they should probably be accelerating their execution. Slower decision making leads to lost opportunity and increases the likelihood the organization will fall out of step with competitors—at best temporarily, and in the worst cases, permanently.

Reinforcement of Inertia

Inertia is defined as "the indisposition to motion, exertion, or change." In rapidly changing situations, where managers are unable to detect changes that are occurring in their environments—and unable to rapidly respond with plausible course corrections—they will by choice or by default maintain a steady course when their best course of action may be a change in direction.

Most people resist change. It stands to reason, then, that groups of people—such as management teams—comprised of individuals who themselves are change resistant will collectively be change resistant. Case research has shown this to be true. Throughout the twentieth century, renowned firms such as U.S. Steel and IBM rose to industrial prominence and near total domination in their markets. Yet they failed to see—or at least acknowledge—major changes occurring in their business. U.S. Steel was unable to accurately assess the impact of both foreign competition and new mini-mill technology on their business. IBM fell prey to the shift from mainframe computing to personal computing. Both firms struggled for almost two decades to return to more competitive positions. IBM has returned to prominence by focusing on services and evolving the mainframe business. U.S. Steel continues to generate losses and today is not considered among the world's top 10 steel manufacturers.

Confusion Regarding Sources of Performance Issues

As turbulence impacts the performance of an organization, the cause or source is often unclear to managers. Despite years of research and implementation of balanced performance measurement systems, traditional financial performance measures still dominate the landscape. Furthermore, managers feel that they lack the information needed to capture bona fide performance insights for their performance measurement systems.

Recently, Cranfield School of Management conducted a study with Oracle Corporation to ascertain the global performance measurement practices of various organizations. The study found, among other things, that in over half of all organizations, financial performance measures still dominate performance evaluation. Also, the data revealed a significant "insight gap"—that is, a failure to understand what leads to performance in an organization. According to the report, today's performance measurement systems "do not accurately assess the effect management's choices have on operations until well after the actions are completed." In a fast-moving environment, a clear understanding of performance issues is critical to the successful navigation of a changing environment.

What We're Seeing in Practice Today

Every day, in the course of our research, teaching, and consulting, we encounter organizations struggling to meet their performance goals in today's operating environment. As an example, one of us recently asked a group of CEOs if they thought the pace of today's business environment was increasing. The answer was a resounding "yes." Indeed, the effects of turbulence that we present are converging to make performance management within organizations more challenging than ever before. What we are seeing from practice has us both concerned and eager to help.

Organizations Are Struggling in Today's Environment

Information now flows faster than it ever has before, thanks to the Internet and other technological advancements, the latest of which—social media—is revolutionizing the way consumers communicate. Managers are continuously connected to their work through e-mail, instant messaging, texting, as well as the traditional channels of personal phone calls, face-to-face meetings, and the like. The workday is now continuous as leaders work nonstop, given that technology has blurred the lines between office and home. Moreover, as the pace of technology introduction quickens, new technologies develop, new companies emerge, and long-standing technologies and business practices become swept up into a pounding sea of competition where traditionally dominant firms no longer have the advantage. Companies such as Google, Facebook, and Amazon, which were not even participants in the business landscape just a few short years ago, are now global giants that have dramatically impacted the way we search for information, share it, and even read it.

The instruments we use to track firm progress just can't keep up with these developments. In the 1980s people predicted a measurement revolution, in which nonfinancial measures would supplement financial measures. We now predict a management revolution where turbulence will drive the need for radically new ways of monitoring and managing organizational performance.

Existing Performance Measurement Approaches Do Not Work in Turbulent Environments

We know from existing literature, as well as our own research, that many traditional performance management practices do not work well in turbulent environments. In turbulent environments the need for timely information grows significantly. Managers must detect and interpret information much more rapidly. They have to make faster decisions. They have to execute more quickly with a narrower margin for error. And they must embrace new ways of operating versus exclusively focusing on exploiting core businesses. Management teams must work together more effectively, sharing information broadly and making sense of their environments while accepting challenges and executing with focus and speed. What enables these critical activities is a performance management system designed for effective functioning in highly turbulent settings.

Doing More of the Same No Longer Works

CEOs are having a difficult time adapting their thinking and actions to the turbulent times in which we all now live. What we see many doing is focusing on things that we know are not working—exclusive emphasis on financial management, continuous reorganization, reexamination of internal organization, and reduction in the most potent investments available to the organization. Leaders cannot expect to navigate themselves and their organizations out of turbulence by doing more of those things that got them there in the first place. A new approach to organizational performance management is needed, one that has the flexibility and adaptability to deliver best in class results.

Summary

Sufficient evidence exists to conclude the business world is more turbulent and volatile today than ever before. In some settings, the regulatory environment has changed dramatically. In others, product demand has declined precipitously, new technology is sweeping entire industries away, and competition is as intense as ever before. All of this is happening in an incredibly short period of time. Like an aircraft buffeted about by air turbulence, many public and private organizations are now being tossed around by unanticipated forces at work in their environments. The effects can be significant and painful, and can persist for long periods of time. Tried-and-true performance management approaches and management responses now have limited efficacy. New tools and techniques are needed to help managers not only endure, but thrive in this setting. We introduce these in our next chapter.

Case Study: The Decline of the Handleman Company

The Handleman Company is a startling example of how turbulence can impact an organization and further, it illustrates each of the four effects described earlier.

Founded in 1934, Handleman grew to a $1.3-billion-plus category manager and distributor of compact discs, music DVDs, and video games by 2006. With operations throughout the United States, the United Kingdom, and Canada, the company serviced notable clients, such as Wal-Mart and Kmart, providing in-store merchandising and promotions to maximize the value of purchases made from within the music category.

But the emerging digital music technology, which started in the late 1990s, and with it the ability of computer users to share files over the Internet, began undoing Handleman's business within a very short time. In 2006, the company's best year from a revenue standpoint, there was virtually no mention of digital audio in the company filings. In the annual 10K report, in which the company highlighted specific risks to its operations, there is one reference to music piracy, the only indication that Handleman was aware of the impending change. In fact, just as the world was about to dramatically change, the company made the following statement regarding their key elements of success in the future:

COMPETITION

Although Handleman Company cannot make any assurances, it believes that the distribution of home entertainment products will remain highly competitive and that customer service, sales to consumers and continual progress in operational efficiencies are the keys to growth and profitability in this competitive environment.

But within two years, the company had begun to feel the dramatic effects of the digital music revolution, with sales falling to under $500 million from the high of $1.3 billion in 2006. The following is an excerpt from their 2008 Form 10K filing, where the company acknowledges the significance of the change:

RECENT DEVELOPMENTS

In recent years, music industry sales have declined at double-digit rates as the industry was impacted by digital distribution, downloading and piracy. In addition, the Company's gross margins were compressed because lower-margin promotional products became a greater proportion of annual sales. This level of continued erosion of CD music sales is expected to continue into the foreseeable future. In response to this dramatic decline, the Company implemented significant cost reduction plans to reduce expenses and streamline operations. These plans included work-force reductions; the consolidation of the operations of two U.S. automated distribution facilities into one facility; the reduction of benefits programs and realignment of medical plans; initiatives to reduce customer product returns; and various other cost cutting initiatives. However, the reduction in music sales volume and the loss of gross margin outpaced the Company's ability to reduce overhead costs; as a result, the Company experienced steep operating losses in the past two fiscal years.

Clear from the excerpt is the fact that managers—even when faced with what obviously is a tectonic shift in their industry—continued to respond with traditional tactics intended to preserve their core business franchise. Unable to navigate the changes within the industry, the company subsequently filed for bankruptcy and was dissolved on May 5, 2009.

Notes

1. A. Greenspan, *The Age of Turbulence: Adventures in a New World* (New York: Penguin, 2008).
2. P. Kotler and J. Caslione, *Chaotics: The Business of Managing and Marketing in the Age of Turbulence* (New York: AMACOM, 2009).
3. D. Sull, *The Upside of Turbulence* (New York: HarperCollins, 2009).
4. "Strategy through Turbulence: An Interview with Don Sull," *McKinsey Quarterly*, December 2009.
5. Economist Intelligence Unit, *Organisational Agility: How Business Can Survive and Thrive in Turbulent Times* (London, 2009).
6. Diego Comin and Sunil Mulani, "Diverging Trends in Aggregate and Firm Volatility," *Review of Economics and Statistics*, May 2006, 88, no. 2: 374–383.
7. M. S. Olson, D. van Bever, and S. Verry, "When Growth Stalls," *Harvard Business Review* 86, no. 3 (2008): 50–61.
8. New Generation Research, Inc., "20 Largest Public Company Bankruptcy Filings 1980–Present," 2009.
9. A. Henderson, D. Hambrick, and D. Miller, "How Quickly Do CEOs Become Obsolete? Industry Dynamism, CEO Tenure and Company Performance," *Strategic Management Journal* 27, no. 5 (2006): 447.
10. F. E. Emery and E. L. Trist, "The Causal Texture of Organizational Environments," *Human Relations* 18, no. 1 (1965): 21–31.
11. G. Dess and D. Beard, "Dimensions of Organizational Task Environments," *Administrative Science Quarterly* 29, no. 1 (1984): 52–73.

2

Performance Management Today

There is nothing more frightful than ignorance in action.

—Goethe

Organizations have been managing performance since their inception. Performance management practices have, in large part, been the product of specific tools designed to monitor organizational performance. Until recently, the budget has been the dominant tool, and for many organizations, it still is. Newer performance management developments, such as the Balanced Scorecard and operational dashboards, have contributed to significant advancements in the field. Yet work remains to be done, especially in turbulent environments. This chapter discusses the basic performance management process, highlights the challenges of using existing performance management approaches in turbulent settings, and explains a set of principles that we believe underpin a system designed to function in a high-velocity environment.

Performance Management—Still an Emerging Discipline

Many of the best-known and most widely used performance management tools and approaches were developed within the past two decades. Consistent with our belief that performance management is an evolving field, we provide in this chapter background on performance management, definitions for it, and challenges with it, as well as shape our own contribution to its practice. We also ask that readers evaluate—at a summary level—the effectiveness of their own performance management practices.

A Primer on Performance Management

As discussed in the outset of the chapter, performance management is an evolving discipline. As would be expected with any emerging field, research on performance management is rapidly evolving, too. Our research shows that a new article on performance management is published on average every five hours—and this has been the case since 1994. Countless conferences, training sessions, and industry events are held each year to help organizations at all levels improve their performance management practices. The performance management revolution, which started in 1991 with the seminal *Harvard Business Review* article "The Performance Management Manifesto," has spawned consulting services and software firms in all sectors focused exclusively on improving business results through better performance management.[1] Today, the industry of performance management is well into billions of dollars.

To help put this book in context, this section provides a brief primer on the performance management within an organization. Although performance management can be looked at through many different lenses, we find the perspective outlined in this chapter useful both for our research and for the work we do with organizations.

Understanding and Defining Performance Management

Performance management is by its very nature a broad term. To better understand what it can mean, and to add some precision to our understanding, it is useful to define its constituent terms. The two words—*performance* and *management*—are defined as follows in the *American Heritage Dictionary:*

> *Performance (noun):* the execution of an action; something accomplished; the fulfillment of a claim, promise, or request.

Management (noun): the act or art of managing; the conducting or supervising of something; judicious use of means to accomplish an end.

By combining these terms, we can conclude that performance management is a process or practice concerned with the management or supervision of the execution of actions.

The actions we're concerned with are those taken by managers within the confines of the modern-day organization. Inside an organization, performance management has a more specific meaning. It is about determining what an organization's objectives are and ensuring that the actions the organization takes achieve those objectives. Setting objectives and ensuring that they are achieved requires managers who effectively set goals, synchronize actions, measure progress, align individual employees with the organization's strategy, and reward performance. This is why most organizational performance management systems are viewed from the standpoint of where they occur in an organization.

Individual Performance Management At the most granular level, performance management is concerned with ensuring that individual employees in an organization work on the priorities aligned with the overall organizational objectives and achieve the results consistent with those objectives. Once hired into an organization, employees are first made to understand their specific job responsibilities and the corresponding goals for their positions. They should also learn how their performance will be evaluated by their supervisor. Depending upon their job-specific responsibilities, employees are typically provided with training, mentoring, or coaching as well as the specific tools to conduct their daily work.

Performance management—at this individual level—is effectively the process of determining what individual work requirements are, ensuring the right training and coaching are given, and evaluating the degree to which specified goals are being achieved consistent with job responsibilities. In instances where individual performance is not meeting expectations, supervisors take action to improve performance. Job descriptions, personal development plans, performance appraisals, and incentive schemes are the typical tools used to manage performance at the individual level.

Operational Performance Management   While individuals in an organization may work alone, more often they are organized into work groups. These can vary from loosely structured teams to highly formalized departments and functions. In a team capacity, groups execute the key processes across an organization. While organizations can have many different processes at all different levels, APQC, the best practices consultancy, developed a Process Classification Framework[SM] that identified 12 major processes in organizations—5 operating processes and 7 support processes.[2] These cross-functional groups managed major processes by engaging in process-based performance management. Performance management at this process level is called *operational performance management.*

Performance management at the operational level consists of determining process performance requirements, setting process objectives, allocating resources to groups to manage processes, and monitoring process performance to determine the extent to which their specific goals are being achieved consistent with the intended objectives of the organization. In cases where process performance is not meeting expectations, work teams labor to understand the source of performance deficiencies and eliminate ongoing occurrences while putting procedures in place to maintain required performance levels. Tools such as budgets, forecasts, dashboards, and process improvement techniques like Six Sigma and business process reengineering are commonly used to manage performance at the operational level.

Strategic Performance Management   Individuals take action and work groups operate processes in organizations to compete effectively with other organizations that provide products or services similar to their own. Competing effectively requires an organization's top management team to set specific objectives that, if achieved, guide the organization to a location in its environment where it can achieve its mission and maintain its profit or funding level. Performance management at this level is known as *strategic performance management.*

Strategic performance management is the process of determining an organization's overall objectives, aligning work group processes and individual actions on the overall organizational objectives, measuring performance toward the achievement of those objectives, and making decisions regarding the achievement of overall objectives. Strategic performance management is largely the domain of the top management team. These managers not only take collective action to ensure the organization overall is working to achieve its highest objectives; they are chartered with determining precisely what the right objectives are. While all tools and information housed in the previous two levels—individual and operational—are at the disposal of top management, these leaders tend to focus their attention on the strategic plans and tools like the Balanced Scorecard and the annual budget to determine whether strategic performance is on track.

Our Concept of Performance Management

Given the broad and far-reaching nature of performance management, we must necessarily narrow our scope to something more manageable and pertinent for the reader. The most influential group in an organization is the top management team. As pointed out in the first chapter, leaders' ability to understand and adapt their plans and actions to turbulent environments is a source of great concern. While we provide insights into operational and individual performance, our performance management approach for turbulent environment has been specifically geared for use by senior leadership teams. We believe that if leaders can improve basic strategic performance management practices, then they can drive the changes necessary in operational and individual performance required to align their entire organization.

Shortcomings of Today's Performance Management Systems

To be sure, performance management in a turbulent environment is a complex and challenging task. It has been a complex and challenging problem for almost 20 years at this writing. To be fair, many noteworthy advancements have been made, some of which we have incorporated into this book. But in the main, we believe methodologies today do not adequately address the challenges associated with managing performance in turbulent settings. Our review of existing performance management practices and strategic performance management systems in particular shows that they demonstrate several common errors.

They Assume a Static State

Each of the models we analyzed relies on a sequential construction approach where one stage "logically" builds on the previous one. From a systems perspective, this is a rational approach, and one that would normally be effective in constructing a strategic performance management system. However, these sequential stages assume that the underlying external environment is not appreciably changing during the development period. The problem is that there are very few industries today—if any—that remain unchanged over a period of years. Most industries undergo significant, if not dramatic, changes in a matter of months. Again, simply looking back over the events of the recent recession show us just how turbulent conditions can become even in industries that have not been prone to wide fluctuations previously. The assumption of a static state is simply unrealistic.

They Don't Acknowledge Time

Related to the assumption of a static state is the acknowledgment of, or rather failure to acknowledge, time as a key dimension of the model. Some of the performance management approaches we examined can require upward of three years to fully implement. Though some results certainly might be seen in less time than that, a full-scale implementation can take almost three years until all aspects of the system are mature. In an environment where the pace of technological change is increasing, product life cycles are being compressed, and capital is moving in and out of the global market in what can be a matter of hours, organizations simply do not have that kind of time to produce results. If this seems unrealistic, ask the CEO of a large company what the average tenure is in a top job today. According to Booz & Company, CEO tenure has dropped from 8.1 to 6.3 years over the last decade.[3]

They Fail to Account for Turbulence in the Model

Turbulence can vary in intensity and persistence, but the reality is that it emanates from a variety of areas and can persist for long periods of time. Turbulence does not lend itself to a gradual evolution of business practices or processes that can be easily identified, internalized, and then addressed within the context of a business system.

Executives today cannot always identify the sources of turbulence since the real thing is difficult to predict, hard to fully comprehend, and even more challenging to internalize and respond to in a manner that successfully confronts the challenge. Again, think about the effects of turbulence on airplane passengers. Even the most basic task, such as pouring a soft drink from a can to a cup, requires an incredible amount of focus when the aircraft is really bouncing. Now imagine similar effects on an organization. Existing strategy execution approaches do not meaningfully address the need to sense and respond to environmental turbulence. They cannot be sped up. They cannot be effectively skipped over. They are insufficient for the task. There are occasions where strategy is reviewed and discussed, but these are more prescriptive than adaptive. Changing the existing strategy when turbulence arises is not addressed with any clarity.

They Address Complexity by Adding More Complexity

Perhaps the greatest shortcoming of today's performance management models is their complexity. Strategy execution and performance management in general are complex. However, the solution does not have to be. Extant strategic performance management processes attempt to meet complexity head on with solutions that are as complex as the very problem itself. These approaches attempt to harmonize every dimension of an organization into a linked, multistage, multi-imperative model. Not only are these models complex—containing upward of 30 steps and substeps—as stated previously, they can take upward of three years to set up in an organization. As shown in Figure 2.1, the disconnect is obvious.

Leaders cannot expect to capably manage strategy with a system that takes three times longer to develop than the strategy it is intended to support. Our point of view isn't that these execution systems aren't useful—clearly they are in some contexts. Our concern is that change is now occurring at a rate considerably faster than existing processes are designed to address. And this pace will only increase in the future. We have built our approach to adopt the stronger points of each of the existing systems while delivering a faster, more flexible process for use in any organization regardless of industry speed.

The Time It Takes for:

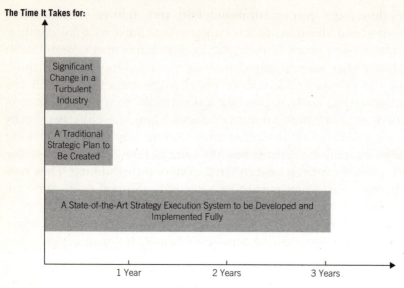

Figure 2.1   Time Comparisons

Principles of Managing Performance in Turbulent Times

With both turbulence and performance management understood, we can identify a set of logical and consistent principles that should underpin any performance management approach in turbulent settings. Organizations are typically founded on a set of values that are in effect principles. While more abstract than practices or guidelines, principles are essential to outline because they govern the thinking and, in effect, the functioning of the model. The Marine Corps, for example, rests its entire war-fighting philosophy on nine principles of war. We have constructed our performance management approach for turbulent times based upon four key principles:

1. Keep it simple.
2. Every activity is NOT created equal.
3. Faster is better.
4. Use the best of the best.

Keep It Simple

As discussed in the "Primer on Performance Management" section, organizations typically conduct performance management activities at all levels in an organization. The very nature of managing performance in a multifaceted entity is a complex task. As might be expected, performance management systems can quickly become very complex.

However, just because a problem is complex does not mean that the solution has to be. We believe that in a turbulent environment, where change happens rapidly and sometimes invisibly, a simple solution to managing performance has a higher likelihood of succeeding than a complex one. Our research of companies in the high-technology arena bears this out. Our model and concept of performance management are designed with simplicity and parsimony in mind. We strictly apply the premise that in order for practicing managers to be successful, they needed a model that they could quickly understand, communicate, construct, and refine within their entire organizations.

Every Activity Is NOT Created Equal

We are brought up to believe that as human beings, we are all created equal. Given the value of human life, this is undoubtedly true. In terms of organizational activity, however, this is definitely not the case. Italian economist Vilfredo Pareto uncovered this principle in the early 1900s when he found that 80 percent of the land in Italy was owned by 20 percent of the population. This theory has been applied in many different settings, management being one of them. Our concept of performance management is no different—in most organizations about 20 percent of the performance management activities undertaken deliver 80 percent of the value.

In the performance management models we reviewed, we found no distinction among the activities in terms of importance. In some instances, some activities were performed more frequently than others; however, we did not find mention of certain activities being elevated as more important. This is not unusual, but it is unfortunate because the simple fact is that very few activities are created equal within an organization. Which bring us to our second principle—not all activities in performance management system are created equal.

Take rolling forecasts for example. Rolling forecasts are useful tools in helping organizations maintain a constant focus on their future financial performance. Are they important to organizations that are improving their forecasting and financial management process? Absolutely. Are building effective rolling forecasts as important as making good decisions? They are not. The bottom line is that there is a set of critical performance management activities that rise above all others. Our performance management model for turbulent times is built to support that critical set.

Faster Is Better

In the Conference Board's 2010 research report on the top 10 CEO challenges, execution took both the No. 1 and No. 2 spots—for general execution and for company strategy execution, respectively.[4] This fact receives a lot of attention in the popular press and, to be fair, is a driver behind this book. Of vital importance is the ability of organizations to operate their performance management systems quickly and adaptably. How do we know this? In the same report, CEOs also ranked speed, flexibility, and adaptability to change in their top five of challenges. We believe that challenges in execution are being affected by difficulties coping with increasing turbulence levels. While organizations have performance management systems in place, they are often not geared toward functioning in high-velocity environments. Furthermore, redesigning performance management systems can take up to three years, especially when technology enablement is part of the equation. As one high-tech CEO told us, that much time to improve a system "is just too long." Organizations today are experiencing change on a scale of months, not years. Our model was designed to be constructed quickly—well within a single operating cycle or a fraction thereof. Moreover, it can be manipulated to operate at greater and greater speeds depending upon the level of executive focus. Since there is no speed limit on the road to excellence, we propose that getting there faster is the best way to travel.

Use the Best of the Best

As we examined existing performance management processes with a critical eye, we recognized that all of them contain elements that are highly effective. With that in mind, our last principle encompasses using the best of what we found.

Few people would argue with the maxim, "a picture is worth a thousand words." Published research supports the proposition that most people are visual learners—we interpret the world largely in terms of what we see. We found several approaches to performance management that draw heavily on visualization of the strategy itself as well as organizational performance. This viewpoint is backed by research, which we discuss later in the book.

We have synthesized in our approach elements of other models that reflect the best thinking available. We feel we have been cautious and judicious in our selections so as not to override our other principles. But we do believe we have worked to take the best of what we learned and combine it in a model that is simultaneously relevant, useful, and above all, flexible.

Performance Management for Turbulent Environments: The PM⁴TE Process

With the preceding principles in mind, we developed the Performance Management for Turbulent Environments (PM⁴TE) process model, depicted in Figure 2.2. While the process has broad applicability, it is specifically engineered for use in turbulent settings where simplicity, speed, and adaptability are at a premium. The process comprises three distinct components: the Performance Management cycle; the Execution Management cycle;

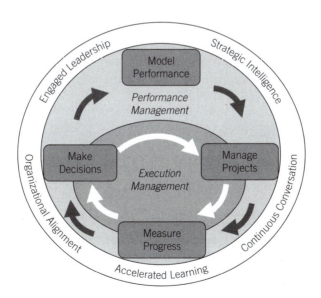

Figure 2.2   PM⁴TE Process Model

and the Model Enablers, which consist of five distinct elements. The Performance Management cycle and the Execution Management cycle work together in what we call the Core Process. We briefly describe the process and its elements next. The rest of the book explains each of them fully and in detail in separate chapters.

The Core Process

The Core Process is the centerpiece of the PM^{4}TE process. It provides four steps in two cycles that can be performed at varying times and with increasing speed in order to ensure the system is maintained in response to a changing external environment. From our observations, we find organizations are typically working on most of the steps in the model in some way. However, the steps are often fragmented, at different maturity levels, and not well integrated into an overall process.

Model Performance   While the process is dynamic, it begins with modeling organizational performance. In the organizations we have studied, the better ones operate from a well-understood model of performance.

A model of performance is typically a visual representation of what the organization is trying to accomplish. In some cases, it is a strategy map. In others, it is a model that explains the financial drivers of performance—a value driver map. We have also seen performance models that identify how the performance of individuals can contribute to organizational outcomes. Regardless of the specific performance sought, we have found it useful to address the following questions:

1. What critical performance objectives are we trying to achieve?
2. How will the objectives fit together in a way that drives overall performance?

The purpose of modeling an organization's desired performance is not just to document or clarify what the organization is trying to achieve, but also to help managers create a shared view of how critical objectives work together to produce the performance outcomes to be achieved by the organization. We discuss the various modeling techniques and the specific tools we advocate later in the book.

Manage Projects Once organizational performance is identified, managers must align key ongoing activities in the organization with that performance. Typically, these activities are referred to as *major initiatives.* Initiatives are discrete projects of specified duration intended to drive improvement in key objective areas. Based upon our observations, as well as research within organizations, we find that initiatives are often poorly managed. In the Manage Projects step, we address the questions:

1. Which projects are vital to achieving performance desires?
2. What is the best way to capture and manage these projects?

If these vital projects or initiatives drive progress, then they should be managed with more attention and more care than other ongoing activities. We are interested in those initiatives that are directly targeted at driving improvement in critical strategic areas, such as reskilling the workforce, making dramatic improvements in business process performance, or having order-of-magnitude impact on delivery of the customer value proposition. Chapter 4 provides guidance on how to capture, evaluate, organize, and drive initiatives for maximum impact.

Measure Progress Within the PM^{4}TE Core Process, measuring performance entails two types of measurement: (1) measurement of initiative or vital project progress and (2) measurement of performance objective achievement. As discussed previously, vital projects and initiatives are the drivers of performance. However, progress toward completion of projects is not sufficient in terms of ensuring that performance is achieved. As projects are completed, their impact must be gauged in terms of desired performance with respect to the critical objectives developed during the model performance stage. In essence, each of the individual objectives contained in the performance model must be measured to determine whether the projects are having the desired effect. With that in mind, we pose two questions regarding measuring performance:

1. Are we completing vital projects on time and on budget as planned?
2. Are we making progress toward our critical performance objectives?

The degree to which the vital projects are having the intended effect on the performance outcomes assists in determining which part of the model the leadership team should focus on in the future.

Make Decisions   In turbulent environments, leaders feel they have difficulty making effective decisions. These are not routine, everyday operational decisions, but rather major decisions, the kind that impact the performance of the organization developed during the model performance step.

Since performance is measured at both the Manage Projects and Model Performance phases, course corrections or full-scale changes to the model may be needed. Both of these fall into the area of the Make Decisions step. The primary decisions, for PM^{4}TE model purposes, pertain to project management and the performance model overall and are captured in the following questions:

- Should we make adjustments to our vital projects?
- Are we achieving our objectives in our model and if not, why not?
- Should we be resetting our performance objectives?

These decisions, when thoughtfully carried out by informed executives, lend themselves to a dynamic, adaptable model of performance.

The Performance Management Cycle   The Core Process is divided into two cycles: the Performance Management cycle and the Execution Management cycle. The Performance Management cycle is typically executed when the organization formulates or updates its strategy. Depending upon industry velocity, this means the Performance Management cycle may fall anywhere between six months to two years. The key point here is that the model of performance should be flexible and adaptable contingent on environmental conditions and coupled with business performance. There is no prescribed time for executives to pass through the Performance Management cycle; an important feature of the model is that it can be adapted to meet the needs of leaders.

The Execution Management Cycle   The Execution Management cycle is the faster operating portion of the model and the ultimate driver of performance. The Execution Management cycle is where performance in the organization is accelerated by the completion of vital projects needed to meet the overall performance goals of the organization. An organization working to better cope with turbulence must be able to move through the Execution Management cycle with ever-increasing speed. The key to making the PM^{4}TE process deliver results is operating each loop at a pace consistent with the rate of change in the external environment. When the rate of change increases, so too should the speed at which the organization operates the appropriate cycle in the Core Process.

Model Enablers

Underlying the Core Process are Model Enablers that make up the enabling foundation. It is important to understand that these are not steps or phases and, as such, are not sequenced in the model. They are necessary elements that must be present for the Core Process to function. If they are not present, executives run the risk of operating the Core Process in the absence of current environmental information or with a misaligned organization, both of which will likely lead to highly unfavorable outcomes. Each of the five enablers is introduced next.

Strategic Intelligence   As highlighted in the opening chapter, organizations operating in turbulent settings face highly dynamic and complex environments. Competitors are jockeying for better positions at a time when technology is changing the very playing field upon which they are competing. New products are being introduced as regulations are being drafted. Operating any performance management process without the benefit of an intimate understanding of what is happening in the external environment can, as the Handleman case in Chapter 1 highlighted, prove fatal.

In order to maintain a full level of preparedness, organizations must detect, interpret, synthesize, process, and share information culled from their environments. Therefore, the first and, perhaps, most critical model enabler is strategic intelligence.

Continuous Conversation   In a fast-moving, high-turbulence environment, ongoing multidirectional conversations are critical to ensuring the best information is flowing up and down and even around the organizational hierarchy. Findings from Stanford researcher Kathleen Eisenhardt indicate that in order for top teams to make fast (and good) decisions, they need to process more information, not less, more broadly throughout their organization at a faster pace than more stable industry counterparts.[5] Information flow does not have to be strictly vertical or horizontal; it also should cycle from network to network to get in the hands of the leaders who can interpret meaning and make changes or adaptations as necessary. This is why maintaining a continuous conversation, informed by strategic intelligence, is so essential to success.

Accelerated Learning   Given that organizational environments change so rapidly, organizations are only as competitive as their leaders' ability to learn and adapt. Unfortunately, as the research discussed in the first chapter shows, experienced leaders are often at a significant disadvantage in this regard.

We feel that leaders and leadership teams should be committed to improving their own performance. In constantly shifting conditions, leaders at all levels must detect changes, interpret them correctly, and then modify behaviors and actions accordingly. Accelerated learning is a critical aspect of the PM^4TE process because without it, essential changes and adaptations cannot occur. When they do not occur, the performance will be compromised.

Organizational Alignment   For the PM^4TE process to work effectively, each part of the organization must be aligned with the overall performance objectives. Work group and individual goals must be consistent with the direction set by the top management team and those objectives must be measured and improved during their execution. The process of developing alignment is discussed later in this book, as well as the concept of what alignment looks like in a fully aligned organization.

Engaged Leadership   The last enabler, Engaged Leadership, is perhaps the most critical of them all. Leaders are responsible for driving results in organization. Not only do they set the high-level direction, they are responsible for achieving the alignment discussed in the previous section as well as driving the performance management process. Our research shows that the performance management approach in organizations is much less a function of the environment than one of the individual leader's preference. This

My organization . . .	Disagree	Neither	Agree
1. Has a model of performance that expresses our critical objectives.	1	2	3
2. Manages vital projects closely.	1	2	3
3a. Measures progress toward completion of vital projects frequently.	1	2	3
3b. Measures progress often for achieving critical objectives.	1	2	3
4. Has a good decision-making process for nonroutine decisions.	1	2	3
5. Does a good job collecting strategic intelligence.	1	2	3
6. Maintains a stream of continuous conversation through the entity.	1	2	3
7. Accelerates learning in key performance areas.	1	2	3
8. Is closely aligned from top to bottom and across the organization.	1	2	3
9. Has top managers that are fully engaged in managing performance.	1	2	3
Sum and total score (*Excellent* > 23, *Good* 18–23, *Opportunity to Improve* < 17)	Total:		

Figure 2.3   Current Performance Management for Turbulence Process Short Self-Test

implies that for those top management teams willing to suspend their existing modes of thinking in favor of adopting a more adaptive performance management process, they may in fact enjoy a competitive advantage. The bottom line is that leadership engagement in the PM^{4}TE process is vital for success. Maintaining harmony between the internal focus of the organization and the outside world will always be a central task of the top management. We believe teams can accomplish this by driving the PM^{4}TE process throughout their organization.

How Effective Is Your Current Performance Management Process for Turbulence?

Before we go any further, let's stop and complete the short self-test in Figure 2.3, which assesses how well your organization manages performance. The questions were designed, not surprisingly, with the PM^{4}TE process in mind. We encourage you to assess your performance candidly in order to reap the insights we share throughout the rest of the book.

Summary

We hope participants fared well on the short PM^{4}TE survey. If not, the rest of the book will help focus readers' energy and attention where improvement is most needed. As discussed, we believe performance management as a discipline is still being shaped. The tools and techniques developed recently have helped organizations make major advancements in performance management. That said, there are still shortcomings with these methods, specifically in the context of turbulent settings. Based upon our research and consulting, we have developed a model for any organization to improve performance, especially those operating in turbulent environments, and the remainder of the book digs deeply into each phase of that model.

Notes

1. R. G. Eccles, "The Performance Measurement Manifesto," *Harvard Business Review* 69, no. 1 (1991): 131–137.
2. APQC, *Process Classification Framework*[SM] (Houston, TX: 2010).
3. K. Favaro, Per-Ola Karlsson, and Gary Neilson, "CEO Succession 2000–2009: A Decade of Convergence and Compression," *Strategy+Business*, May 25, 2010, www.strategy-business.com/article/10208?gko=9345d.
4. L. Barrington, *CEO Challenge 2010 Top 10 Challenges*, Report R-1461-10-RR (New York: Conference Board, 2010).
5. K. Eisenhardt, "Making Fast Decisions in High-Velocity Environments," *Academy of Management Review* 32, no. 3 (1989): 543–576.

THE PERFORMANCE MANAGEMENT CORE PROCESS FOR TURBULENT ENVIRONMENTS

CHAPTER 3

Model Performance

The purpose of science is not to analyze or describe but to make useful models of the world.

—Edward de Bono

The first step in the Performance Management for Turbulent Environments (PM⁴TE) process is Model Performance. A performance model enables managers to understand how their organization creates value for its customers and service recipients. Recent research and contributions from the practice indicate that visualizations of performance help leaders better understand how their organizations create value as a system. Models of performance are not new. In fact, they are used in a wide variety of settings to enhance the understanding of actions related to performance. In turbulent settings, their use is of particular value. This chapter discusses the value of visualizing performance, defines a model of performance, and illustrates various models in use today. The steps necessary to create a performance model in practice are presented along with a case study highlighting effective use of a performance model.

We begin the PM⁴TE process with a picture—a picture of performance. As most people are visual learners, this represents the ideal way to improve performance in a turbulent setting. Distilling an organization's performance objectives to a critical few and showing how they fit together using a graphic model provides an excellent way to not only analyze but communicate key performance goals. It also helps the organization think through how to best achieve them. There are a variety of models available and we review some of the main ones here. We also present the steps necessary to construct an effective performance model in practice. The rest of the PM⁴TE process is predicated on developing a sound performance model. Therefore, readers should pay particular attention to how they might work through this phase in their own organizations.

In the Model Performance step of the PM⁴TE process, check-marked at the top of Figure 3.1, top managers evaluate different ways to graphically depict organizational performance as a series of cause-and-effect relationships. To aid in this step, we provide in the body of the chapter a review of the common models used today. Once a model has been selected, leaders then identify the primary performance objectives or outcomes they wish to achieve. Often these objectives are derived from or developed in conjunction with an organization's strategic planning activities. Performance objectives are then organized into the framework of the selected model and refined so that managers can begin the process of aligning vital projects with their critical performance objectives. This leads to the next phase, Manage Projects, which is discussed in Chapter 4.

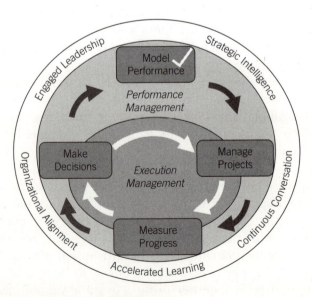

Figure 3.1   Core Process, Step 1: Model Performance

Why Model Performance during Turbulent Times?

As lateral thinking expert Edward de Bono's quote at the outset of the chapter points out, performance models are tools that help managers make sense of the world. In turbulent environments, information flows from a variety of sources quickly and is often difficult to interpret, let alone act on. Interpretation and action are made more difficult when there is no shared understanding of how the organization is supposed to create value consistent with its environment.

Modeling performance is a way to help managers transform their modes of thinking and specific assumptions into something that is simultaneously tangible, communicable, and ultimately testable. By taking the time to think through outcomes to be achieved and the mechanisms that will likely drive those outcomes, managers make explicit their thinking in a way that facilitates shared analysis and ultimately improvement. When employees in an organization understand what main objectives are to be achieved, they can align their actions without too much interdiction from management. It is true that models help leaders make sense of the world. With that in mind, the last thing leaders want is to operate on a model of the world that is inaccurate.

State of the Art

An increasing number of organizations that we work with begin their performance management activities with a model that describes or visualizes the performance they seek. In some cases, it is a simple business model. In others, it is a financial model that shows how long-term financial value is created. In still others, it is a graphic depicting how their strategy works. Regardless of the specific type of performance model chosen, we find that modeling desired performance has many important benefits that improve the performance management process, especially for those organizations operating in environments of uncertainty.

A variety of different performance models exist that can be used to explicate an organization's performance goals. These vary from simple graphical representations and driver models to complex visuals that show integrated systems processes. As is the case with any model, which by its very definition is a limited representation of reality, each one has strengths and weaknesses. More important than the selection of any specific model is that your organization finds a model that it is comfortable with. In the next few sections, we present the current thinking on performance models as well as examples of several different performance models that managers can select to commence the Model Performance step.

Visualization in General

In 2008, researchers Martin Eppler and Ken Platts, in an article published in the journal *Long Range Planning*, make the case that visualizing strategic performance during strategic planning not only helps improve communication, it also enhances management team effectiveness. "It is a powerful process that can enable strategizing as a joint managerial practice," the authors note.[1] We have found that visualized models of performance help managers share and adapt their mental models of how the world operates and, in so doing, increases both understanding of and commitment to desired performance. To help illustrate the concept of visualization, we present a series of commonly used models next.

Business Model   In 2002, Joan Magretta, a former McKinsey consultant and then editor at Harvard Business Publishing wrote an oft-cited article for *Harvard Business Review*, "Why Business Models Matter." The term *business model* emerged during the heady days of the Internet boom as a summarization of how organizations founded during that time would create value. Since few did so with good effect, Magretta provided a description of what the term came to mean either inside or outside of the dot-com bubble and, more importantly, what one actually is comprised of in practice. "A good business model answers Peter Drucker's age-old questions: who is the customer? And what does the customer value? It also answers the fundamental question every manager must ask: how do we make money in this business? What is the underlying economic logic that explains how we can deliver value to customers at an appropriate cost?"[2] More recently, Alexander Osterwalder has proposed a business model template for defining a firm's business model shown in Figure 3.2.

Driver Model   Sometimes referred to as *value trees*, value driver models are diagrams that show how specific factors in an organization link together in a cause-and-effect chain to drive desired outcomes.

Key Partners	Key Processes	Value Proposition	Customer Relationships	Customer Segments
Who are your key partners? Consider strategic alliances, co-opetitors, joint ventures, and key suppliers.	What are your key processes? Consider product development, revenue generation, order fulfillment, and after-sales support.	What is your value proposition? Why will customers buy from you?	What relationships are you building with your customer: acquisition, retention, and cross-selling or upselling?	Which customer segments are you going to deal with: mass market, niche market, segmented?
	Key Resources		**Channels**	
	What are your key resources? Consider physical, financial, intellectual, human, and information-based resources.		What are your channels to market? Direct or indirect? Stores and offices or web based?	

Cost Structure	Revenue Streams
What are the major drivers for your cost structure? What scope for economies of scale? Can fixed costs be converted to variable?	What are the revenue streams: sale of assets, usage fees, subscription fees, leasing or rental fees, licensing, brokerage, advertising?

Figure 3.2   Osterwalder's Business Model Template

Source: Alex Osterwalder & Yves Pigneur, *Business Model Generation: A Handbook for Visionaries, Game Changers, and Challengers* (Hoboken, NJ: John Wiley & Sons, 2010). Reprinted with permission of John Wiley & Sons, Inc.

Value trees are often financially oriented; however, they can be used to articulate anything, from business operations to human capital performance. As researchers Chris Ittner and David Larcker of the Wharton School point out, "The starting point [for value creation] is understanding a company's value drivers, the factors that create stakeholder value. Once known, these factors determine which measures contribute to long term success and so how to translate corporate objectives into measures that guide managers' actions."[3] The value driver model was designed expressly to assist in this process.

Consider that most managers take for granted the simple relationship of how profit is driven by both revenue growth and expense management. To grow revenue, managers can increase prices or volume or do both in various combinations. To control expenses, they can reduce selling, general, and administrative expenses; improve the cost of goods sold; or minimize what they pay in cash taxes. They

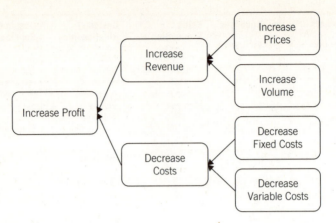

Figure 3.3   Driver Model for Increasing Profit

can also reduce the physical asset base of the organization, restructuring to offer a leaner business. Each main category is made up of a set of drivers that can be sequentially broken down into increasing levels of detail. Once the detail is sufficiently granular, managers can identify their own revenue or cost drivers and then work to start improving them. Figure 3.3 provides an example of a driver model for increasing profit.

While the driver model in Figure 3.3 is straightforward and financially oriented, driver models can be created to improve performance everywhere, from inefficiencies on the factory floor to key activities that a work team needs to accomplish in order to develop their skill level. Driver models have broad applicability and are especially useful in terms of improving business performance. They can even span an entire enterprise value system.

One of the most widely used driver-based models today is known as the Service-Profit Chain (see Figure 3.4). The Service-Profit Chain was introduced in 1994 in the best-selling *Harvard Business Review* article "Putting the Service-Profit Chain to Work," by the service management faculty at Harvard Business School. Since then the concept has been extensively adopted by service-oriented institutions around the world.[4] The model articulates the empirical relationships between internal service quality, employee satisfaction, employee retention and productivity, external service value, customer satisfaction, customer loyalty, and, ultimately, revenue growth and profitability. It highlights how organizations can drive the creation of value

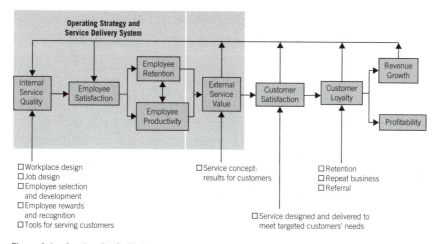

Figure 3.4   Service-Profit Chain

Source: J. Heskett, T. Jones, G. Loveman, W. Sasser, and L. Schlesinger, "Putting the Service-Profit Chain to Work," *Harvard Business Review* 72, no. 2 (1994): 164–174.

by articulating and improving the links between each of the variables in the model.

In addition to this model, there are several books and publications that provide examples of different types of value driver models. Regardless of the originality of their concept, value driver models are powerful tools in creating a shared understanding of business performance that can be broadly understood and improved.

Success Map   The success map—developed by one of this book's authors—is similar to a driver model and is typically specific to an organization's strategy.[5] Like a value driver model, it shows cause-and-effect relationships that contribute to business improvement. However, the relationships are derived from an organization's unique capabilities and processes to the outcomes the organization is seeking to achieve. As is the case with most business performance models, these outcomes are financial, but they can be mission-based as well in the case of public sector or nonprofit organizations.

The success map is designed to be more free flowing than value driver models because it is less restrictive than the strategy map and is more like a mind map than a systems model. Structural particulars aside, the success map accomplished the main goals of depicting a series of strategy subcomponents (e.g., objectives) in relation to one

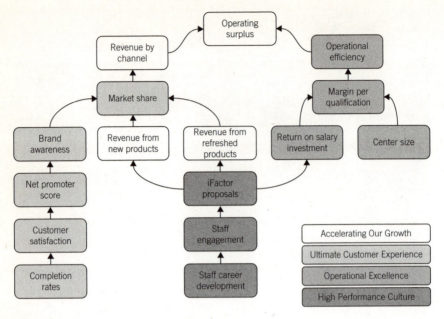

Figure 3.5   Success Map for City and Guilds

another so that they drive toward a unified end state. An example of the success map of a U.K. charity, City and Guilds, is shown in Figure 3.5.

Strategy Map   Created in 2000, the strategy map was developed by Drs. Robert Kaplan and David Norton as a means of structuring and articulating an organization's strategy.[6] The strategy map is a systems model that shows the specific objectives that an organization is trying to accomplish through four interrelated performance perspectives: the financial perspective, the customer perspective, the internal process perspective, and the learning and growth perspective. While typically built from the top down (by starting with a question), the strategy map is usually read from the bottom up as follows: Organizations hire people, build their skills, and provide them with technology inside the organization. Those employees in turn operate key business processes that deliver on the organization's value proposition and so deliver financial outcomes. As its name implies, the strategy map is built using the organization's strategy as the source of its main inputs and desired performance outcomes.

The strategy map is not as comprehensive as some value driver models. Yet one key strength is that a strategy map is considerably easier to create and understand. It is typically created by a leadership team during strategy development and reflects a strategy unique to the team that constructed it. This can be seen in the strategy map shown in Figure 3.6, an example from an industrial products company. For the strategy map to be fully effective, it must be paired with a Balanced Scorecard or measurement approach of some sort to ensure that the outcomes sought on the map are measured and managed in practice. Building measures is covered in more detail in Chapter 5.

While there are many other types of performance models in practice, the ones described here are some of the more commonly used and, in our opinion, most useful models available today. Although we have preferences in terms of the models we use in our practice, we are actually agnostic when it comes to which model business leaders select. What is important is that they select one as the first step to improving performance.

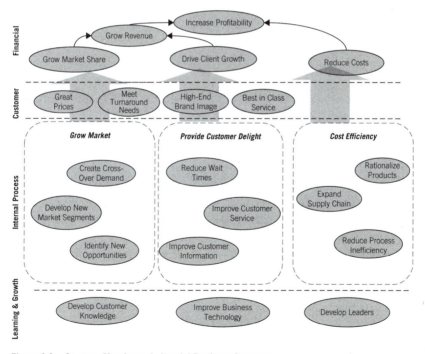

Figure 3.6   Strategy Map for an Industrial Products Company

Enterprise Value Map Developed by Deloitte Consulting LLP, the Enterprise Value Map (EVM) is one of the most broad performance models that we know of. The model shows how shareholder value is enabled by four main drivers: revenue growth, operating margin, asset efficiency, and expectations. The value drivers in the EVM are the metrics by which shareholders, analysts, and potential investors assess company performance—in specified terms and relative to that of competitors. Each of the drivers depicts the potential tactical actions and strategic changes that companies can take to improve performance and thus create more value for their organizations. The full model is a three-by-five-foot wall chart and is too big to show in its entirety in this book. An excerpt is contained in the appendix. Hard copies of the map can be ordered online at www.deloitte.com.

Benefits of Modeling Performance in the PM⁴TE Process

Although building a good model can take managers some time, modeling performance has many important benefits. These benefits significantly outweigh the costs. Here are a few of the most important benefits we've seen inside of organizations that have developed and used robust performance models.

Builds a Shared Understanding of Performance

When we ask management teams to describe their strategy or what their organization's critical performance objectives are, we often find ourselves working with unclear and conflicting answers. A set of strategy objectives can be hard to articulate, let alone link together in a fast-moving environment, given how quickly objectives can change. Further, it is hard to understand how activities performed in certain parts of a complex organization contribute to overall outcomes. Using a common framework to develop and describe performance aids managers in developing a shared understanding of how their actions and decisions, seen in aggregate, drive performance. Research shows that one key value of activities such as strategic planning is to create "prepared minds," a shared understanding of issues facing an organization. The process of developing a model of performance among top leaders helps them gain a better understanding of how their organization works as a system and how each of their unique functions contributes to it. Once that system is broadly understood, then the process of aligning key activities becomes clearer and easier.

Improves Communication

If managers have difficulty agreeing among themselves about how their organization creates value, then they will have a difficult time explaining it to employees in a consistent, coherent manner. Once a performance model has been created and internalized by top managers, they can use it to improve their communication across the organization by showing and describing what actions need to occur to drive desired results. The process of socialization also builds commitment to the main result areas. This practice helps employees better understand how they fit into the organization and provides a context for aligning their individual activities with those of the entire enterprise. As was mentioned in Chapter 2, alignment is a key enabler for the PM^{4}TE model.

Provides a Mechanism to Manage Performance

To effectively manage performance, it is essential to first define and understand what performance is to be achieved. The process of modeling performance not only helps identify objectives but, equally importantly, provides the context for the development of measures that can be used to evaluate performance toward those objectives.

Testing a performance model also lets managers evaluate whether their model is correct. As Joan Magretta points out, "Business modeling is the managerial equivalent of the scientific method—you start with a hypothesis, which you then test in action and revise when necessary."[7] This is true of all performance models—they represent a theory of how the organization functions. Rapid evaluation and revision of that theory is critical in a turbulent setting. Even if managers decide not to test the model—and to be clear we strongly recommend they do—the process of simply articulating performance will aid significantly in building a shared concept of what is to be achieved.

Steps to Modeling an Organization's Performance

Effectively modeling your organization's strategy is the first step to improving and then accelerating your performance management process. Despite the straightforward logic of the models presented thus far, creating one can be difficult. The following section presents a "how to" guide for quickly creating an actionable, comprehensive performance model.

1. Select a Model

The first step in modeling performance is having a template or framework from which to start. The models covered in the previous sections provide a good starting point for organizations, but they are by no means exhaustive. If there are other models more pertinent to the organization and its work, they can and should be used to get a better handle on performance management.

Identify Your Main Purpose   The model chosen depends upon the purpose being addressed. For start-up or growing organizations, a simple business model will be sufficient if the main purpose is to clarify how value will be created. Where a strategy is being planned or created, a success map or strategy map will be more applicable. For larger, more sophisticated enterprises looking to identify specific actions that will lead to performance improvement, success and strategy maps are useful, too, but a value map may be a helpful starting point since it can provide a comprehensive view of the enterprise. In cases where specific aspects of performance, such as financial or operational performance in particular are being improved, value trees may be particularly helpful. The main point here is to select a model that matches the organization's main purpose. The most sophisticated model will be of little value if it goes unused.

When in Doubt, Start with Strategy   The PM[4]TE process typically begins with the development of an organization's overall strategy. Every organization executes some sort of game plan, whether or not it is documented. It is important to get that game plan out of the minds of managers and into a framework that facilitates structured, holistic thinking.

2. Identify Your Key Performance Objectives

Once a performance model template has been selected, leaders in the organization must identify their performance objectives. Identifying the right performance objectives is critical to the success of not just the PM[4]TE process but the organization's mission overall because most, if not all, of the actions in the organization will be aimed at achieving key performance objectives.

Table 3.1   Sample Primary Performance Objectives

Organization	Primary Performance Objective
Electrical wholesale business	Continue to deliver sustainable profit growth
Consumer goods manufacturer	Deliver sustainable growth of 8 percent per annum by increasing consumer demand for products
Charitable agency	Support the delivery of the national and international targets to reduce income inequality and poverty
University research group	Achieve a reputation for through leadership while simultaneously creating sufficient income to ensure financial sustainability
Military branch	Develop a lighter, more flexible fighting force
Economic development agency	Make high-payoff investments in the communities we serve

Identify Your Primary Performance Objectives   Every organization has a primary objective or a small set of primary performance objectives (usually no more than two or three). In for-profit organizations, the primary performance objectives are driven by revenue or profit growth. For public sector organizations and other not-for-profits, the objectives are associated with mission achievement. Table 3.1 shows sample primary performance objectives in both public and private organizations.

Regardless of the specific content, top managers need to ensure that everyone in the organization is working to achieve the most critical performance objectives. Accomplishing this requires that they first understand what the critical objectives are, and it is top management's job to define those objectives as clearly as possible.

While at first glance, identifying the primary performance objectives in an organization may seem easy, in practice it is not. We have attended sessions where some managers think the primary objective is market share growth, while others believe it is profit generation. Some believe that both must be managed simultaneously. Others think they are weighted or sequenced differently. We have also attended sessions where everyone agrees the objective is growth, but differences of opinion emerge at the next level of detail. Some managers think growth means growth in volume—shift more product—while others think growth comes from growth in value—increase margins. Specifics aside, managers need to meet with their lieutenants to discuss what the top performance objectives might be and then come to agreement on what they are.

Identify Contributing Performance Objectives Reaching the primary performance objectives requires achieving a series of underlying, subordinate objectives. These objectives are no less important than the primary objectives; however, they will likely have to be accomplished first to reach those main performance objectives originally identified. As is the case with every organization, outcomes are the result of activities—and achievement of primary objectives is the result of subordinate objectives attainment.

If the primary objective is profit growth, then, in some combination, revenue growth and cost control will contribute to it. Furthermore, revenue growth may be generated by a set of subordinate objectives such as developing new products or penetrating existing markets. There is a logic chain that needs to be followed throughout the organization if the primary objectives are to be achieved. At this stage, it is not important to have the logic entirely correct; what is important is that leaders take the time to work with their teams to identify a range of objectives that contribute to the primary performance objectives.

When developing an organization's strategy, objectives typically originate from most, if not all, areas. Many performance objectives may already be contained in the organization's strategic plan, so the existing strategic plan is the best place to start. When focusing on improving a single process, performance objectives may be limited to the process area. Regardless of the specific content of each objective, at this point, simply getting performance objectives "on the table" is more important than getting all of them right.

At the end of this step, managers and their teams will have identified a single or small set of primary performance objectives with a host of contributing objectives. A good number is probably 20 to 30 objectives in total. In the next step, we will show how these are organized into a logic chain.

3. Build the Linkages

With the full set of objectives identified, the performance model can now be built. Typically, the top team, or a team working for the top team, accomplishes this. The purpose of this step is to organize the contributing objectives in a cause-and-effect chain that ends with achievement of the primary objectives.

Keep in mind that each manager in an organization already has a preexisting model of performance before beginning this step. The value of building the model is that these unseen mental models are revealed during discussions and accommodated or adapted during the modeling process itself. This is why it is perhaps the most important activity in the modeling performance step. While this process can be completed in a few days, we recommend spreading the building of the model over a few separate sessions to ensure participants have time to fully internalize the thinking.

Understanding the Organizational Ecosystem   Regardless of whether the model is being used to improve human capital development or implement an organization's strategy, using the model effectively begins with an understanding of the where it fits within the organizational ecosystem.

The organization ecosystem represents the full set of objective areas within an entity. Its five activity areas are depicted in Figure 3.7. As can be seen from this figure, the ecosystem itself reflects a series of cause-and-effect relationships at the enterprise level. The logic of the ecosystem—and the structure of strategic performance—can be seen by reading the diagram from bottom to top.

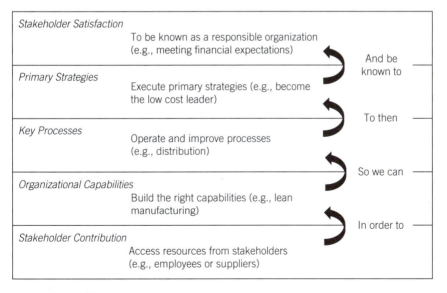

Figure 3.7   The Organizational Ecosystem

The following sentence articulates how a set of objectives—at a high level—flow from bottom to top across the ecosystem:

> Hire and develop people (stakeholder contribution), in order to build our manufacturing capabilities (organizational capabilities) and improve our distribution process (key processes) becoming the low cost leader (primary strategy) to meet financial objectives and be known to act as responsible citizens (stakeholder satisfaction).

With that in mind, models of performance can be developed across the entire system or within a single area. Ideally, a model and strategy should have critical objectives across all five areas of the ecosystem. A model designed to improve only organizational capabilities, however, might include critical objectives from only the stakeholder contribution and organizational capabilities areas. Regardless of the model being developed, all critical objectives should fit within at least one area of the ecosystem.

The brainstormed performance objectives from the previous step should be sorted within the five areas identified above. The process of simply grouping them within the ecosystem framework will help teams gain a better understanding of how their objectives fit together. Once they are grouped together, they can be joined using arrows from bottom to the top to show how contributing objectives at the bottom of the model drive toward the primary objectives at the top. The strategy map and success map discussed and illustrated earlier in this chapter can also be structured across the ecosystem to reflect not only individual objectives but also the relationships between objectives within the ecosystem.

Identify Cause-and-Effect Linkages   More than helping organize the performance objectives in a common structure, the main value of the performance model is to depict the relationship between the objectives. When we refer to the relationship between the objectives we mean each objective should be organized in the structure of the model to show visually the cause and effect the contributing objectives have on each other and then, ultimately, the primary performance objectives.

In a simple cause-and-effect relationship, an action is taken that, in turn, causes something else to happen, as shown in Figure 3.8.

Effects

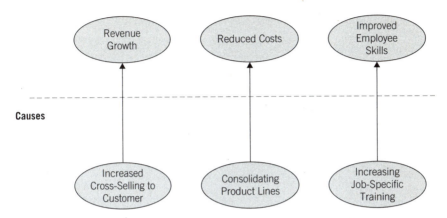

Causes

Figure 3.8   Simple Cause-and-Effect Relationships

Within the model—whether it be financial, operational, or strategic—actions are taken that drive specific outcomes. Managers can work together to organize the objectives they have developed into a chain of cause-and-effect relationships that reflect the area to be improved or the strategy to be implemented. Another simplified cause-and-effect chain, depicting the entire organizational ecosystem, is presented in Figure 3.9.

The process of organizing all of the objectives quickly becomes challenging and managers have to work at creating an overall set that represents their strategy. But there is great value in the struggle. Expressing performance objectives this way enables managers to see gaps in their thinking that, in turn, can be fixed in real time. Furthermore, it builds a shared model of how actions drive outcomes at whatever level the organization is working at. The model in Figure 3.9 would ultimately depict the organization's entire strategy when complete. A different model may only focus on the development of human resources. Regardless of the scope of the performance model, the practice of building performance models helps managers comprehensively think through how their specific actions improve business performance.

4. Check the Logic

What should be clear from the previous steps is that managers, through the performance modeling process, improve the logic

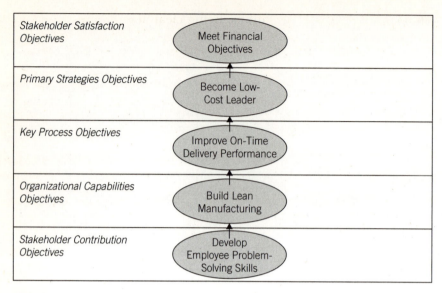

Figure 3.9   Cause-and-Effect Relationships within the Organizational Ecosystem

underlying how their organization creates value. Many managers say that they fully understand the process of how their organization creates value. We challenge that assumption. We know that there are both standard ways to express value and organizationally specific ways. The modeling process forces managers to make their thinking explicit in a way that can be challenged and ultimately create a clearer performance model for the organization to use.

Share with Employees   Once the complete performance model is built managers can share it with one another—and with employees, to challenge their assumptions. The performance model expresses the theory behind the business or, in plain English, shows how actions fit together in the organization to create value. With assumptions made explicit, they can be challenged and refined. The practice of challenging assumptions both helps managers think critically and strengthens the performance model overall.

Share with Customers and Suppliers   Some organizations go further and share their performance model with key customers or suppliers, asking them to validate the model. Clearly this can have benefits in terms of strengthening your relationships—but there are risks in terms of raising expectations. Being clear about the relative pros and cons of sharing your performance model with external stakeholders is important before you decide what to do.

Your Model Will Never Be Perfect   Remember, all models will be inaccurate, no matter how thoughtfully developed. Organizations are complex systems that cannot be represented on a single sheet of paper or computer screen. *Socializing* the model ensures that key details or elements are checked, assessed, and revised where necessary. Nevertheless, the model will always be incomplete. Still, checking the logic enables other contributors who have not directly participated in the process to begin the internalization of the objectives. This activity directly helps overcome the comprehension barriers that so often hamper execution in organizations. In cases where there are improvements to be made to the model, make them and then continue the process of sharing throughout the organization.

5. Communicate Expectations

When the model is complete, it should be shared and socialized in the organization to the extent possible. One of the main barriers in achieving results is failure to communicate performance expectations. The process of modeling performance not only identifies objectives, builds linkages, and checks logic, it also aids in the process of communication. As we pointed out in the beginning of this chapter, a picture is still worth a thousand words—maybe more.

First the Model, Then the Objectives   Leaders and managers at all levels should be given time to learn how the performance model works. Before going on a road trip, it's essential to understand how to read a map. The same is true when trying to drive organizational performance—understanding how a model works must precede taking action on specific objectives. Once employees understand how the model works, they can be exposed to the particulars of the performance to be achieved (e.g., the objectives and their linkages).

Constant Communication   Most people are exposed to hundreds if not thousands of advertising messages every day. They're so ubiquitous that most people are completely unaware of them. In organizations, employees are bombarded with a high volume of messages as well. Even though top leaders say that all this communication is important, the simple fact is that these messages often pass right by employees due to the sheer volume.

To be effective, the performance model needs to be communicated more than once or twice. We believe it must be referred to regularly, if not continuously. The assumption that employees will understand the logic of the strategy or performance objectives after only one or two exposures is simply false. It takes continuous messaging to get their attention. As we point out later in the book, continuous conversation is essential in turbulent settings.

Critical Success Factors

Through our work helping all kinds of organizations build maps and driver models, we have identified several factors critical to success that need to be considered when modeling performance. These factors must be present for the modeling process to pay off.

Begin with the End in Mind

In his best-selling book, *The Seven Habits of Highly Effective People,* Steven Covey presents seven habits or principles of personal effectiveness. His second habit is "Begin with the End in Mind."[8] While it takes the first habit—*being proactive*—to get this entire performance management process started, it is the second one that initiates building the performance model. While having the right model is important, a critical factor for success is identifying the primary performance objectives. Extra time should be given to unearthing the main objectives of the organization. They may seem easily identifiable at first, but being precise about what they are will make the balance of the development process easier.

Work in Teams

Creating a performance model is a team effort. While it may be appealing to busy senior managers to simply set time aside to develop the model themselves, the temptation to do so must be resisted. An essential aspect of the process is melding disparate managers' perspectives into a single commonly held view of organizational performance. Working in isolation may be faster, but the value of independent viewpoints is lost for the sake of speed. In a fast-moving organization, everyone needs to be operating from a common paradigm.

Think Process, Not Just Product

Dwight D. Eisenhower, former Army general and thirty-fourth president of the United States, is often quoted as saying, "Planning is everything, the plan is nothing." While we would not go so far as to say the performance model is nothing, we do agree that there is tremendous value to the process of developing one.

Most senior managers move into their roles with deep functional expertise. What is lacking is a common understanding of the overall performance objectives of their organization as well as the critical pathways to achieving them. The team-based process of building a performance model lets managers work together to develop a common view of performance they can all agree on. Further, it helps synthesize their functionally based perspectives into a single view, wherein each manager can understand how their individual actions contribute to the team overall.

Adapt Your Model

Many teams work to create the perfect model. As noted previously, performance models are, by their very nature, incomplete and therefore inaccurate representations of the world. To further the quote at the outset of the chapter, de Bono notes that "models are useful if they enable us to get use out of them." A good performance model should be used—and adapted—to changing conditions within the eternal environment.

Most strategies today have a shelf life of less than three years. In turbulent industries, the time may be even shorter—a year or less. Managers can and should expect to review and refresh their performance models when conditions change. In fact, that is one of the values of the model—it can be changed and adapted as needed. Prepare the model for use and then continue to make it useful for the organization.

Summary

In this chapter, we discussed the first step in the PM⁴TE process: Model Performance. Understanding what drives results in an organization is not simply an academic question, it is an important prerequisite to achieving critical outcomes. Managers need to take the time to understand how various performance models work and how they can be adapted to many purposes within an enterprise. Once a model is chosen, primary and contributing objectives can be selected and organized within the framework of the performance model as a series of cause-and-effect relationships within the organizational ecosystem. As important as using the model is building it. In this process, leaders make their assumptions plain and challenge them in the process of developing the model. Furthermore, it helps executives developed the skills needed to be effective in a rapidly changing, highly dynamic environment.

Case Study: Ricoh Corporation

Company Background

Tokyo-based Ricoh Company Limited was founded in 1936. The company's first product was sensitized paper used in the fledgling process of developing photographs. Today Ricoh Corporation, the American division of the global entity, has grown into a leading supplier of copiers, office automation, and electronic equipment. The company provides a full line of integrated hardware and software products aimed at helping businesses manage and share information more efficiently, including black-and-white as well as color multifunctional copiers and printers, scanners, and wide format and digital duplicators. At the end of its 2011 fiscal year, the global entity employed over 109,000 people with turnover in excess of $24 billion.[9]

Turbulent Situation

Ricoh competes in the almost $30 billion copier market with well-known heavyweights such as Canon, Konica-Minolta, and Xerox.[10] Over the past decade the industry has undergone not only technological change but significant consolidation. Digitization has replaced traditional imaging technology as print output volumes have increased. Acquisition activity has become a fixture throughout the value chain as firms jockey for improved position and profit. In 2001, Ricoh purchased Lanier Worldwide, a global office automation product distribution organization. In 2006, the global firm added the European operations of Danka—now known as Infotec—to supply toner and ink for copiers, printers, and fax machines. In 2007, Ricoh acquired a majority stake in IBM's U.S.-based printing-systems business. And in 2008, Ricoh purchased Ikon Office Solutions, a distributor of copiers and printers. As Shiro Kondo, Ricoh Company Limited's current president and CEO, noted in a recent interview with *Barron's*, "The current business environment has been challenging, to say the least."[11] Given moves to expand aggressively into services by all competitors, these challenges will only intensify.

Description of the Performance Modeling Process

To help with the management of a rapidly growing and increasingly complex U.S.-based organization, senior managers at Ricoh Corporation adopted the process of developing performance models for their business. The U.S. business—like many Japanese subsidiaries—engaged in a long-term planning effort called the Mid-Term Plan. This three-year strategic directions document was developed centrally in Japan and distributed to all operating companies throughout the organization. It specified high-level strategic objectives complete with financial targets for the businesses. The process of translation into the format of the strategy map was initially directed by senior managers within the quality function under the guidance of the chief financial officer. Eventually, the process became the responsibility of the strategic planning organization.

The development of the performance model—specifically a strategy map—commenced with strategy and performance modeling training for senior leaders and project managers through the North and Latin American businesses. After teams of managers were established and fully skilled, they deployed throughout the organization to create strategy maps of critical objectives for the corporate-level entity and each of the four operating businesses at the time—Lanier, Ricoh-U.S., Ricoh Canada, and Ricoh Latin America. In addition to the existing mid-term plan document, senior leaders from each business were interviewed to ensure their specific objectives—along with corporate-level objectives—were included in their specific business unit model. Despite reaching across the entire U.S. enterprise, it took just a few weeks to develop integrated performance models for the business. The corporate strategy map is depicted in Figure 3.10.[12]

The map identifies the company's top priorities (e.g., critical objectives) in a set of cause-and-effect relationships across its organizational ecosystem. Stakeholder expectations in the form of financial objectives are identified at the top. Customer expectations are shown in the customer area. Key internal process objectives are in four major strategy areas:

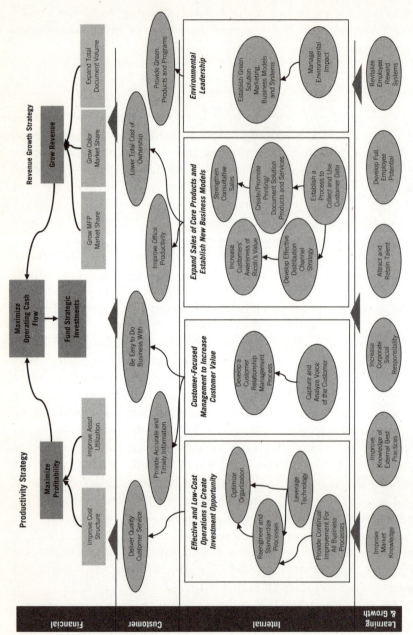

Figure 3.10   Ricoh Company Strategy Map

Source: Edward Barrows, "Ricoh Corporation: Becoming a Strategy-Focused Organization," Palladium Group Case Study, 2007.

1. Effective and low-cost operations to create investment opportunity
2. Customer-focused management to increase customer value
3. Expand sales of core products and establish new business models
4. Environmental leadership[13]

All of the objectives in the first three areas of the strategy map rest on the stakeholder contribution or Learning and Growth objectives. This succinct, one-page articulation of the critical performance objectives, formatted in a causal model, enabled managers to focus their energies and project work on those business areas most critical for success. Ricoh leaders were so committed to the achievement of the objectives contained within the map that they held a map-signing ceremony where large-scale versions of the strategy map were printed and signed by each member of the senior management team. One copy was framed and hung in the lobby of the company's headquarters in West Caldwell, New Jersey.[14]

Interpretations from Key Managers

Throughout the process managers from the top to the bottom of the organization were highly engaged. Senior leaders participated in interviews with project managers and external advisors to discuss and engage in interactive dialog about their strategies and critical performance objectives. Project leaders worked to synthesize information from all parts of the business into one integrated strategy. Employees, through the individual performance management systems, were able to align their daily activities to key objectives on the strategy map. Throughout the organization there was a sense that the strategy was well understood and supported. As then-CEO Sam Ichoika noted at the time of development, "Everyone in the company must be able to answer the question: 'What does the strategy mean in terms I can act on?'"[15]

Tangible Benefits and Outcomes

Over the three-year period from 2001 to 2004, Ricoh Corporation enjoyed an overall revenue increase of 8.7 percent. At the same time, the company's U.S. copier/multifunctional market share grew to 25 percent from 17 percent, helping the company move into the top spot for market leadership for both black and white as well as color multifunctional products in those retail channels where Ricoh actively competed. The most significant performance improvement, however, came in the area of increased profitability. From 2001 to 2004, the company's profit almost doubled, increasing by 175 percent.[16] The company won not only industry accolades but recognition in the realm of performance management when they were inducted into Palladium Group's Balanced Scorecard Hall of Fame for Strategy Execution. The process of developing a clear, comprehensive performance model helped Ricoh articulate and then achieve significant results in a highly dynamic and competitive business environment.

Notes

1. M. J. Eppler and K. W. Platts, "Visualizing Strategy: The Systematic Use of Visualization in the Strategic-Planning Process," *Long Range Planning* 42, no. 1 (2009): 42.
2. J. Magretta, "Why Business Models Matter," *Harvard Business Review* 80, no. 5 (2002): 86.
3. C. Ittner and D. Larcker, "Coming Up Short on Nonfinancial Performance Measures," *Harvard Business Review* 81, no. 8 (2003): 88.
4. J. Heskett, T. Jones, G. Loveman, W. Sasser, and L. Schlesinger, "Putting the Service-Profit Chain to Work," *Harvard Business Review* 72, no. 2 (1994): 164–174.
5. A. Neely, C. Adams, and M. Kennerley, *The Performance Prism: The Scorecard for Measuring and Managing Business Success* (London: Financial Times Prentice Hall, 2002).
6. R. Kaplan and D. Norton, *Strategy Maps: Converting Intangible Assets into Tangible Outcomes* (Boston: Harvard Business School Publishing, 2004).
7. Magretta, "Why Business Models Matter."
8. S. Covey, *The Seven Habits of Highly Effective People*, 2nd ed. (New York: Free Press, 2004).
9. Ricoh Company Limited. Web page, available at www.ricoh.com/about/company/data/.
10. N. Martin, "Ricoh: Getting Ready to Rumble." Web page, available at http://online.barrons.com/article/SB124908694002798273.html
11. Ibid.
12. Barrows, E. "Ricoh Corporation: Becoming a Strategy-Focused Organization," Palladium Group Case Study, August 2007.
13. Ibid.
14. Ibid.
15. Ibid.
16. Ibid.

CHAPTER 4

Manage Projects

In organizations, most notably in meetings and group discussions about projects, most time and attention is given to trivial issues rather than important ones.

—Parkinson's Law of Triviality

The second step in the Performance Management for Turbulent Environments process is Manage Projects. Effective project management within the PM⁴TE process requires considerable thought and activity, and going beyond managing a project plan toward the achievement of key milestones and deliverables. Project management is one of the key drivers of organizational results. Vital projects stimulate continuous improvement of core processes but also serve as the basis for transformational change. Strategy execution largely resides in key projects. This is especially true in turbulent settings where effective project management can make or break organizational performance. This chapter discusses the challenges associated with project management today, the value of aligning projects with key objectives, and the steps necessary to improve the effectiveness of project management in an organization. The chapter ends with a case study that demonstrates effective management of strategy projects.

The words "project management" often bring to mind detailed project plans, excruciating milestone reviews, and painful budget overruns. While project management is essential to organizational effectiveness, many organizations shudder at the thought of digging into the particulars of how they manage vital projects. We continue our discussion of the PM⁴TE process with one essential thought: *Projects are the drivers of change in organizations.* Fixing a process, introducing a new product, assessing an adjacent market, and the like are all activities that require project management skills. Because success is so closely linked to effective project management, we address it in a detailed way as part of the PM⁴TE process. At the executive level, project management is about keeping initiatives on track—not excessive documentation. With that in mind, we now focus on improving project management oversight and execution at the top team level.

The Manage Projects step of the PM⁴TE process is shown on the right side of Figure 4.1. In this step, within the framework of the performance model created in the first phase, managers identify vital projects that accelerate the accomplishment of objectives. To provide the framework for this phase, we review some common viewpoints on project management today, in particular, strategy project management. This review will result in steps and tools managers can use to better understand and improve key project management in their own organization. After the vital projects have

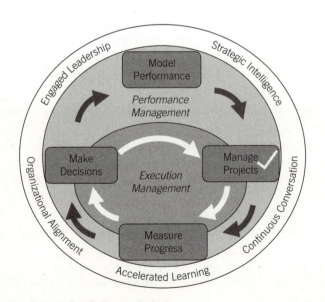

Figure 4.1   Core Process, Step 2: Manage Projects

been designed and or refined, they can then be measured in the next step, Measure Progress (covered in Chapter 5).

Why Manage Projects during Turbulent Times?

As highlighted by Parkinson's Law of Triviality, organizations spend an inordinate amount of time focusing their energies on trivial instead of important activities. One might be tempted to conclude that this is not the case in performance management—but sadly, even here, the law of triviality exists in full force. Not only is time given to nonurgent matters; worse, top management attention, the scarcest of all resources, is frequently focused on areas that have the highest likelihood of achieving the smallest results in an organization.

In turbulent environments, managers have no time to waste. Conditions are changing rapidly and with a high degree of uncertainty. To cope, managers need a smaller set of vital projects that are managed more closely and executed more quickly than during stable times. Organizational direction may have to change quickly, too, a process that becomes considerably more difficult when a high volume of diffuse projects are underway with spurious linkages to critical performance objectives. Every year, organizations spend massive amounts of time and energy on key projects. What is needed is not just better project management; organizations need better project focus as well.

State of the Art

While project success has improved over the past decade, it is far from excellent. The Standish Group produces a periodic survey that assesses technology projects in three categories: succeeded, failed, and challenged. Their data, published in *CIO Magazine*, reveals that success rates are edging to just over 32 percent. Challenged projects rates are about 44 percent and failure rates are about 24 percent.[1] Despite incremental improvement, with only 3 out of 10 projects being classified as successful, that translates into a tremendous amount of wasted time and money. This amount is estimated to run into the hundreds of billions in the United States alone. Project management may be getting better but the fact is it has a long way to go.

In one of the more comprehensive reviews, a 2004 PricewaterhouseCoopers survey of project management practices in 200 companies from 30 countries found that these companies in total ran 10,640 projects worth an estimated $4.5 billion. Of those projects, only 2.5 percent were completed on time, within scope, and with the intended business benefits. A clear 60 percent of organizations said they wanted to improve their project management maturity.[2]

Obviously this is not a stunning success rate. But project management improvement is possible. According to researchers Richard Discenza of the University of Colorado and James Forman of Microsoft, seven factors need to be present for project success:[3]

1. Focus on business value, not technical detail
2. Establish clear accountability for measured results
3. Have a consistent process for measuring unambiguous checkpoints
4. Have a consistent methodology for planning and executing projects
5. Include the customer at the beginning of the project and involve them as things change
6. Manage and motivate people so that the project's efforts will experience a zone of optimal performance throughout its life
7. Provide the project team members the tools and techniques they need to produce constantly successful projects.

Discenza and Forman continue to note that the seven factors can further be grouped into three broad categories: people, process, and communication. We will consider these categories as we present some of the best contemporary practices in vital project management.

Business Cases

It is not uncommon for organizations to launch projects without a clear business case. When we say business case, we mean more than just the rationale behind why the project is being started. Almost every project launched in an organization has some rationale—to improve the order fulfillment process, build employee business acumen, improve internal communications, or the like. But what projects often lack are particulars such as a clear purpose, the direct linkage to critical performance objectives, the explicit documentation of intended benefits, and a host of other pieces of information essential to the project's ultimate success.

Business cases are not developed because they are, in a word, difficult. For many managers, it seems easier to launch a project and worry about the benefits later than to take time up front to construct the business case. The problem is that projects consume massive amounts of time and energy, while business cases do not. We have never run across an organization that has complained about spending too much time on business cases. Recall that the PricewaterhouseCoopers survey cited earlier noted that only 2.5 percent of the projects sampled delivered the full intended benefits. Business cases are the best tools available to tip the success scale in favor of project success.

A good business case features a set of critical information. An example of a one-page business case format can be seen in Figure 4.2.

Basic Information																								
Project Name:									Date Submitted:															
Project Description:									Project Owner:															
									Project Sponsor:															
Strategic Information																								
Linked Objective(s):									Impact on Objective(s):															
Financial Information																								
NPV: Time to Payback	Year 1								Year 2							Year 3					Year 4			
Revenue Increase ($)																								
Cost Reduction ($)																								
Cost to Implement ($)																								
Summary Project Information																								
Milestones	Year 1												Year 2											
	1	2	3	4	5	6	7	8	9	10	11	12	1	2	3	4	5	6	7	8	9	10	11	12
TBD																								
TBD																								
TBD																								
TBD																								
TBD																								

Figure 4.2   Business Case Format

As shown in Figure 4.2, a business case contains a section that provides the project's basic information. It also contains strategic information about the project as well as basic financial information such as cost, revenue increase, and net present value (NPV). The business impact should be identified as well in both qualitative and quantitative terms. If there are several different options under consideration, each should be summarized and evaluated at a high level. Actual costs in terms of time and money should be described over the project period along with a high-level project plan. Risks can be discussed along with assumptions and key constraints in the project description. Depending upon the needs of the organization, other fields can be added as well; however, these are the basic fields that we use.

Business cases are not new. Many organizations, however, lack the discipline to fully use them. We find that they are essential to structuring for success in the world of fast-paced performance management.

Project Alignment Tools

Because it is commonplace for managers to launch projects without a business case or other project structuring tools, the result is a proliferation of projects throughout organizations. From the PricewaterhouseCoopers report, 42 percent of the 200 respondents ran more than 50 projects per year and 26 percent ran a whopping 100 per year or more. Only 10 percent of organizations in the sample managed fewer than five. This "peanut buttering," the spreading of finite resources across a large number of projects, is a possible explanation for why project failure rates in organizations are so high.

A way organizations improve project effectiveness, especially in the case of strategic projects, is to align projects with key strategies or, as we refer to them, performance objectives. What this involves is collecting projects and matching or mapping them to high-level objectives. In their book, *The Execution Premium*, researchers Robert Kaplan and David Norton present what they call an *initiative alignment matrix*.[4] An example is shown in Figure 4.3.

What this simple matrix enables organizations to do is see where alignment exists between major projects and critical objectives. Where there are more projects than objectives, an opportunity exists to rationalize projects. Where gaps are present, in the form of

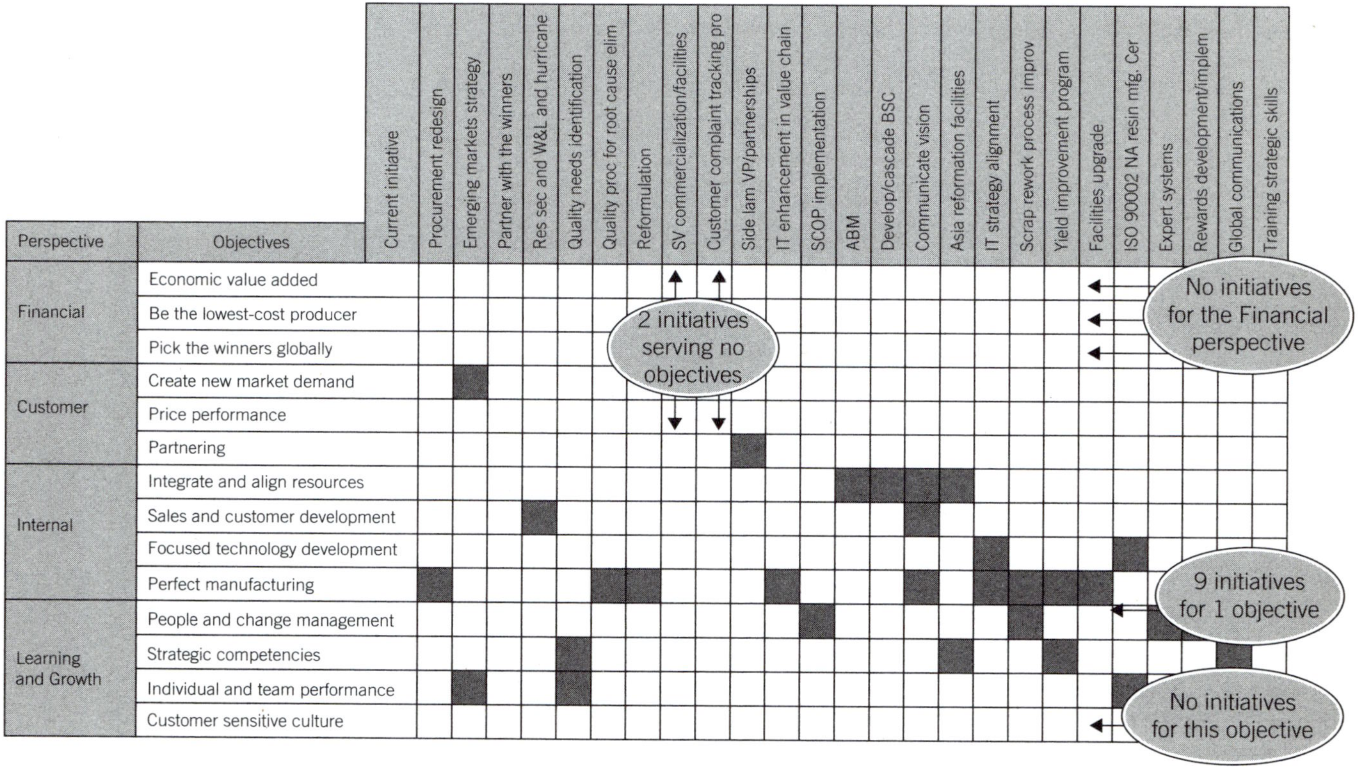

Figure 4.3 Initiative Alignment Matrix

Source: Robert S. Kaplan and David P. Norton, *The Execution Premium: Linking Strategy to Operations for Competitive Advantage* (Boston: Harvard Business School Press, 2008).

Current initiative

Initiatives (columns):
Procurement redesign; Emerging markets strategy; Partner with the winners; Res sec and W&L and hurricane; Quality needs identification; Quality proc for root cause elim; Reformulation; SV commercialization/facilities; Customer complaint tracking pro; Side lam VP/partnerships; IT enhancement in value chain; SCOP implementation; ABM; Develop/cascade BSC; Communicate vision; Asia reformation facilities; IT strategy alignment; Scrap rework process improv; Yield improvement program; Facilities upgrade; ISO 9000Z NA resin mfg, Cer; Expert systems; Rewards development/implem; Global communications; Training strategic skills

Perspective	Objectives
Financial	Economic value added
	Be the lowest-cost producer
	Pick the winners globally
Customer	Create new market demand
	Price performance
	Partnering
Internal	Integrate and align resources
	Sales and customer development
	Focused technology development
	Perfect manufacturing
	People and change management
Learning and Growth	Strategic competencies
	Individual and team performance
	Customer sensitive culture

Callouts:
- No initiatives for the Financial perspective
- 9 initiatives for 1 objective
- No initiatives for this objective
- 2 initiatives serving no objectives

objectives that do not have projects aligned with them, there may be a need to add projects. While this tool will not make the decision, what it does is force managers to consider where projects align to their key objectives.

Executive Project Teams

In a 2006 survey of almost 800 executives, consulting firm McKinsey & Company found that just over half of respondents track execution of their strategic initiatives.[5] This is unfortunate given that the primary drivers of progress in an organization are the vital projects discussed in this chapter. One of the best ways to improve project execution is to develop project teams staffed with key executives. Executives, especially those at the top, need to maintain responsibility for the critical work of the organization and that critical work is its many projects.

The vital projects in this phase of the PM^{4}TE model are often those tied to the organization's strategy. These are projects like entering a new market, accelerating development of a second-generation product, or deepening the bench behind the top team. As such, these represent the most important projects in the enterprise. Projects of this magnitude must be managed by top leaders, otherwise it sends the message to employees that they are not really important. When senior leaders are not involved, midlevel managers and rank-and-file employees quickly lose interest, which dooms the most important projects of the organization to substandard execution—if they are executed at all.

We have found that creating high-level project teams for each major project is a key driver of success. Usually the team is championed by one executive who maintains cognizance and accountability for the project. But other senior leaders can be accountable on the project as well—typically for specific action items. Senior executive monitoring and management of these vital projects are important feeders into the next two phases of the process: Measure Progress and Make Decisions.

Project Portfolios

The last practice we have found effective is organizing projects into discrete, dynamic portfolios of projects with different purposes. While this technique itself is not new, its effective use is.

In his June 2002 article, "Just-in-Time Strategy for a Turbulent World," Lowell Bryan, a director at McKinsey & Company, points out that in the past, managers could analytically determine a company's strategy and then chart a course of action to get there. But in the turbulent world of today, he asserts that this approach is untenable. There are too many variables and the world is far more complex to accommodate a static strategy.

> Strategy today has to align itself to the fluid nature of this external environment. It must be flexible enough to change constantly and to adapt to outside and internal conditions even as the aspiration to deliver favorable outcomes for shareholders remains constant.[6]

In the balance of the article, Bryan highlights what he calls a *portfolio of initiatives approach,* that is, putting projects into groups such that the organization can manage them dynamically depending upon the operational time frame as well as the level of risk.

At the simplest level, organizations can first separate projects into two categories—those that are strategic and those that are operational. They can be subdivided into categories such as high and low risk or rapid or long-term payback. Indeed, portfolios of projects can be created using a host of different criteria. What is important is not the specific factors used, but that projects are grouped using logical criteria that facilitate better management. In cases where projects do not align with the results desired by leaders, their priority should be changed and they should be managed accordingly.

Benefits of Managing Projects in the PM⁴TE Process

No one would question the importance of managing projects in any setting, especially a turbulent one. However, applying the state-of-the-art techniques discussed thus far has particularly valuable operational benefits for today's organizations. These benefits are described next.

Focuses Limited Resources: Time, Money, and Management Attention

A preponderance of most organizations' resources are consumed by what is commonly referred to as operations and maintenance (O&M) activities. Operations and maintenance comprise the work that might be called "business as usual." Paying employees, operating manufacturing processes, and selling goods or services represent activities that fall into the business-as-usual category. What little remains after O&M activities is left to be allocated among vital projects that drive toward the implementation of the strategy. Therefore, it is essential that these limited resources for vital projects are focused and managed in a way that helps organizations garner the best and highest value for its investment.

Accelerates Execution

There are a variety of viewpoints regarding what constitutes effective execution. Systems theorists note that execution is a function of having an execution process. Organizational design experts note that execution is about human capital alignment. These, as well as other views, are right to a degree. But in the final analysis, it is the completion of vital projects that results in performance improvement.

As such, tangible progress in organizations is compelled by the execution of vital projects. Projects that incrementally improve areas, such as ordering through remittance or implementing a new customer management process, are essential to keeping organizations on par with their peers. Because these projects are so important, they must be managed with the utmost care and be given the most attention by senior executives. No effective performance management process can be void of an active project management step.

Provides a Mechanism to Manage Performance

As noted at the outset of this book, results are achieved when performance is managed. Management is a hands-on, active process. If projects are the key drivers of results, especially in the area of strategy, then the project management process is a key performance management activity. Based on our observations, too many organizations leave project management to the vagaries of individual and department leadership. Projects need a consistent methodology for planning and execution. The responsibility for establishing the methodology rests with senior leaders who must ensure that a robust project management capability exists within the organization.

As we discuss in Chapter 5, measuring project performance is an essential step in the PM^{4}TE process.

Steps to Managing an Organization's Vital Projects

Effectively managing projects in an organization is the second step to improving performance management in turbulence. This phase calls for projects to be identified, organized, aligned, and managed to achieve results. The following sections present a series of steps that improve project management in organizations.

1. Capture and Profile Projects

The first step toward improved project management comes from capturing and profiling all of the ongoing vital projects in an organization. We define *vital projects* as those high-level projects designed to drive achievement of critical performance objectives. This step may seem daunting to many leaders. If project proliferation is taking place, it will be. But it is essential if managers want to get control of the activities that are consuming most of their time, money, and attention. Based on our experience, it is not uncommon for this step to reveal scores, if not hundreds, of projects underway. But organizations become inadaptable if they are not able to shift resources among projects quickly and easily, so accomplishment of the step is essential.

Ask for and Identify Vital Projects   To capture vital projects underway in an organization, leaders need to ask their direct reports to provide the details on each project. As simple as this step is, we have found that top managers are often uncomfortable doing this. They believe subordinate leaders have their projects under control and do not want to appear meddlesome. Consequently, top managers assume that projects are being capably managed when, in fact, they are not. Unless the details of each project is captured and understood, there is no way to align them with the organization's critical objectives.

Structure and Profile Vital Projects   As vital projects are identified, they should be profiled. The business case described previously is a useful tool here. If business cases have already been used to justify projects underway, that is good news. A simple review of projects ensures that in-stream projects are driving toward their intended benefits. If business cases were not used, project profiling can establish the discipline of creating business cases in the organization. Beware of managers who see project profiling as too much work. Our experience is that managers would rather execute unproven projects for months, if not years, than take the time to justify what they are doing. This perceived loss of control can contribute to the lack of focus in an organization.

2. Align and Prioritize Projects

Once the full range of projects—especially the most critical ones—in an organization is captured and profiled, they can then be aligned with the critical objectives developed in the Model Performance phase. Linking vital projects with critical objectives is an essential step in the effective management of projects.

Recall from Chapter 3 that primary and contributing objectives are developed and organized within the framework of the performance model. Once major projects in an organization are captured and profiled, they can be compared and aligned with critical performance objectives. The matrix in Figure 4.3 is a useful tool in this regard and shows where alignment exists. We have extended this matrix and included a set of factors to prioritize vital projects. Figure 4.4 shows what we call the *project execution grid* (PEG).

The PEG aligns vital projects with critical performance objectives. It also contains a set of standard factors we regularly use to help determine project priority: cost (or NPV), time to complete, project risk, and interdependencies on other projects. Each project—existing or proposed in business-case form—should be evaluated and scored using each factor for assessing prioritization. While the final alignment and prioritization of projects is a management decision, the PEG can help significantly with the process.

In the Figure 4.4 example, vital projects are listed in the vertical axis to the left. Each of these existing or proposed projects should have a business case associated with it. Across the top the critical performance objectives from the performance model are listed. The top team works to identify the intersection between the vital projects and the critical performance objectives. Then, using the prioritization factors at the end of each row, projects are sorted to ensure those that will likely have the greatest impact are executed and resourced first.

Critical Objectives/Vital Projects

Project	Be a Responsible Citizen	Grow Profits	Penetrate Customers	Expand into New Low-Cost Segments	Improve On-Time Delivery	Enhance Market Process	Accelerate New Product Development	Improve Research and Development	Expand Customer Knowledge	Share Best Practices	Cost	Time to Complete	Interdependence	Risk	Total Score
	Stakeholder Satisfaction		Primary Strategies		Key Processes		Organizational Capabilities		Stakeholder Contribution						
Shipment Automation					■						1	1	1	2	5
Open Innovation Adoption								■			3	3	2	2	(10)
Detailed Customer Study			■	■					■		2	3	1	1	(7)
Knowledge Exchange Project								■		■	2	2	1	1	6
Marketing Benchmarking						■					2	1	2	1	6
Community Day Expansion	■										3	3	3	3	(12)
Margin Management Technology Project		■									1	1	1	1	4
Six Sigma					■	■	■				2	3	3	1	(9)

Figure 4.4   Project Execution Grid

3. Build the High-Level Project Plan

If the first two steps have been followed, managers will have a prioritized set of vital projects aligned with their critical performance objectives. This alone is no mean feat. What needs to happen next to ensure project execution is for each of these projects to be evaluated to determine whether a workable, high-level project plan is associated with it.

We find in the organizations that we advise and research that an assumption often exists that projects are being effectively managed *somewhere* in the organization. Top leaders often believe the details of project management are best left to midlevel managers with the time and skill to run projects. While we would like to believe this is the case, it is not. Top managers must get involved in the details of the vital projects underway in their organization if they are to yield the intended results. This is achieved through a *plan of actions and milestones* (POA&M) paired with the business case. As defined by the United States Office of Management and Budget (OMB), a POA&M is defined as:

> a tool that identifies tasks that need to be accomplished. It details resources required to accomplish the element of the plan, any milestones in meeting the tasks, and scheduled completion dates for the milestones.[7]

We use the POA&M as a summarized project plan that accompanies the business case, which is then used to manage projects at a high level. It is important to understand that the POA&M is not a replacement for a detailed project plan; every project in an organization should still have one of these. The POA&M is a subset of that plan, and specifically used by senior executives to keep their fingers on the pulse of execution of vital projects. An example of a POA&M is provided in Figure 4.5.

Developing a detailed POA&M, along with the business case, facilitates both completion of the business case and transition to effective project execution. Top managers know that the devil is in the details when it comes to getting tasks completed in an organization. They have to be involved in this detail too. Creating and using POA&Ms facilitates both execution planning and accountability at the top team level.

POA&M Productivity Enhancement Project

Item	Actions	Milestone	Resources	Accountability	Due Date	Status
1	Organize Kickoff Meeting	Kickoff Meeting Held	1 FTE for 10 hours	DL	16-Jun	C
2	Establish Improvement Teams	Improvement Teams Chartered	3 FTEs for 4 hours	DS	1-Jul	C
3	Map Key Processes	Four Main Processes Mapped	6 FTEs for 40 hours	KP	16-Jul	C
4	Analyze Key Processes	Measures for Each Process Documented	6 FTEs for 80 hours	SM	31-Jul	C
5	Develop Improvement Actions	Top Improvement Actions Agreed on	3 FTEs for 40 hours	DR	15-Aug	C
6	Develop Training Materials	Training Materials Published	2 FTEs for 20 hours	JI	31-Aug	C
7	Train Process Owners	Process Owners Certified	1 FTE for 10 hours	BB	10-Sep	C
8	Implement Improvements	Top Improvements Implemented	6 FTEs for 80 hours	TB	15-Sep	C
9	Reevaluate Process Performance	Process Evaluation Document Complete	1 FTE for 10 hours	RS	30-Sep	C
10	Identify Best Practices	Best Practices Forum Held	1 FTE for 15 hours	SN	30-Sep	C
11	Communicate Best Practices	Division Best Practice Meeting Held	1 FTE for 5 hours	RS	1-Oct	C
12	Write Case Study	Case Study Complete	1 FTE for 4 hours	BF	1-Oct	C

Key

G	On track
Y	Off track but with solution
R	Off track with no solution
H	On hold
C	Complete

Figure 4.5   Plan of Actions and Milestones

4. Establish Executive Accountability

What must follow project plan development is project plan accountability within the executive team. This step is a sine qua non for effective project management. To be fair, projects are usually subject to some form of executive accountability. Executives are generally aware of projects occurring in their business or function. They may not, however, have all of the details at their fingertips. Assigning vital projects to members of the top management team generates important benefits.

Reduction in Number of Projects   As a rule, top managers are very busy. They do not have time to engage in frivolous activities. The practice of assigning vital projects to top leaders naturally forces the selection of fewer projects by virtue of the simple fact that senior leaders cannot handle much more work than they are already accommodating. Based on our experience, when senior leaders are given direct oversight of projects, they seek to winnow responsibilities down to something manageable—usually by reprioritizing or reducing the number of projects underway. With enforced accountability at the top-team level, the number of ongoing projects in an organization generally declines.

Communication of Importance   When executives champion vital projects, employees at all levels take note. As executives get involved in projects and "own" them, accountability improves not just at their level but at the subordinate level as well. As mentioned earlier, accountability and interest improve in those areas where employees are involved. This is true of senior executives as well. Alignment is driven in part because of the indirect communication that the projects assigned to executives are a priority within the organization.

5. Manage Projects Dynamically

The last step in this phase entails managing projects dynamically. We cover this topic in the next two phases, Measure Progress and Make Decisions. In practice, however, dynamic management starts in this phase.

Managing projects dynamically means more than just following the POA&M to ensure key milestones are reached. It entails executives working on their teams to ensure the vital in-stream projects represent the best and highest use of the organization's resources at every point in time. Remember, the environment for which the PM^{4}TE process is designed is both volatile and highly dynamic. As such, it is very likely projects will need to be accelerated, delayed, or stopped altogether as new opportunities and threats present themselves. Leaders need to set up forums where they can actively discuss vital project progress and performance with the intent of making changes necessary to ensure critical performance objectives are being achieved as quickly and effectively as possible.

Critical Success Factors

In our work with struggling as well as successful organizations, we have identified four factors important to project execution success that should be kept in mind at all points in the PM^{4}TE process.

Realize the Odds Are against You

Despair.com is the purveyor of what they call *demotivator* posters, an antidote to platitudinous success posters present in most organizations. One of their posters is entitled, "Overconfidence." The poster shows two skiers ahead of what appears to be an avalanche rushing toward them from behind. The caption reads:

> Before you attempt to beat the odds, be sure you can survive the odds beating you.

This quote provides a valuable lesson in project management: The plain truth is that the odds are against most organizations when it comes to effective project execution. The data bear this out, too. What managers need to do is accept this fact and then take action to improve their approach to project management. More documentation and technology is not necessarily the key—better project focus is. That better focus starts with the realization that most organizations are probably not beating the odds.

Understand that Strategy Follows Structured Projects

Most managers have heard the phrase, "structure follows strategy." When it comes to strategy, this is usually the case. Organizations need structure to implement the strategy being undertaken.

In terms of project management, we think the opposite is true: Strategy execution follows project structure.

Too many organizations leave their vital projects unstructured. They allow projects to exist in a world of outdated and inaccurate spreadsheets. They allow projects to be launched with very little justification. Structuring projects using a business case format and project plans is an important step toward getting vital projects organized and executed.

Create Executive Accountability

At a basic level, executives are responsible for routine as well as nonroutine activities. Most operational-type work can be considered routine—things that are done day-to-day in the normal execution of business. Managers are generally good at these things. Where they often struggle is in nonroutine activities. Projects are by their very nature nonroutine—they are done once and then considered completed. The process of project management, however, must be a routine skill, and to make it one, executives need to have a higher level of accountability. In our view, every executive on a top team should have accountability for and cognizance of the most vital projects in an organization. This not only focuses effort and signals importance, it also builds top team skills necessary for execution success.

Remember that Less Is More and Quitters Win on Projects

While many people pride themselves on having more and doing more, we find that reciprocal rules serve leaders better when it comes to project management. Two truths illustrate this thinking.

First, less is more in project management. We believe that organizations that reduce their vital projects to a manageable set—typically less than 10 major ones—experience better implementation success than those that let them grow to 50, 100 or more. When there are fewer ongoing projects, more resources and attention can be aligned with each, accelerating their implementation. As projects are finished, new ones can be launched consistent with our view of making project management dynamic. Sadly, many executives believe results are sped up when more and more projects are piled on their teams. The effect is actually the converse—less gets done and more slowly.

Second, quitters may be the ultimate winners in the area of project management. When we say *quitting*, we mean stopping projects that are not really vital or, at a minimum, delaying them while higher priority projects run their course. Again, working on a high number of projects slows execution. The best course of action, when it comes to a project that is not adding the value needed, is to stop it altogether. As learned from the reengineering days, there is little value in improving the way something is done that should not be done in the first place.

Summary

In this chapter, we discussed the second step in the PM⁴TE process: Manage Projects. We presented a set of tools and practices that organizations use to get results today. We also highlighted steps that any organization can use to improve project performance. The bottom line is this: Most organizations execute projects poorly and that is driven in large part by poor project management practices. What we believe is that managers should spend time implementing the five steps in the execution phase to improve outcomes. These steps alone are worth the price of this book. With that, in the next chapter we move on to the next step in the PM⁴TE process, Measure Progress.

Case Study: Hubbell Lighting, Inc.

Company Background

Founded in 1888, Hubbell Incorporated has grown its lighting business into a global leader in lighting fixtures and controls. Hubbell Lighting, Inc. (HLI), a subsidiary of Hubbell Incorporated, headquartered in Greenville, South Carolina, provides indoor, outdoor, and specialty lighting solutions for the commercial, industrial, and residential markets by way of its 23 brands to distributors and consumers in North America and selected regions across the globe. Throughout its history Hubbell Incorporated has enjoyed a rich tradition of product innovation, from its invention of the pull chain socket, which was patented in 1896, to L.E.D. lighting and wireless controls, representing one of its most advanced innovations in new technologies today.

Turbulent Situation

But perhaps at no time in its history has the Hubbell Lighting business experienced the kind of environmental turbulence it faced coming into 2008. Immediately following the housing market collapse, paired with the global financial crisis, Hubbell Lighting found itself facing a significant demand decline in its core business in the span of only a few short months. Worse than a simple short downturn, the reduction in demand was projected by economists to persist for several years into the future. As a significant operating segment of a publicly traded company, the Hubbell Lighting leadership team was forced to act quickly and aggressively to not only adapt the business to the dramatically different conditions but also prepare themselves to manage more reflexively on an ongoing basis.

Description of the Project Management Process

For years HLI had relied on what it called the Long-Range Strategic Planning (LRSP) process to formulate strategy. At the start of 2009 it revitalized the process by incorporating performance modeling and a renewed focus on project management. Concurrent with setting the three-year strategy, the company developed a strategy map to help guide its focus in four main areas: revenue, price realization, cost containment, and productivity. Simultaneously it identified a focused set of 21 strategy projects aimed at specifically driving results in the three areas identified throughout the entire brand portfolio.

The Hubbell Lighting business turned to its operations leadership to spearhead the initial effort. The leadership team had deep experience in process improvement techniques such as lean manufacturing and Six Sigma and had developed a project management methodology specifically for use at the senior executive level. The process took the best thinking from standard project management approaches and simplified and focused it on the most vital projects of the business overall.

The approach works as follows: From the high-level strategy projects identified during the LRSP process, a project initiation is held for each one. In this step a single project leader is assigned, the project is scoped out as completely as possible, and buy-in is created with senior HLI leaders. Next, a project vision session is held with the project manager and six to eight people from the organization, who are not necessarily directly involved with the project. This is done to incorporate fresh ideas and novel perspectives from experienced as well as new employees. It is a major driver of their success. During the half-day visioning event, the project lead helps define the future state of the project as well as identify all the key activities that are essential to complete the project. Each of the activities is then organized into the priority matrix shown in Figure 4.6.

The priority matrix helps isolate those steps that are the most valuable in terms of completing the project. The company notes that approaching projects in this way helps focus efforts on those activities that have the biggest payoff. The teams are told to work the bottom-right quadrant first, then the bottom-left and top-right, and forget about the top-left; the purpose is to front-load those activities that will drive results the fastest. At the end of the visioning session, a detailed project plan is developed that is used to guide the project.

Next, an executive-level action plan is developed, consisting of the high-level milestones excerpted from the detailed project plan. An example of an actual project is shown in Figure 4.7.

This step of developing a high-level action plan for leaders to use was a major contributor to project success in the organization.

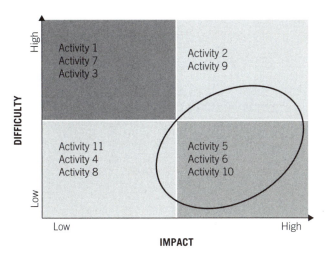

Figure 4.6   Project Activity Priority Matrix
Source: Hubbell Lighting, Inc.

HLI Stategic Projects

"Leadership in Innovation" and "Superior Customer Support"

Initiative Description	Category	Priority	Item #	Action	Accountability	Commitment Date	Status	Comments
Improve Supply Chain Bottlenecks to Drive 10% Improvement in On-Time Service Levels	Planning	A	3	Implement Sales, Inventory, and Operations Planning Process for MTS	SD	5/25/2009	C	
		B	2	Complete Training on SAP Best Practices with All Planners	SD	10/1/2009	C	
		C	4	Expand SIOP Program to MTO Components	PMs	12/1/2010	C	
		B	1	Implement Advanced Planning & Optimization Module for SAP	JP	12/31/2011	C	
	Purchasing	B	6	Complete Training on SAP Best Practices with All Buyers	PMs	10/1/2009	C	
		D	5	Upgrade Buyer Competencies through Top-Grading	PMs	12/31/2010	C	
		A	7	Develop SAP Reports and Standard Work for Daily Metrics	SD	1/1/2011	C	
		A	8	Implement Supplier Scorecard	SD	12/1/2009	C	
	Suppliers	B	9	Utilize Quantity Contracts for Long-Term Commitments	SD	6/10/2010	C	
		C	11	Upgrade Underperforming Suppliers	MM	12/31/2010	C	
		B	10	Establish and Maintain Preferred Supplier Program	MM	12/31/2011	C	

Fabrication	D	14	Develop Redundant Tooling for all Critical Components	PMs	12/1/2009	**C**
	A	12	Implement SMED	PMs	12/1/2010	**C**
	B	13	Implement Total Productive Maintenance Program	PMs	3/1/2011	**C**
Paint	C	15	Develop Outsourcing Partners	MM	12/1/2011	**C**
	A	16	Implement Kaizen Cadence Methodology	PG	7/15/2010	**C**
Assembly	B	17	Implement Plan for Every Part and Material Flow Improvements	SA	10/12/2010	**C**
	A	20	Develop Performance Metrics for all Distribution Centers	MT	6/1/2009	**C**
Shipping	B	18	Implement Bar-Code Capability	MT	12/31/2010	**C**
	B	19	Consolidate Multiple Distribution Centers into Strategic Locations	MT	12/31/2011	**C**

G On target

Y Off target, but have a solution

R Off target with no foreseeable resolution

C Complete

H On hold

Figure 4.7 Action Plan Sample with Single Accountability and Commitment Dates

Source: Hubbell Lighting, Inc.

According to HLI's vice president of operations, "This prevents the problem of executives not developing an action plan and tracking it. For a senior executive, this format is ideal."

Once the high-level action plans are developed, they are executed. For each of the major projects underway, applicable HLI leaders hold weekly review meetings with their single point project leader. That project leader in turn is holding weekly team meetings where the more detailed project plans are reviewed. Project progress measures from the weekly reviews are incorporated into monthly operating reviews with the entire executive team where overall project accountability by functional area is maintained. Hubbell Lighting believes that what gets measured gets done. These metrics are a part of the business' standard monthly operating reviews.

The final step is project completion that—depending upon the project—occurs typically three to six months after initiation. At that point, success has been achieved, and both teams and individuals are recognized for their contribution. Motivation is key to success. With the pace HLI is working at, management has to take the time to let people know that the results are successful and that their efforts are appreciated.

Interpretations from Key Managers

Hubbell Lighting, Inc., is unlike many organizations that struggle with project execution. Success rates are high as is satisfaction throughout the organization. "In the past year we've been able to drive key elements of our strategy—specifically the top projects and priorities—to successful completion" commented HLI's executive leadership. "We believe that we have an effective project management strategy and that we are continuing to increase our competitive position during this challenging time."

Tangible Benefits and Outcomes

HLI's business performance exceeded its operating plan for calendar year 2010 and was a valuable contributor to the total corporation's overall successful financial performance results. In the process, HLI was also recognized as the best company to work for in its home state of South Carolina by research firm Best Companies Group. HLI's executive leadership expresses pride in its employees and the company and continues to strive to distinguish itself in the lighting industry through leadership in product innovation and superior customer support.

Lessons Learned

The managers at HLI reiterated much of what was discussed throughout this chapter—namely that most organizations are deficient in project management, especially at the executive leadership level, and that project management by executives is a key to success. As we said at outset of this chapter, effective project management isn't about detailed reports and painful meetings. Effective project management is about carefully monitoring the vital projects ongoing in an organization and ensuring the impact on the critical objectives is being delivered. Most organizations can gain valuable insight from the Hubbell Lighting example.

Notes

1. M. Levinson, "Recession Causes Rising IT Project Failure Rates," *CIO,* June 18, 2009.
2. A. Nieto-Rodriguez and D. Evrard, "Boosting Business Performance through Programme and Project Management," PricewaterhouseCoopers, June 21, 2004, www.pwc.com/en_BE/be/multimedia/2004-06-21-boosting-business-performance-through-programme-and-project-management-pwc-04.pdf.
3. R. Discenza and J. Forman, "Seven Causes of Project Failure: How to Recognize Them and How to Initiate Project Recovery," in *PMI Global Conference Proceedings,* Project Management Institute, New York, 2007.
4. R. Kaplan and D. Norton, *The Execution Premium: Linking Strategy to Operations for Competitive Advantage* (Boston: Harvard Business School Publishing, 2008), p. 107.
5. R. Dye, "Improving Strategic Planning: A McKinsey Survey," *McKinsey Quarterly,* September 2006.
6. L. Bryan, "Just-in-Time Strategy for a Turbulent World," *McKinsey Quarterly,* Special Edition: Risk and Resilience, 2002, pp. 16–27.
7. M. Daniels, "Memoranda 02-01 (Guidance for Preparing and Submitting Security Plans of Action and Milestones)," October 2001, available at www.whitehouse.gov/omb/memoranda_m02-01.

Measure Progress

Without a standard there is no logical basis for making a decision or taking action.

—Joseph M. Juran

The third step in the PM⁴TE process is Measure Progress. The right set of measures helps managers evaluate performance and then take the actions necessary to improve it. Over the past three decades, significant advances have been made in the way organizations measure performance with quality frameworks such as Baldrige, financial frameworks such as EVA, and balanced systems such as the Balanced Scorecard and the Performance Prism. Contrary to popular thinking, we find that in turbulent settings managers often need to use more, not fewer, measures, which is logical given the demands placed on them. In this chapter, we discuss current practices in performance measurement, highlight tools used in organizations today, and show how managers can improve performance by organizing measures into two essential domains: project measurement and objective measurement. The steps to creating effective performance measures for turbulence are discussed, and a case study highlights the effective use of performance measures in a complex global enterprise.

Common homilies, such as "what gets measured gets done," "if it can't be measured, it can't be managed," and the like reflect the interest in performance measurement, which has grown steadily over the past several decades. Despite this interest, effective performance measures and measurement systems are lacking in organizations. We believe that performance measures contain additional value well beyond simple management control. This chapter expands our thinking on performance measurement to include measures as means to clarify strategy, communicate expectations, and challenge assumptions—all important aspects of managing performance in turbulent environments. And, as discussed later in the book, measurements provide the basis for accelerated learning, one of our key model enablers. Because choosing the right measures is so integral to successful execution, we have added a specific step to our PM⁴TE process expressly for measuring progress. Top management teams don't need more information—what they need is the right information to tell them what is going on in their environments and their organizations.

The Measure Progress step of the PM⁴TE process is shown at the bottom of Figure 5.1. In this step, managers develop and use two sets of performance measures to evaluate whether their critical performance objectives and vital projects are on track. In support of our thinking, we review the state of the practice with respect to performance measurement today. These tools can be used to set the stage

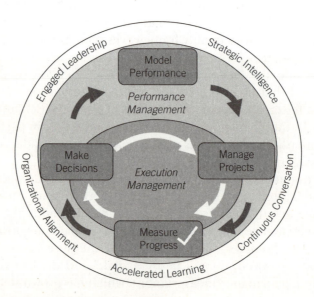

Figure 5.1   Core Process, Step 3: Measure Progress

for effective performance measurement within an organization. Some of these measures will already be in place from existing measurement systems. However, it is likely they will need to be rationalized and aligned to create a better focus on the critical performance objectives. Performance measures are organized into a framework for monitoring by senior leaders as well as provided as input to the next phase, Make Decisions, which is covered in Chapter 6.

Why Measure Progress during Turbulent Times?

Joseph Juran's quote provides the ideal context for our discussion in this chapter. If managers are not clear about what they are trying to achieve—and how well they are achieving it—there will be little basis for effective decision making and action within an organization. This thinking comes at the ideal place in the PM^{4}TE process— between managing projects and making decisions.

In the preceding chapter, we showed how to capture and align vital projects with critical performance objectives in the organization. But in order for the projects to be managed and critical performance to be evaluated, both the projects themselves and the critical objectives must be measured. In turbulent environments, leaders must measure regularly to ensure that projects stay on track *and* objectives are being achieved. Measuring the projects and performance objectives simultaneously is necessary in execution of the strategy.

Measuring performance is a basic activity in most organizations. The age-old truth still stands: "What gets measured gets done." Unfortunately measurement in most organizations is not done particularly well. Like with projects, which can be created for seemingly any improvement, managers create measures to evaluate just about anything. The challenge is to create measures that have meaning and provide the kind of insights that the organization needs. As one CEO told us, "I have more data now than I've ever had before. I still don't feel like I have what I need, however." In the following section, we explore some key developments in the field of performance measurement that can be used immediately in organizations to improve results.

State of the Art

The CEO quoted above reflects how many managers feel today— they have more information but know less about their performance than ever before. In a study that coauthor Andy Neely led for Oracle Corporation in 2007, the global performance management practices of over 600 companies in five countries revealed some sobering information. Despite all of the advancements made over two decades, performance measurement (and, more broadly, management) is not delivering the benefits promised.[1] Some of the more persistent challenges found by the Cranfield University–Oracle Corporation Global Enterprise Performance Management Survey include:

- Measurement is still tactical, not strategic.
- Financial measures are still the dominant means of measurement.
- Measures are still internally focused (e.g., focus inside, not outside the organization).
- There is still a major gap between vision and execution in most organizations.

These findings support observations made by other researchers and practitioners. Organizations still use mostly financial measures, and use them in highly tactical ways that are focused largely internally. As a consequence, the broader aim of performance management improvement still has a long way to go and, as a result, organizations are still struggling with execution. Again, this is why execution came out in the Conference Board's CEO survey as not only the first, but also the second among the top 10 challenges facing organizations today.[2]

Understanding Measurement Today

Despite the widespread performance measurement initiatives in organizations today, many managers are still not clear why they need to measure performance, what constitutes performance measurement, and, just as important, how it should best be accomplished. In his book, *Transforming Performance Measurement,* Dr. Dean Spitzer highlights 17 different reasons organizations measure performance.[3] Performance measurement can:

1. Direct behavior
2. Increase the visibility of performance
3. Focus management attention

4. Clarify expectations
5. Enable accountability
6. Increase objectivity
7. Provide the basis for goals setting
8. Improve execution
9. Promote consistency
10. Facilitate feedback
11. Increase alignment
12. Improve decision-making
13. Improve problem-solving
14. Provide early warning signals
15. Enhance understanding
16. Enable prediction
17. Provide motivation

With so much riding on effective measurement, it is easy to see why doing it well is so important and why doing it poorly has such profoundly negative effects on organizational performance. The relative ease of measuring belies a complexity that many managers are simply unaware of. Two simple pieces of information should facilitate improvement in this regard.

First, let's start with a basic definition of *performance measurement*: the quantification of the efficiency and effectiveness of an action. Quantifying is an essential aspect in determining whether the action had, or will have, its intended effect. Managers need to be able to compare their actual results against their expected standards—as Joseph Juran pointed out—to determine what to do next and to what degree it must be done. Quantification alone, however, does not constitute a complete performance measure.

Which brings us to our second point: Simply stating what is to be measured and then quantifying it is still not a comprehensive performance measure. In actuality, a performance measure consists of nine separate elements necessary for a complete performance measure (see Table 5.1).

Whether loaded into an automated reporting system or maintained separately in a spreadsheet, organizations need to define every element listed in Table 5.1 for each performance measure—especially those linked to critical performance objectives. If this seems like a lot of work, that's because it is. But as one client told us, "When we started documenting and defining our performance

Table 5.1   Elements of a Performance Measure

Elements or Attributes	Description
Measure name	A clear, self-explanatory title describing what the measure is
Measure purpose	Defines why the measure is going to be used
Objective supported	Explains which main objective the measure is supporting
Target level	Defines the expected performance level for this measure—can be broken into time periods
Formula	Provides the calculation for the measure
Frequency	Specifies how often measured data is to be collected and calculated
Source of data	Identifies the system or source input for the measure data
Who acts on the data	Identifies an individual/department/area that acts on the results

Source: Adapted from Andy Neely, Huw Richards, John Mills, Ken Platts, and Mike Bourne, "Designing Performance Measures: A Structured Approach," *International Journal of Operations & Production Management* 17, no. 11 (1997): 1131–1152.

measures, I thought it would be an activity of limited value. But by the time we were finished (three weeks later), it was one of the most useful things we've ever done at our company." Why is this the case? There are several reasons.

First, filling out the template forces organizations to clarify (not just quantify) the thinking behind the measures—what the measure is, what its purpose is, and what is supposed to happen given the results. Second, it provides the means to analyze the range and types of measures used in an organization. Although managers regularly lament that they do not have the measurement data they really need, they never challenge the data they have in any structured way. If they did, they would likely find rafts of measures that have limited value. This would lead to stopping much of the performance measurement currently underway. Lastly, it provides a basis for the managers to communicate the particulars of measurement to one another. In organizations today where roles and responsibilities are changing often, this type of documentation provides the basis for smooth transition in the area of performance management.

Performance Measurement Frameworks

In the late 1980s and early 1990s, groups of individual measures, known as *performance measurement frameworks*, came into use in

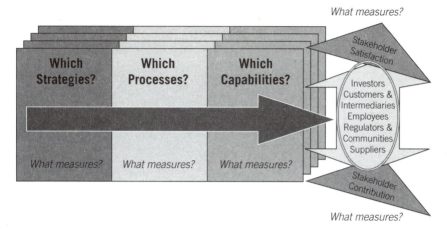

Figure 5.2 The Performance Prism

Source: Andy Neely, Chris Adams, and Mike Kennerley, *The Performance Prism: The Scorecard for Measuring and Managing Business Success* (Upper Saddle River, NJ: Financial Times Prentice Hall, 2002).

various organizations. Performance management frameworks are sets of performance measures, such as financial and nonfinancial measures organized to give more comprehensive views of organizational performance. There are literally dozens of these frameworks ranging from the Baldrige framework for quality to the Stern Steward framework for economic value added. Over time, these frameworks have migrated into balanced views of performance. The Performance Prism, developed by coauthor Andy Neely and two of his colleagues, is one of these (see Figure 5.2).[4]

The most popular and widely used framework is the Balanced Scorecard developed by Robert Kaplan and David Norton in 1992.[5] According to Bain & Company's 2011 Management Tools and Trends report, the Balanced Scorecard was being used by 47 percent of firms among the 1,230 surveyed.[6] Most organizations manage performance within some type of balanced framework, although in many cases, the balanced scorecards in use are little more than a repackaging of existing measures into a four-quadrant measurement framework. An excerpt from a state-of-the-art, complete Balanced Scorecard is shown in Figure 5.3.

With advancements in spreadsheets, along with automated reporting packages, more and more organizations are developing some type of a dashboard or scorecard. Most organizations have

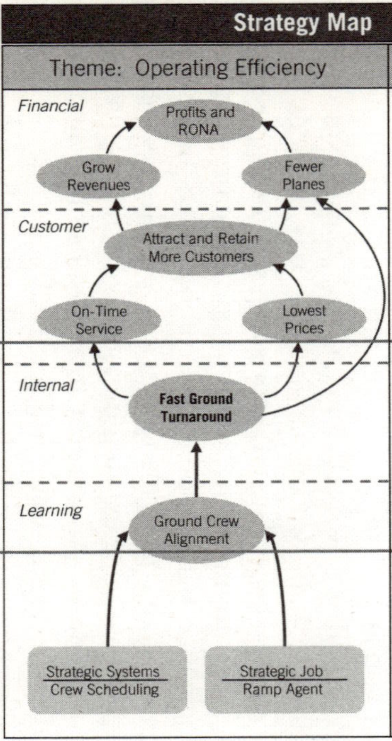

Figure 5.3 The Balanced Scorecard Management System

Strategy Map		Balanced Scorecard		Action Plan	
Theme: Operating Efficiency					
Objective	Measurement	Target	Initiative	Budget
Financial					
• Profitability	• Market Value	• 30% CAGR		
• Grow revenues	• Seat Revenue	• 20% CAGR		
• Fewer planes	• Plane Lease Cost	• 5% CAGR		
Customer					
• Flight is on time	• FAA On-Time Arrival Rating	• #1		
• Lowest prices	• Customer Ranking	• #1		
• Attract and retain more customers	• # Repeat Customers	• 70%	• Customer Loyalty Program	• $XXX
	• # Customers	• Increase 12% annual		
Internal					
• Fast ground turnaround	• On-Ground Time	• 30 Minutes	• On-Ground Cycle Time Optimization	• $XXX
	• On-Time Departure	• 90%	Quality Management	• $XXX
Learning					
• Ground crew aligned with strategy	• % Ground Crew Stockholders	• 100%	• ESOP	• $XXX
• Develop the necessary skills	• Strategic Awareness	• 100%	• Ground Crew Training	• $XXX
	• Strategic Job Readiness	Yr. 1: 0% / Yr. 3: 90% / Yr. 5: 100%	• Crew Scheduling System Rollout	• $XXX
• Develop the support system	• Information System Availability	• 100%	• CRM System	• $XXX
			Total Budget	**$XXX**

Strategy Map diagram:

Financial: Profits and RONA; Grow Revenues; Fewer Planes

Customer: Attract and Retain More Customers; Lowest Prices; On-Time Service

Internal: Fast Ground Turnaround

Learning: Ground Crew Alignment; Strategic Job — Ramp Agent; Strategic Systems — Crew Scheduling

Communicate   **Measure**   **Execute**

Figure 5.3 The Balanced Scorecard Management System

Source: Adapted from Robert Kaplan and David Norton, *The Execution Premium: Linking Strategy and Operations for Competitive Advantage* (Boston: Harvard Business Press, 2008).

multiple dashboards and scorecards throughout the enterprise, from the top team down to front-line teams and sometimes individual employees. The top management team will often use its dashboard to measure high-level performance, while regular employees may have personal scorecards to track individual development.

We make a simple, useful distinction between dashboards and scorecards. *Scorecards* are used for measuring and managing strategy, whereas *dashboards* are used in measuring and management of operations. Both of these frameworks—balanced or otherwise—contain sets of financial and sometimes nonfinancial measures. But dashboards contain more granular information that is looked at more frequently—daily or weekly—than scorecards. Scorecards typically contain measures linked to strategic objectives that are examined less frequently, such as on a monthly basis.

This distinction is useful because managers need to become aware that, despite looking the same, measures in organizations are actually quite different. Much of that difference is owed to their use. Tracking strategy and individual human capital development is very different from meeting a budget or controlling manufacturing process variation. We talk more about this later in this chapter, in the section "Learning Instead of Control."

Correlation Analysis

Organizations today generally stop evolving their performance measures once they have their frameworks together. They are content to measure performance—either operational or strategic—and check to see if progress is being made. They use those measures to challenge the strategy too. What they tend not to do, however, is examine any relationships between performance measures.

When we speak of relationships, we mean the "if-then" or causal relationships introduced in the Model Performance step. The purpose of developing critical performance objectives within the performance models discussed in Chapter 3 was to test whether empirical relationships within the model exist—not just hypothesized relationships (although documenting these was the point of the model), but actual relationships based on real data. That real data are collected through the quantification of performance for each critical performance objective. Stated simply, we can analytically test performance through performance measurement. Let us provide an example.

In the early 1990s, the longstanding U.S. retailer Sears, Roebuck, and Co. experienced losses in the billions of dollars. A new management team arrived that focused on turning the company around. They made a host of changes, such as discontinuing the home catalog business that the company was founded on. But one of the most significant changes came in the area of performance measurement.

The company launched a strategy around making Sears a compelling place to work, shop, and invest. Over the course of a year, senior managers collected data on employee attitudes, customer satisfaction, and financial performance. As they homed in on more precise performance measurement, they developed what they called *total performance indicators*. These were described by A. J. Rucci, S. P. Kirn, and R. T. Quinn in their *Harvard Business Review* article as "an econometric model . . . delineating causal connections along a pathway from employee attitudes to profits."[7] In other words, as we have pointed out previously, a performance model. Sears tested this model—using performance measurement data collected from two quarters—and found the correlations shown in Figure 5.4.

Managers then went on to align their management activities with the model and communicated to employees what they could do to better align their own behaviors with it. The results were impressive. From 1992 to 1993, the merchandise group went from a $3 billion loss to over a $750 million profit in one year.

We use this example for two reasons. First, it demonstrates very clearly the type of analytics that can be accomplished using the right measures within a clear performance model. Rucci et al. refer to this *causal pathway modeling* as a step beyond simple regression analysis. Second, Rucci et al. note that they wanted to take the Balanced Scorecard beyond its use as a simple performance management framework:

> We wanted to assemble the company's vast body of interview and research data . . . then analyze it, draw connections across the data sets, and construct a model to show pathways of actual causation all the way from employee attitudes to profits. We wanted a set of nonfinancial measures that would be every bit as rigorous and auditable as financial ones. To make that happen, we had to take this first version of the employee-customer-profit model and elaborate and refine it until we had tested and proved the measures it was built on.[8]

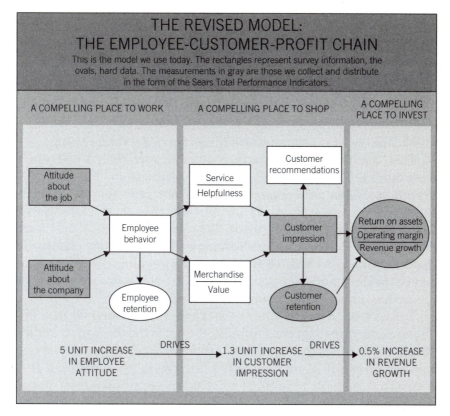

THE REVISED MODEL:
THE EMPLOYEE-CUSTOMER-PROFIT CHAIN

This is the model we use today. The rectangles represent survey information, the ovals, hard data. The measurements in gray are those we collect and distribute in the form of the Sears Total Performance Indicators.

A COMPELLING PLACE TO WORK   A COMPELLING PLACE TO SHOP   A COMPELLING PLACE TO INVEST

Figure 5.4   The Employee–Customer Chain Model

Source: A. J. Rucci, S. P. Kirn, and R. T. Quinn, "The Employee-Customer-Profit Chain at Sears," *Harvard Business Review* 76, no. 1 (1997): 82–97.

We think the power in this type of approach is self-evident. It is used at many different organizations today, although it is clearly not mainstream in terms of performance. We hope it soon will be.

Learning Instead of Control

A final activity that best-in-class organizations are doing today is using measures for the purpose of learning rather than for control. While we do not advocate stopping the use of measures to control performance in areas such as cost management, the performance we focus on in this book has more to do with evaluation of strategy than day-to-day operations.

As pointed out earlier in the chapter, organizations use measures for a variety of purposes. We find that in the strategy area, measures are used more commonly to check progress, clarify strategy, communicate strategy, and challenge assumptions. The last of these—challenge assumptions—requires that managers establish a context in which employees feel comfortable discussing performance progress free from criticism regarding whether performance objectives were fully achieved. This prerequisite is important for several reasons.

First, the critical performance objectives we refer to here are most often linked to the strategy of the organization. They are only hypotheses when first created; they do not represent empirically proven relationships. In order for the objectives themselves, as well as the relationships among them, to be evaluated, employees must feel they can do so in an environment where information can be shared without the risk of negative interpretation. Attempting to control performance in instances where the performance objectives themselves are still unclear undermines learning.

Second, because this entire PM⁴TE process is situated in a turbulent setting, managers must build the capability to work together effectively. If colleagues are constantly levying criticisms against one another, an unwillingness to share information will emerge. If that occurs, information pertaining to changes in critical performance variables may be withheld at a time when the organization would be best served by the sharing of this information—even if it runs contrary to expected performance. Critical conversations will not occur if fear of criticism, or worse, retribution, is present.

Lastly, testing the measures and the models discussed in this book requires an approach by executives that is exploratory in nature. Most managers think that they need to know everything going on in their organizations. When testing assumptions and hypothesis, the approach requires that executives accept that they may *not* know what is going on in their organizations. Challenging assumptions means that leaders have to be comfortable with the thought that their assumptions may be wrong.

Benefits of Measuring Progress in the PM⁴TE Process

Given the multitude of purposes for which organizations measure, the benefits of measuring performance should be clear. That said, there are stark differences between organizations that measure performance well and those that do not. For those that do it well, especially when it comes to measuring critical performance objectives and project performance, we see the following benefits.

Focused Management Attention

Managers know that they live in a world of limited resources. Certainly money and time are in short supply. What we see in our work is that the scarcest of all resources is management attention. Not only are managers limited in the amount of time they have, they are constrained in their ability to process ever-increasing amounts of information.

Research indicates that in high-velocity environments, managers need to process more information—not less—more quickly than their counterparts in stable environments. But that does not mean they must process all information or that information being processed is of equal importance. We believe that managers need to extract from day-to-day information a subset that is better aligned to the vital projects of the organization as well as the performance model they are using to drive results. Our observation is that when managers operate from a model of performance that is accurate and well understood, they are better able to assimilate and process all other performance measures in a way that provides both meaning and insight.

Improved Execution

One of the main reasons we wrote this book was to help managers improve execution of strategy. The right set of measures—those focused around vital project management and critical objective testing—helps managers not only test assumptions, but use measures better in each of the other essential ways: checking progress and clarifying and communicating strategy.

By winnowing projects down to a narrow, focused set aimed at improving a manageable number of critical performance objectives, managers can feel comfortable that they are working on the highest priorities of the business. When those measures are then are organized into a performance model framework, they naturally work to clarify the strategy. And when they are shared with employees at all levels, the strategy is effectively communicated. Better measurement means better execution.

Early Warning Signs

In turbulent settings, change happens quickly and unpredictably. The right measures can provide useful early warnings regarding the nature and extent of the change.

If managers have developed a shared understanding of performance objectives, and have measures associated with each objective paired with aligned projects (which have projected benefits), then they have a basis for knowing what to expect in the future. If actual performance starts to deviate in a significant way, managers will know that something is occurring that is out of the ordinary. Using the performance model and measures, they will have the basis for examining actual performance with an eye toward signals that something unexpected—and maybe unplanned—is occurring.

Steps to Measuring Progress

We recognize that managers reading this book are measuring progress in their organizations already. For that reason, we are not recommending a wholesale redesign of performance measures but rather a review and reevaluation of measures as they pertain to critical performance objectives and vital projects. The five steps in this section are for that process.

1. Review Critical Performance Objectives and Vital Projects

The first step in improving measurement entails reviewing each of the primary and contributing performance objectives within the performance model framework as well as reviewing the plans of actions and milestones (POA&Ms) and detailed project plans for vital projects. These two dimensions of the PM^{4}TE process represent the critical areas where performance must be managed closely to better align with the external environment.

Reviewing Critical Performance Objectives   While performance models vary in complexity, a typical performance model contains between 15 and 25 critical performance objectives. A handful—say, 3 to 5—will be primary objectives and the remainder—about 12 to 22—will be contributing objectives. These are arrayed in the main areas of organizational performance—stakeholder, capabilities, processes, primary

Table 5.2   Sample Objectives and Objective Descriptions

Sample Objective	Objective Descriptions
Grow profit	Ensure profit growth exceeds historical averages.
Provide great service	Deliver a customer experience that exceeds their service expectations.
Reduce manufacturing waste	Drive down process scrap and waste generated in the extruding process.
Create capable successors	Develop capable successors for all key positions in the company.

strategies, and satisfaction. As a guideline, management teams should review each of the objectives and document what each one means in detail. Examples are provided in Table 5.2.

This documentation should be performed for each of the critical objectives within the body of the performance model. The purpose of writing two- or three-sentence detailed descriptions is to help managers develop better measures to be associated with each objective. Effective measurement starts with a clear understanding of the performance objectives to be achieved.

Reviewing Vital Projects   Vital projects should be reviewed after critical performance objectives. Each vital project should contain a POA&M for use by senior managers as well as a detailed project plan for the project manager. No more than a dozen vital projects should be aligned with an organization's strategy. Remember that additional projects can be added as projects are completed; however, at any one time, the top management team should maintain focus on no more than 12 or so projects. The purpose of reviewing vital projects is to better understand the key milestones, time frames, and deliverables that have to be managed sucessfully.

2. Align or Develop Measures

The second step to improving performance measurement is assessing the measures that are currently used to evaluate performance. During the course of our advisory work, neither of us has been asked to design a performance measurement system because the client is not yet using one. Organizations normally have extensive measurement systems in place. The problem is that these systems do not give managers a complete picture of performance. That said, we start with the existing performance measures already in place.

Align/Develop Key Measures for Critical Objectives With a detailed under-standing of performance areas from the first step, we align—or create if necessary—measures with critical performance objectives. Our experience tells us that financial measures as well as many process measures can be readily aligned to performance. What we see fewer of are measures that provide insights regarding customer satisfaction, that is, customer value proposition, or measures that assess the capability of the workforce. Typically, new measures are developed in these areas. The main idea, however, is to develop one or two key measures for each of the critical performance objectives. If the objective is clearly described, one measure should suffice.

If a host of measures are needed to quantitatively evaluate per-formance relative to the objective, then the objective is likely too vague and it should be simplified. At the end of this step, there should be about the same number of key measures—15 to 25—as there are critical performance objectives. These measures will be used to determine if critical performance objectives are being achieved. The template in Figure 5.1 can be used for this.

Align/Develop Key Measures for Vital Projects Vital projects also must be measured. But the measures used to assess project progress are dif-ferent than those used to evaluate objective performance. Whereas measures paired with critical performance objectives assess objec-tive achievement, project measures gauge project progress. Project measures are effectively the milestones within the POA&M and the detailed project plan. Managers need to assess how realistic the milestones are as part of the overall measures review. In cases where the organization keeps missing important deadlines or deliverables, milestones are not realistic and must be reset.

3. Set Targeted Performance

Once existing performance measures are aligned to each objective and project milestones are reviewed with an eye toward realistic achievement, then targets can be set. Target setting is a three-step process, which is described next.

Baseline Performance For each measure associated with a critical performance objective or a vital project, a current performance baseline must be established. Before something can be improved, current performance must first be understood. For each measure and each project, current performance must be determine and documented. This provides managers with a comprehensive set of information that gives a snapshot of current performance. It also serves to begin the process of quantifying the relationships within the model.

Benchmark Performance Once baselines have been developed for each measure, then current performance for each measure should be benchmarked where possible. Benchmarking gives managers a sense of how they are faring relative to either internal standards or external competitive performance. It does little for a team to work diligently to improve a critical performance objective only to learn as they complete their work that their performance is still far behind their peers'. Benchmarking helps avoid this problem by providing a realistic basis upon which to assess progress. Interestingly, consultants Bain and Company found that benchmarking was the number one management tool in use in their 2011 survey.[9]

Progress on vital projects can be assessed as well. Internal performance standards, such as actual to expected completion time, exist in most organizations but are often not checked with any rigor. Furthermore, organizations such as PMI and other project management associations can provide input regarding the time taken and the processes used by best-in-class organizations to complete projects. This, too, should be assessed.

Set Targets by Reporting Period When current performance has been documented and benchmarks determined for both objectives and projects, then managers should set targets by reporting period. If progress is reported monthly, then monthly targets should be set. The sum total of the targets should equal the performance requirements for the duration of the strategy period or operating cycle— whichever managers use to pace performance. For example, if there is a three-year strategy in place, with quarterly reviews, 12 targets should be set over the reporting period for each measure. If the reporting period is dynamic, targets should be dynamic as well. Targets should be set for performance objectives and vital projects.

4. Gauge Progress

As the work of the organization is executed and vital projects are advanced over time, progress should be gauged. The faster the turbulent environment changes, the more frequently progress should be evaluated. Progress needs to be evaluated in the areas of vital projects and critical performance objectives.

Gauging Vital Project Progress Projects need to be kept on track—or altered appropriately as conditions change. This is an area where organizations tend to struggle. Project management is left to the discretion of individual functions, individual departments, or individual managers. Driving progress in the PM⁴TE process comes largely from project execution.

Top managers need to evaluate project progress frequently. We suggest a weekly review. This may seem excessive, but it isn't. If the vital project set has been narrowed to a manageable number—the dozen or so recommended previously—the evaluations will be simple and straightforward. Using updated POA&Ms, top managers can hold vital project meetings to see whether milestones are being met. They can also shift and allocate resources in a rapid and dynamic way to keep the project portfolio aligned with top priorities. This lever—vital project progress—is not used as well as it should be in organizations today.

Gauging Critical Objective Progress As vital project progress is made, progress toward achieving targets for each individual objective must be evaluated. This process should be frequent too, though not as frequent as project reviews. We would assert, however, that the review of measures and objectives should become more frequent as turbulence levels increase.

As data is collected for projects and measures, the assumptions underpinning the performance model can be tested. Top managers need to set up meetings exclusively to review the critical performance of the organization—chiefly the strategy—to see whether their hypothesis of the model is accurate or needs to be changed. That is the main work of executives in an organization. We cover this in more depth in Chapter 6, "Make Decisions."

5. Test Assumptions

As progress is gauged and data collected for each of the measures, leaders can begin the process of testing assumptions.

Initial assumption testing determines whether completing a vital project contributes to the achievement of the target for each critical objective's performance measure. Executives review the projects at the same time they review actual measurement data. Managers then have the basis for making decisions about shifts in project priorities or project resources. Adjustments to critical objectives can be made as well. This happens at all points during the execution process.

When more data is collected—typically six to eight performance periods, either quarterly or monthly—then managers can start the process of determining the correlation between objectives in the performance model. The objectives become variables in analytical models that test the relationships between them. This type of testing is critical for assessing of the value of the model. In cases where little to no relationship exists, managers should review the model, going back to the first phase, Model Performance, and reset if necessary.

Critical Success Factors

Measuring progress is a critical step in the PM^{4}TE process. Done poorly, it can have significant detrimental effects on an organization. Done well, it becomes one of the fastest routes to improved execution. Here are recommendations based on the organizations we have studied that get the most out of performance measurement systems.

Focus the Measures

Measures tend to proliferate in organizations much like projects do. Getting the measure of your organization first requires an understanding of the current measures in place, along with knowledge of how they are used. Once that is accomplished, managers can pare down the measures to a number that is more manageable and meaningful. The answer to measure problems in most organizations is not more measurement, but better measurement. While turbulent environments call for a whole host of signaling devices, managers must first ensure that the signals they get are the right ones. Otherwise, time and attention will be paid to false signals that diffuse rather than unify management efforts.

Seek Understanding

Measures are important tools in controlling performance. But they play an even more critical role in helping managers assess what is working and what isn't in their organizations. As Gandhi famously said, "Seek first to understand, then be understood." This thinking should be applied to measurement in general and certainly within turbulent settings. The purpose of the measures here—project measures and objective measures—is to provide leaders with insight into two essential questions:

1. Are we completing our vital projects in a timely, effective manner?
2. Are we achieving the critical performance objectives necessary to win in our environment?

In our estimation, winning requires a high degree of comfort with asking—and answering honestly—these difficult questions. A genuine desire to learn what is working and what is not is needed here. We discuss this point in depth in the second half of the book.

Test the Relationships

The PM⁴TE process starts with the development of a performance model intended to show the relationships between critical performance variables in an organization. In the first phase of the model's development, a set of assumptions is given about which actions cause specific outcomes to occur. These relationships are not proven at this time—they are only hypothesized. What has to happen over time is for the assumptions to be tested using actual quantitative measurement data. While challenging, this is the only real way to gain true insight as to whether the focus and efforts of management are the proper ones.

Align Management with Measurement

Our last, and perhaps most important, success factor is aligning management with measurement. We are not referring simply to using measures as a basis to control, evaluate, or even learn in an organization. Certainly, most measures are already used in these ways. What we mean is that managers start to take action based upon *known* relationships resident in the measures. Managers know that profit is increased by increasing revenue, reducing costs, or some combination of both. But in more complex situations, what managers do not always know are things like the benefit for an incremental training dollar or the additional revenue potential directly related to an increase in customer loyalty. These are the real nuggets of knowledge that managers must find. Once they do, they can make dramatic improvements in performance because they know what actually enhances performance.

Summary

In this chapter, we covered the third step in the PM⁴TE process—Measure Progress. Managers measure progress every day, for many different purposes, and with varying levels of effectiveness. Improving the measurement aspect of performance management in turbulent settings comes in two forms: measurement of vital activities and measurement of critical performance objectives. These areas reflect the critical drivers and critical results in organizations and, as such, they should be managed much more thoughtfully, effectively, and dynamically than other areas. Measurement has much room for improvement, but in keeping with our philosophy, improving these 20 percent of the measurement activities should yield 80 percent of the results.

Case Study: British Airways

British Airways, Plc, which traces its roots back to 1919, is currently one of the world's leading premium global airlines. Together with its alliance partners, the company flies to over 400 destinations around the world. For the fiscal year ended March 31, 2010, the company earned £7.9 billion in revenue, down from £8.9 billion for the prior year. As of the close of 2010, British Airways transported over 24 million passengers with its fleet of 240 aircraft.

Turbulent Situation

The commercial airline industry today is one of the most volatile industries in the world. Competitors—who freely enter and exit the market while constantly consolidating—compete largely on price. Airlines are further buffeted by a bevy of unfavorable factors, many of which are beyond their control, the most significant being fuel costs and employee expenses, respectively. In the case of a global carrier such as British Airways, not only is it impacted by recurring weather patterns, such as inclement conditions during winter months, but it is at the mercy of natural disasters as well. In 2010 air travel in and around Europe was restricted for five days due to ash from the Eyjafjallajökull volcano in Iceland. This translated to a loss of millions of pounds per day. When asked to describe the airline industry, strategist Michael Porter notes, "[I]t's among the least profitable industries known to man."[10] According to his research, which began in the late 1970s, this has been the case for decades.

Description of the Measuring Progress Process

British Airways's measuring process has historically flowed from its strategy, which since 2008 has been to become the world's leading global premium airline.[11] This strategy is manifest in a series of objectives that are documented in their business plan. The company's seven critical performance objectives from its 2010 annual report are listed in Table 5.3.

Linked to these critical objectives are a number of vital measures. While British Airways tracks scores of measures, it tracks particularly closely and often those associated with what it calls the eight "moments of truth." These are service interactions that, based on market research, British Airways has found to be particularly

Table 5.3   British Airways Critical Performance Objectives

Critical Objective	Objective Descriptions
Synergies	Generate synergies from the merger with Iberia.
Deliver outstanding customer service and continue to invest in our products	Make investments in the employees who deliver services as well as the aircraft that are flown.
Grow revenue with our airline partners	Help alliance partners grow their businesses.
Secure the right assets and infrastructure	Add new aircraft and IT infrastructure.
Achieve a cost base that enables us to compete and grow	Manage costs through the airline.
Create the culture and capabilities to succeed	Implement a new people strategy which improves training, leadership, compensation and engagement.
Set the standard for responsible aviation	Reduce carbon emissions; campaign for a single, appropriate and competitively nondistorting regulatory regime; and minimize local community impacts from air quality and noise.

Source: British Airways, *Report and Accounts to December 2010* (London: 2011).

Table 5.4   British Airways Sample Measures

Vital Measure	Measure Descriptions
Financial performance	Quarterly data on sales revenue. Monthly data and net yield per revenue passenger kilometer.
Customer retention	Intention to repeat purchase and willingness to recommend.
Customer satisfaction	Customer perspectives on service.
Answering calls quickly	Percentage of calls answered in less than 20 seconds.
Check-in service	Overall measure of services offered to customer during the check-in process.
Departure time	The industry's standard measures as the percentage of flights departing within 15 minutes of schedule.
Aircraft condition	Results of regular investigation of the interior condition of the aircraft.
Cabin crew service	Covers three main cabin services: manner of crew, attitude toward customers, pace of crew service.
Meal rating	Measure of the taste of the food and quantity offered.
Short-handed baggage	Loss rate of baggage per 1,000 passengers.
Executive Club	Feedback obtained from users of the British Airways club.
Employee satisfaction	Employee survey containing over 70 questions.

Source: A. Neely and M. Al Najjar, "Management Learning Not Management Control: The True Role of Performance Measurement?" *California Management Review* 48, no. 3 (2006): 101–114.

important to driving performance. A sample of measures British Airways uses to gauge progress related to moments of truth is highlighted in Table 5.4.

Historically, British Airways tracked and examined these measures in a largely functional manner within its business functions (e.g., financial measures in finance, human capital measures in human resources, etc.). In 2005, researchers working with management began examining the measures in Table 5.4 to challenge the assumptions inherent in the business model—namely that higher levels of service would lead to increased customer satisfaction and thus lead to retaining customers and driving profitability. Over a two-year period, data related to the measures in Table 5.4 were collected and tested to determine where significant relationships existed among measures. Researchers found that, contrary to management's beliefs, not all measures impacted customer satisfaction

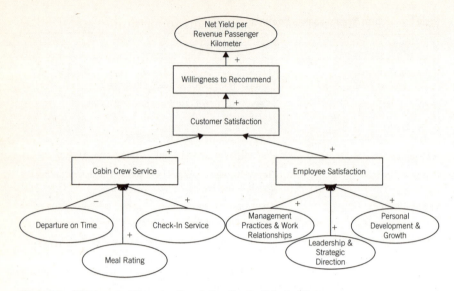

Figure 5.5   BA Integrated Measures Correlation Map for Selected Measures

Source: A. Neely and M. Al Najjar, "Management Learning Not Management Control: The True Role of Performance Measurement?" *California Management Review* 48, no. 3 (2006): 101–114.

equally. The relationships of the measures examined are depicted in Figure 5.5 and discussed in the next section.

Interpretations from Researchers and Managers

What researchers found when they examined these relationships was that willingness to recommend did impact net yield per revenue passenger kilometer. However, only two factors examined—cabin crew service and employee satisfaction—were directly correlated with customer satisfaction. Cabin crew service was positively correlated to check-in service and meal rating. If check-in was smooth and meals were satisfying, customers felt cabin crew service was good. However, departure time was negatively correlated to cabin crew service. Researchers discovered that the later the flight left, the better the service was, presumably because the crew worked harder to compensate for the lost time. As for employee satisfaction, it was impacted most significantly by three factors: management practices and work relationship, confidence in leadership and strategic direction and personal development and growth. When employees felt empowered in their jobs, had faith in leadership, and believed they were being provided with development opportunities, satisfaction followed. Thus, British Airways should expect that as each of the three drivers improved, so too should overall employee satisfaction. The researchers examined other more granular relationships but, in conclusion, they found that not all measures among those originally thought to be equal in fact were.

Tangible Benefits and Outcomes

Over the past few years, British Airways has faced a particularly challenging environment both externally and internally. The global recession, labor challenges, and the credit crisis, in conjunction with other challenges, have placed significant operating pressure on the company. In 2009, while it recorded a £231 million loss, British Airways did stay the course of working to become the world's leading premium airline. As of December 31, 2010, the company reversed the trend and significantly exceeded their annual operating profit targets. Per its 2010 report and accounts:

> For 2010/11, we set ourselves a target operating result of £150 million, this equated to £160 million for the nine months to 31 December 2010. Our operating profit was £342 million for the nine months compared to a loss of £231 million for the 12 months to 31 March 2010. This significant improvement reflects the increase in revenue combined with the permanent structural changes we made to our cost base over the past two years.[12]

While the company clearly has more work to do, its focus on key performance measures—and the relationships among them—is having a positive effect on business performance.

Lessons Learned

There are several key findings researchers and managers learned from the measures analysis. First, British Airways, like most companies, looks at performance measurement in a narrow manner. Measures analysis is relegated to functional snapshots and a holistic picture of performance is not maintained. Second, regardless of whether a performance model is constructed, one exists. In this instance, the researchers uncovered it through retrospective analysis—analysis that would have been better performed up front. Third, organizations many times do not have employees with the requisite analytical skills necessary to perform analysis, as was done in this case. To be competitive, organizations must invest in these capabilities. Finally, managers must make a commitment to managing performance in a more analytical and insightful way. When they do, the true drivers of performance can be uncovered and ultimately, managed to the best effect.

Notes

1. A. Neely, B. Yaghi, and N. Youell, *Enterprise Performance Management: The Global State of the Art* (London: Cranfield School of Management/ Oracle Corp, 2009).
2. L. Barrington, "CEO Challenge 2010 Top 10 Challenges," Report R-1461-10-RR (New York: Conference Board, 2010).
3. D. Spitzer, *Transforming Performance Measures: Rethinking the Way We Drive Organizational Success* (New York: AMACOM, 2007).
4. A. Neely, C. Adams, and M. Kennerley, *The Performance Prism: The Scorecard for Measuring and Managing Business Success* (London: Financial Times Prentice Hall, 2002).
5. R. Kaplan and D. Norton. "The Balanced Scorecard: Measures That Drive Performance." *Harvard Business Review* 70, no. 1 (1992): 71.
6. D. Rigby and B. Bilodeau, *Management Tools and Trends 2011* (Boston: Bain & Company, 2011).
7. A. Rucci, S. Kirn, and R. Quinn, "The Employee-Customer-Profit Chain at Sears." *Harvard Business Review* 76, no. 1 (1997): 82–97.
8. Ibid.
9. Rigby and Bilodeau, *Management Tools and Trends 2011.*
10. T. Stewart and M. Porter, *The Five Competitive Forces that Shape Strategy* (Boston: Harvard Business Publishing, 2008).
11. British Airways, *Report and Accounts to December 2010* (London: Author, 2011).
12. Ibid.

CHAPTER

Make Decisions

Decision making is the specific executive task.

—Peter Drucker

The fourth step in the Core Process for Performance Management for Turbulent Environments is Make Decisions. Decisions, among other things, set direction and ensure proper resource allocation. Virtually all activities in an organization start with a decision. Even those where no conscious decision is made involve the decision not to decide. Despite major advances in information gathering and analytics, organizations still struggle to make effective decisions. In this chapter, we will discuss current thinking on decision making and present processes organizations use today to improve not only the decision process but decision outcomes. Steps to improving decision making in organization—a critical activity in turbulent environments—are presented along with a case study highlighting an effective decision process.

Make Decisions is the final step in the Core Process of the overall PM⁴TE process, as shown at the left of Figure 6.1. In this phase, managers synthesize information pertaining to vital project progress and critical performance objective improvement and make decisions regarding course corrections that are necessary to keep the organization moving toward its desired results. Decision making in organizations has significant impact at all levels; organizations that

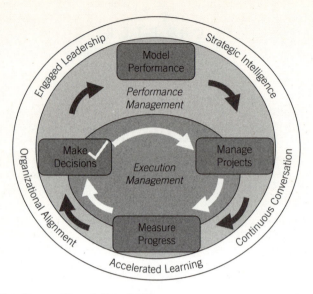

Figure 6.1   Core Process, Phase 4: Make Decisions

make better decisions perform better than those that make poor ones. The good news is that decision making is a learned skill. By understanding how decisions get made, knowing how biases creep into the process and how the decision process itself can be strengthened, performance can be improved. Decisions made as part of the PM^{4}TE process drive action with respect to critical performance objectives and vital projects. The virtuous cycle that we have described in each chapter of this book so far then speeds up and becomes synchronized with the external environment to maintain high performance during turbulence. We discuss how the PM^{4}TE process functions overall in Chapter 12, "Making It Work."

Why Make Decisions during Turbulent Times?

As this chapter's opening quote by Peter Drucker says, decision making is the specific executive task. Effective decision making is perhaps the most important job of top managers in organizations today. All of the efforts identifying performance objectives, developing a performance model, aligning projects, and measuring progress are of limited value if good decisions are not made from the information provided by those activities. Therefore, to expressly omit decision making from any performance management process seems irresponsible to us. Core Process steps to this point are performed as part of this process for the specific purpose of enhancing decision making. In turbulent environments, decisions must be made quickly with a high success rate; poor decisions are not rewarded. Although it is the last phase in the Core Process, it is arguably the most important.

In the last chapter, we described how to measure progress in the areas of vital projects and critical performance objectives. Gauging progress is necessary to determine whether the strategy is working. All strategies, no matter how well conceived, require adaptation, not least because changes in the external environment necessitate changing strategy. This is where decision making comes in. In turbulent environments, leaders must ensure the decisions they make are made rapidly, are rooted in reality, are well thought out, and, in the final analysis, effective. As Bain & Company consultants Marcia Blenko, Michael Mankins, and Paul Rogers point out in their June 2010 *Harvard Business Review* article, "The Decision-Driven Organization":

> An army's success depends at least as much on the quality of the decisions its officers and soldiers make and execute on the ground as it does on actual fighting power. A corporation's structure, similarly, will produce better performance only if it improves the ability of the organization's ability to make and execute key decisions better and faster than competitors.[1]

While we do not address the concept of organization structure, we do cover what is known about decision making today and what can be done in organizations to improve it at all levels.

Before a decision can—or rather, should—be made, the issues or problems underlying the decision need to be addressed. Based upon our observations, this is one of the weakest skills of most managers. There are two reasons for this.

First, in the main, managers are not taught critical thinking, decision making, or problem-solving skills. What managers have learned is how to solve problems using incomplete approaches or ad hoc methods. For straightforward decisions, incomplete approaches are generally sufficient. For complex decisions, however, where the causes of performance shortfalls are not known and the range of options are not easily identifiable, this quickly proves insufficient and will lead to behaviors such as trying to remove symptoms or failing to identify the best choices available.

Second, managers are prone to taking action versus conducting analysis. The desire to take action trumps analysis more often than not. If there is a problem or decision, the prevalent thinking surrounds making a choice or doing something first and thinking about it later. One of this book's coauthors has a client that has been unable to gain market share for four years despite valiant attempts to do so. When its managers are asked for the reason or cause behind this inability to grow share, they cannot provide a clear answer. What they can do is explain how the next project they are working on will certainly increase share. If history in this organization has any predictive power, the next project too will fail.

What organizations need today is better thinking and better processes when it comes to both problem solving and decision making. This chapter focuses on both.

State of the Art

One of our colleagues, Tom Davenport, a professor at Babson College and coauthor of the book *Competing on Analytics* (Harvard Business School Press, 2007), noted recently that "decision making is the last frontier of performance management." It's hard to disagree with his thinking. We too see this area as ripe with opportunity for improvement given the content of this chapter. Despite all the technology available to executives today and the hundreds of reports supported by sophisticated analytical techniques, decision making seems, at best, modestly better today than it was decades ago. This claim seems unfathomable in today's world, where more information is available faster and with more accuracy than ever before. But it has merit.

In 2007, the Economist Intelligence Unit conducted a survey of 154 business executives coupled with in-depth interviews with practitioners.[2] They made some useful observations:

- Poor data leads to poor decisions.
- As organizations grow, decision making becomes more challenging.

- Decision support tools need to be easier to use.
- Decisions today may involve too much art and not enough science.

The last point is derived from some interesting information from the survey. The majority of organizations surveyed, 55 percent, have decision processes that are largely informal. The authors assert that "common metrics and greater use of automated information tools such as dashboards would help support better quality decisions." Based on the first three phases of our model, we absolutely agree. Most interesting was that 77 percent of respondents believed that decisions made by senior management were either sometimes or frequently *wrong*.

McKinsey & Company found the same to be generally true. In a survey of over 2,200 executives, only 28 percent said the quality of their decisions was good; 60 percent said bad decisions were as frequent as good ones, and 12 percent noted that good decisions were infrequent at best.[3] In a turbulent environment, where fast, accurate decision making is at a premium, these surveys do not present encouraging information. Understanding how to improve the problem-solving and decision-making processes, we believe, helps top managers looking to improve results.

Most importantly, the stakes for decision making have proven to be high. In the same data cited by Bain in its 2008 survey of 760 companies across all industries with revenues over $1 billion, those firms that were most effective at decision making and execution generated average total shareholder returns almost six percentage points higher than those of other firms. They also found that the average organization they examined had the potential to "more than double its decision effectiveness." This kind of evidence is why we include decision making as one of our essential PM^{4}TE steps.

Decision Making Today

Despite the gloomy picture the data paint, not all organizations, obviously, make poor decisions. Many organizations routinely make effective decisions. In the same survey discussed above, McKinsey & Company also analyzed good decisions. They gathered responses from managers across all industries and regions in an effort to identify common features of good decisions and then asked respondents to identify a decision that the organization had made. They then asked respondents to identify the decision makers involved in the decision, as well as the analysis, the politics, and the goodness of outcomes. Some of the components of good decision making identified by McKinsey are:[4]

- Include people with the right skills and experience in the decision making.
- Make decisions based upon clear criteria and facts.
- Ensure the parties accountable for the decision are included in it.
- Build consensus and alliances across the organization to aid in implementation.

These findings may seem basic, but in our experience managers often fail to incorporate them into their basic decision activities.

A decision is defined simply as "the act of reaching a conclusion or making up one's mind." Consistent with the definition, managers tend to think of decisions in term of the efficacy of the conclusion. "Was the right decision made?" is the primary consideration when it comes to decisions. But in this step of our process, we are interested in the act of making the decision or the decision-making process. Simply reviewing the outcomes of decisions will do little to improve organizational performance if the underlying process to make those decisions is not considered as well.

At this point in our PM^{4}TE process, we have provided organizations with the fundamentals to help improve their decision-making activities—even before we present a basic process. If managers have been working in teams, as suggested in Chapter 4, then the right people with the right skills should be at the table when decision making occurs. If they are not, expand the team for purposes of making the decision. Better to have the right people than the right titles at the table.

The performance model, the vital projects, and the key measures identified to this point should provide both the criteria and data necessary to facilitate effective decisions related to critical objectives. The documentation of desired performance (e.g., critical performance objectives, measures, and targets) provides managers with standards against which actual performance can be judged.

If managers have been organized into project teams, as suggested in Chapter 4, and if there is executive accountability at the top, by design the managers responsible for executing the decision are included in the process itself. The age-old rule that people buy in to those activities in which they are involved holds as surely with decision making as it does in other areas. Alliances and consensus can be developed, provided that the team process exists to vet and make an effective decision. With this firm foundation in mind, the joint processes of problem solving and decision making can now be explored.

Problem-Solving Processes

As mentioned, one of the main challenges we encounter when we work with executive teams is the absence of a formal problem-solving process. Again, we believe that for many top teams it seems easier to just take action than work to analyze and resolve a problem.

We define a problem for our purposes as a *deviation from a standard of performance.* Thus, if critical objectives have been assigned measures and targets, and vital projects have milestones and deliverables as previously discussed in Chapters 3 through 5, we have created a set of standards by which we can gauge performance. When we see variances from our expected standards, we now have a problem that must be resolved for the desired performance levels to be achieved. While problems are rarely viewed positively in organizations, the process of understanding, analyzing, and correcting problems can yield significant value. Figure 6.2 shows a basic problem-solving process that any executive team can use.

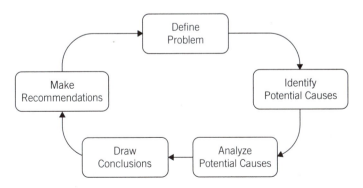

Figure 6.2   Basic Problem-Solving Process

The first and most important step in analyzing a problem is finding exactly what the deviation from a standard is. Managers need to be clear on what was expected to happen and what actually happened. Using market share as an example, if share growth was expected to be 5 percent and over the reporting period it was 3 percent, this creates the variance. At this point, the problem is actually quite simple and should be defined as narrowly as possible. In this case, there is 2 percent unfavorable deviation from what was expected. While it is tempting to try to identify solutions at this point, it is not useful to do so. Managers often jump at solving the problem, but, at this point, it is not clear what the causes are. It may be, for example, that the market has shrunk unexpectedly over the same reporting period. Hence a 3 percent growth is actually a good outcome, albeit not as good as the planned 5 percent growth.

Before moving to solutions, managers must think through what the potential causes of the variance are. Teams usually will brainstorm at this point and stop when they think they have come across the most likely cause. The problem is that biases strongly influence our selection of choices, so a better method must be used.

Similar to the performance modeling discussed in Chapter 3, we recommend using *issue trees* to identify the potential causes of problems. An example of an issue tree related to making strategy part of an organization's everyday routine is shown in Figure 6.3.

The issue tree helps to structure and think through the issues or causes associated with a problem similar to the way a performance model does. Instead of putting the primary objective(s) as the main outcome, the problem to be addressed is used. Issue trees are not new. Issue-based problem-solving techniques have been used for years by management consulting firms and investment analysts. Yet they are not routinely applied by management teams, despite their proven value.

Next, the likely causes from the issue tree are selected and analyzed. In this step, managers collect data in order to determine if the potential cause being analyzed is the actual cause. It is likely several of the potential causes listed in the issue tree will have to be analyzed. While this may appear to take considerable time, it is much more efficient than adding new project after new project with the hope (versus the knowledge) that the problem will be solved. Once all the likely causes have been analyzed, conclusions can be drawn as shown in the next step. The cause that addresses the most facts in the problem will likely be the root cause.

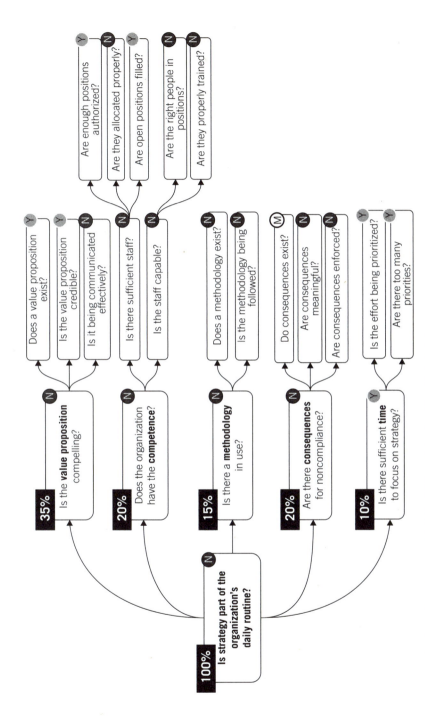

Figure 6.3   Issue Tree: Drivers behind the Failure to Make Strategy Part of Daily Operations

The final step in the process is making recommendations. The managers who worked on the analysis should aggregate their findings and make a recommendation to the top team regarding what the potential courses of action might be. This work feeds into the decision-making process we discuss next.

Decision-Making Process

Decision making can proceed in the absence of the underlying problem-solving process, but we would not recommend that. The analysis done during the problem-solving process forms the basis for better decision making. We encourage managers to keep in mind two of the findings from the survey data previously highlighted when preparing to make decisions:

1. Decisions today involve too much art and not enough science.
2. Make decisions based upon clear criteria and facts.

A decision-making process should be employed when addressing challenges associated with accomplishing critical performance objectives. A basic decision-making process is presented in Figure 6.4.

The first step in making a decision is to confirm the objective to be achieved. As mentioned, the critical performance objectives identified in Chapter 3 provide the context for the decisions we are discussing. Carrying our example through, the 2 percent shortfall in performance would likely be related to an objective such as "increase market share." The performance measure would be

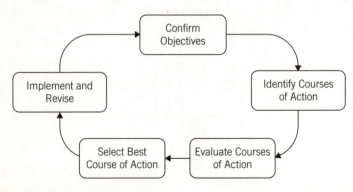

Figure 6.4   Basic Decision-Making Process

market share in percent and the targeted level was 5 percent. The variation to the standard was 2 percent.

If the problem-solving process was used prior to engaging the decision-making process, it is likely courses of action already exist. If not, the top team should generate courses of action that help it reach the critical performance objectives. Many organizations do not perform this step well (if they perform it at all). Often there is the development of a preferred course of action and the creation of a set of lesser, unrealistic courses of action. Generating real options helps challenge the status quo and force managers to think through a range of implications, not just the ones associated with the main course of action. After the courses of action are developed, they need to be evaluated. Criteria such as complexity, speed to impact, and cost, which are similar to those used when prioritizing vital projects, can be used here as well. While these criteria facilitate good choices, it is managers who ultimately need to choose the best option.

Once the best course of action is chosen, it must be implemented. This may require adjusting a vital project, realigning resources, or making some other adaptation needed to achieve the desired results. In the market share example, if the chosen course of action was to accelerate a product already under development, then that decision would be made by the top management team as part of the decision-making process.

We deliberately associate the decision-making process as well as the problem-solving process with structured reviews of critical performance objectives. But in general, the problem-solving and decision-making processes can be used at any time; they need not be limited to the PM^{4}TE process.

Decision Biases

Before moving to the specific steps to implementing improved decision-making activities, it is worth discussing *decision biases*. Everyone likes to believe he or she is a good decision maker, especially the members of top teams. But some biases that consistently creep into decision making can undermine even the best processes. These are presented in Table 6.1.

In addition to these common biases, there are two other unfavorable practices managers often engage in that hamper their ability to make good decisions. The first is *plunging in*. Managers often

Table 6.1   Common Decision Biases

Bias	Description
Availability bias	Placing too much importance on information or data that is recent or available
Anchoring bias	Limiting the scope or extent of the analysis based on the starting point
Commitment bias	Adherence to a previous decision despite knowledge of information contrary to the prior decision
Confirmation bias	The belief that the solution has been decided or is known before any data is collected or the analysis is completed
Hindsight bias	The belief that the occurrence of an event was caused by a previous action that in fact has little to do with the outcome
Overconfidence bias	The practice of being overly optimistic, often in the face of data to the contrary
Representative bias	The practice of assessing the likelihood of an event or outcome by drawing parallels to other events or outcomes that are unrelated

plunge into decisions, drawing parallels and offering solutions before an effort is made to properly define the problem. The second is *framing*. Decision information is sometimes presented or framed in a way that makes choices seem more favorable than they really are (by positioning the choices as positive) or by making them seem unfavorable (by positioning them as negative). What is important for managers is to realize that many biases exist and to establish a process that minimizes them.

Benefits of Making Decisions in the PM⁴TE Process

Managers make decisions every day. The decisions we are focusing on as part of the PM⁴TE process enable an organization's critical performance objectives and vital projects to deliver desired results. That makes these decisions especially important. Improving the processes to analyze and make these decisions will have immediate and significant payback for the organization. There are other important benefits as well, which are discussed next.

Building Critical Skills

As Peter Drucker's quote at the beginning of this chapter says, decision making is the specific executive task. Doing it well is an essential activity. The consequences of doing it badly can be significant. By focusing on problem-solving and decision-making process improvement, leaders build their most critical skills. That is important to keep in mind because both problem solving and decision making are skills. Skills can be developed. World-class athletes are masters of the fundamentals—they have highly developed basic skills upon which their game is played. The same is true of senior leaders. Their skills are problem solving, strategy making, execution, and decision making. Top management teams must build and master these fundamental skills if they are to be effective.

Improving Organizational Capabilities

While it is true that decision making is the specific executive task, everyone in an organization makes decisions. Managers at all levels address problems and take action daily. In turbulent environments, action is often decentralized. This means that leaders at all levels are responsible for making decisions independent of specific senior level guidance. Therefore, the organization needs to develop the capability to solve problems and execute effective decisions from top to bottom. High-quality thinking cannot solely be the domain of the top team. Organizations like Google and McKinsey have gone to great lengths to hire and cultivate employees with the best analytical skills. But make no mistake, they have well-developed processes to ensure employees think and act effectively. Any organization can improve these processes. Training people at all levels will improve the outcomes to the organization overall.

Improving Performance

The entire PM^{4}TE process focuses on improving performance. Improving project execution, measurement, and objective achievement are what we seek with this book. In the final analysis, improving each of these areas requires good decision making. All the guidance of the previous chapters will be of little value if the organization lacks the skills to make better decisions. Keep in mind the activity that resides between all of the aforementioned analyses and improved outcomes is decision making. We cover this topic because many organizations do not have effective decision processes. Furthermore, most performance management approaches do not address it at all.

Steps to Making Decisions

Following the two processes highlighted earlier will eventually improve decision effectiveness. That said, we know that skills to improve decision making and problem solving are not built overnight. In addition to following the processes highlighted, we recommend taking the next steps to improve decision making.

Identify Major Problems

The first step to improving decision making seems obvious, but in our experience it is anything but. Top management teams need to spend their time focusing on the major problems of the organization. These problems tend to be strategic in nature. In a study of strategic decision making, Bain & Company found that companies, on average, make 2.5 strategic decisions a year. For major organizations in turbulent environments with high stakes, this number would be relatively low.

Despite their agreement that they should focus on major decisions, managers routinely get caught up in the details of day-to-day challenges and lose sight of the big picture. Hours of meetings are held to review low-priority items like the status of the employee work-from-home policy or long-term leases while critical technology projects fall behind, profitability erodes, and product launches are delayed. It is the job of the top team to identify and take action on the most pressing problems facing the organization. The PM⁴TE process facilitates this focus.

Hold Ongoing Reviews of Vital Projects   Vital projects represent the most important initiatives in an organization. While leaders can and should review these projects regularly using the POA&M (discussed in Chapter 4), the project managers should be constantly reviewing progress. Executives accountable for these projects should be highly involved in these reviews so that problems can be addressed before they become intractable. While problems can emerge anywhere in the organization, the problems with the biggest impact are likely to be associated with vital projects.

Hold Frequent Reviews of Critical Objectives   Critical objectives reflect the critical performance areas of the organization. As such, these objectives should be monitored frequently—monthly, at the least—to ensure progress is being made. In the Bain study cited previously, organizations that continuously reviewed their strategy managed to make 6.1 decisions per year, almost a threefold increase over annual planners.[5]

If monthly reviews of these objectives are held, the meeting agenda should be developed around the critical objectives where performance is falling short. Developing this discipline—to maintain a focus on the most important objectives—ensures that the executives are focusing on the areas where major problems exist.

Analyze Selected Problems Completely

Isolating and focusing on major problems does not necessarily mean that they will be analyzed completely. Analyzing problems completely involves applying the entire problem-solving process to problems as thoroughly as possible. The problem needs to be defined, data needs to be gathered, and root causes must be identified. There is little benefit in identifying major problems if those problems are not analyzed as completely as possible.

Half solutions (or no solution) stemming from failures in analysis only cause problems to persist long after they should have been solved. As we discussed previously, this is a real challenge in organizations—allowing problems to continue due to a failure to apply effective problem-solving techniques. A commitment to analyzing problems as thoroughly as possible improves decision making.

Generate Realistic Options

Organizations often do a poor job of developing viable choices for major decisions, even after analysis has been completed. Often choices are biased toward one dominant point of view—with the analysis sometimes skewed in favor of that point of view—or the option that seems the most acceptable to the decision maker. This thinking does little to help top managers make better choices. It inhibits the quality of thought by limiting options to those that seem palatable.

Structured decision-making processes, such as those used by military commanders, generate different options for the very purpose of challenging preconceived notions about which option is the best. In this activity, subordinate commanders are put into teams and forced to develop different courses of action. Each of these actions can then be war-gamed to determine which is the most plausible. Private sector organizations can do the same thing by setting up groups of managers to analyze different options for major decisions under consideration. Not only does this co-opt more people into the process, as was recommended by the McKinsey study, it provides realistic assessments of a greater number of choices.

Drive Implementation of Selected Option

Once an option has been selected or a choice made, the focus needs to shift rapidly to implementation. Implementation can take many forms, but it is usually centered on changes in vital projects. The major project activities in organizations are top management teams' most powerful levers for change. Where leaders emphasize activity and where they allocate resources, results will be generated. The more focus and attention are given, the more rapidly results follow. In high velocity environments, leaders need to be sure they are pushing the organization to complete those actions that have the highest payoff potential.

To make implementation successful, top managers must identify specific actions, time frames, deliverables, and accountabilities. Successful implementation is not complex, but it should be comprehensive. It is good practice to have the implementation areas just mentioned captured, documented, and monitored at the top-team level. During each executive review of key performance objectives, a team member should be designated to track this information for purposes of monitoring implementation going forward. Accountability drives implementation.

Reevaluate Progress

Finally, leaders must be sure to periodically reevaluate progress on the problems solved and decisions made. Leaders must develop the discipline to ensure actions taken are not only fully implemented but achieve the desired results.

Periodic review meetings of vital projects and the critical objectives themselves provide the ideal forum to assess the effectiveness of the actions taken. Since many of the actions taken by leaders entail project modifications or become new projects themselves, it is appropriate to start any review related to the strategy with a review of previous actions. This not only ensures accountability is maintained, it provides for a continual reevaluation of previous decisions with an eye toward their ultimate effectiveness.

Critical Success Factors

Making decisions is the final step in the PM^{4}TE core. We have found—in concert with the research findings presented earlier—consistent factors that top managers should keep in mind as they make decisions in an organization. The factors—such as the use of problem-solving or decision processes presented earlier—will tip the scales of decision effectiveness in favor of top teams.

Commit to Improved Decision Making

It may sound peculiar that one of our critical success factors is encouraging leaders to commit to improving decision making. Simple logic would suggest that executives focus on making good decisions whenever they make them. We certainly believe they do. What we don't see very often are commitments to the *process* of decision making or problem solving. As pointed out by the Bain study, an opportunity exists for many organizations to improve their decision effectiveness by 200 percent. Further, this translates directly into financial results for private sector firms and mission results for public sector organizations. But what is required to capture those results is a willingness by top teams to commit to improving their decision processes.

Inject Contrarians into the Process

It was General George S. Patton who said, "If everyone is thinking the same way, then someone isn't thinking." Groupthink in organizations can be a real stumbling block to making effective decisions. One way to counter this challenge is to deliberately inject contrarian views into the decision-making process.

Seeking out, listening to, and handling contrarian views can be exceptionally frustrating for some managers. It takes time to understand and reflect upon challenges to conventional thinking. Moreover, it requires skill in managing these viewpoints in a way that encourages them, rather than punishing managers for providing them.

In our observations—and the data support this view—the value exceeds the cost. Contrarian views force refinements and clarifications in thinking. They also promote the open and honest dialog necessary to fully vet issues. Some of the best organizations—such as the United States Marine Corps—are adept at incorporating contrarian views into difficult decisions.

Don't Ignore Good Science

Many managers—Western managers in particular—pride themselves on their view that good decision making is an art form. Keen intuition and sound judgment—honed over years of executive experience—are prized possessions. Exacerbating this problem is popular business literature. Books from corporate chieftains such as *Straight from the Gut* by former General Electric CEO Jack Welch and *Doing What Matters* by former Gillette CEO James Kilts glamorize the wisdom of top-tier CEOs while downplaying the processes that make for effective top management teams. While we too like an entertaining CEO story, we also know the value of good thinking.

Good thinking is not dependent upon a smart or charismatic CEO. What it requires is a top team that is committed to using proven methods to run their organization. The techniques we present in this chapter can be used by any team—large or small—to improve performance in difficult times.

Summary

In this chapter we discussed making decisions the fourth and final step in the Core Process. Making effective decisions is the sine qua non of excellent top management teams. Results follow managers skilled at understanding and addressing the most pressing challenges facing their organization. But most managers were not born outstanding decision makers—they developed their skills over time. And virtually all managers can improve their decision making effectiveness if they commit themselves to learning how to make better decisions. By employing the problem-solving and decision-making processes we present in this chapter, managers can hone their own skills and those of their organizations. Most important, they can measurably improve the performance of their organizations, even in the most difficult environments.

Case Study: 1st Marine Logistics Group, United States Marine Corps

The 1st Marine Logistics Group (MLG)—part of the 1st Marine Expeditionary Force—provides direct logistics support to Marine ground combat forces operating within a single theater. They do this by establishing beach, landing zones, and other combat service support areas that maintain all types of supplies, which they send forward to equip and sustain the ground units they are supporting. The size and composition of the 1st MLG varies depending upon the nature and duration of the operation underway. In mid-2010, under the command of then-Brigadier General Charles "Chuck" Hudson, 1st MLG deployed over 4,000 men and women to Afghanistan's Helmand province in support of the 19,000 Marines in the region.

Turbulent Situation

Marine Corps Doctrinal Publication-1 (MCDP-1), titled "Warfighting," defines war as "a violent clash of interests between or among organized groups characterized by the use of military force." It continues noting, "Portrayed as a clash between two opposing wills, war appears a simple enterprise." However, for those in practice, it is anything but simple. One of the principle features of war is "friction," which is "the force that resists all action and saps energy. It makes the simple difficult and the difficult seemingly impossible." Friction is typically comprised of external actions taken by enemy forces, challenges posed by impassable terrain, or harsh weather conditions. But friction can also stem from internal sources. Again, from MCDP-1:

> Friction may be self-induced, caused by such factors as lack of a clearly defined goal, lack of coordination, unclear or complicated plans, complex task organizations or command relationships, or complicated technologies.

The war in Afghanistan consists of many of these features, making it one of the most friction-filled operations in United States history. The enemy is irregular in nature and dispersed across a wide and unforgiving geography. Their relationships and integration with the local populace make them particularly difficult to identify. They employ unconventional technologies such as improvised explosive devices, which have claimed the lives of combatants and noncombatants without discrimination. The war's duration—over a decade—has itself had significant impacts on the morale of soldiers, sailors, airmen, and Marines. In many respects, it is perhaps the most turbulent environment any organization could ever encounter.

Description of the Decision-Making Process

Given the speed at which situations on the ground change, the Marine Corps has developed an integrated planning and decision-making process that enables sound, structured decisions to be made under virtually any condition even those of great uncertainty. The process is shown in Figure 6.5.

Regardless of the nature of the situation, this same planning and decision-making process is employed. When time permits, more

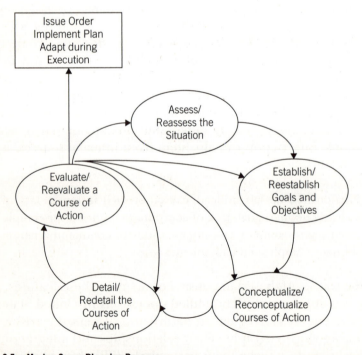

Figure 6.5   Marine Corps Planning Process

Source: Marine Corps Doctrinal Publication 5, *Planning.*

deliberate steps and evaluations are made. When time is constrained, the steps in the process are compressed and developed in rapid sequence.

On the night of May 16, 2010, the 1st MLG's main supply area, a huge supply warehousing facility housing approximately $72 million worth of repair parts, caught fire. As the uncontrolled blaze spread throughout the night, it consumed almost half the inventory on hand. Of immediate concern to leadership, in addition to the safety of personnel working in the facility, was the ability to rapidly reconstitute this capacity in order to maintain the materiel readiness of Marine forces. "In the span of a few short hours our operational capability was severely degraded, jeopardizing our ability to support all Marine units in the country," said General Hudson. "We needed to act to reconstitute our capability as fast as possible."

While firefighters were still fighting the blaze, Hudson determined the courses of action available to him to rebuild the supply base in a location 7,000 miles away from the United States industrial complex. His first action was to convene a working group—called an *operational planning team*—consisting of leaders, planners, and material managers under his command. These seasoned leaders had the joint responsibility of reconstituting the critical capability while avoiding a further decline in material support and equipment readiness. Somehow they had to rapidly source supplies and parts from a variety of organizations ranging from the Marine Corps Logistics Command in Albany, Georgia, and the Defense Logistics Agency in Alexandria, Virginia, to the closest Defense Depot in Kuwait, along with myriad suppliers in the United States.

As they began their work, the team realized they faced a series of integrated challenges, each of which would require linked decisions. First, the team had to avoid overloading the Defense Logistics Agency's supply chain management system, which is responsible for providing logistics support to all U.S. military agencies, not just the Marine Corps. To avoid this, only selected parts were identified by the top for priority requisition. Second, Hudson and his staff needed to ensure their shipments did not overburden the Defense Transportation System as his high-volume resupply requests would lead to the rerouting of aircraft from other missions in order to source replenishment stocks from the United States to Afghanistan. Again, a prioritization process was used to determine which parts would require the most immediate transport. Finally, the team had to weigh how to further decentralize their warehousing capability by moving more of it into major supply nodes throughout the battle space, placing it closer to forward units while protecting it from disruption by Taliban forces. To accomplish this, they examined the volume and mix of remaining parts as well as their criticality to the operating forces.

As the team considered the constraints posed above they entered into the planning and decision-making process. "For each of the challenges we identified, we needed to develop separate courses of actions which could then be evaluated in the context of the known constraints." Over the hours that followed the team created, analyzed, detailed, and revised a series of integrated actions that ultimately provided them with a comprehensive capability in a matter of a few short days.

Interpretations from Key Leaders

Previously in his career, Hudson served as an instructor at Marine Corps University teaching, of all things, rapid planning. His deep doctrinal knowledge was pushed to its limits as he and his staff worked around the clock to contain one of the most catastrophic incidents in his 30-year military career.

"The rapid planning process was specifically designed to help commanders orient to the facts and circumstances of the current situation and generate realistic courses of action that can be assessed and ultimately turned into an actionable decisions," noted Hudson. "As chaotic as the situation on the ground became, all of us—including the Marines and sailors at the supply center—were able to remain rooted in a process that we were confident would yield results—quickly."

Tangible Benefits and Outcomes

In the span of 48 hours, 1st MLG was able to initiate a $45 million replenishment replacing the losses of critical stocks. Over the next 96 hours, the supply center was fully reestablished and reconstituted to provide mission-critical supplies. Continuing into the execution phase, 1st MLG planners pressed forward and ultimately reestablished the full supply center within 60 days. The events that occurred over the few days in May were profiled in the *Marine Corps Gazette* to serve as a lesson learned for all future Marine commanders. Hudson himself returned after a successful tour and was promoted to Major General.

Lessons Learned

The quote from MCDP-1 presented earlier bears repeating with an eye toward its applicability in most commercial enterprises:

> Friction may be self-induced, caused by such factors as lack of a clearly defined goal, lack of coordination, unclear or complicated plans, complex task organizations or command relationships, or complicated technologies.

Based upon our observations, the tendency for managers to avoid structured planning and decision making in turbulent environments is high. A strong sense persists that plans and process are best relegated to slower environments, where the time and resources exist to cautiously work through detailed analysis and calculated decisions. As this example shows, structured thinking, problem solving, and decision making can be applied in any setting. We might argue that this kind of thinking is, perhaps, ideally suited for application in this situation. Every day executives work tirelessly to impose some semblance of structure to make chaos manageable. The tools, concepts, and examples, including those of the 1st Marine Logistics Group, presented in this chapter are effective in the most challenging situations.

Notes

1. M. Blenko, M. Mankins, and P. Rogers, "The Decision-Driven Organization," *Harvard Business Review* 88, no. 6 (2010): 52–62.
2. P. Kielstra, *In Search of Clarity: Unraveling the Complexities of Executive Decision Making* (London: Economist Intelligence Unit, 2007).
3. R. Dye, O. Sibony, and V. Truong, "Flaws in Strategic Decision Making: McKinsey Global Survey Results," *McKinsey Quarterly,* January 2009.
4. Ibid.
5. Blenko, Mankins, and Rogers, "The Decision-Driven Organization."

PART 3

PERFORMANCE MANAGEMENT FOR TURBULENT ENVIRONMENTS MODEL ENABLERS

CHAPTER

7

Strategic Intelligence

You cannot convert the absence of information into a conclusion.
— Tom Clancy, *The Sum of All Fears*

The first enabler supporting the core Performance Management for Turbulent Environments process is Strategic Intelligence. For an organization, up-to-date intelligence from the external environment is essential to making informed decisions within the Core Process model. In turbulent settings, the external environment changes rapidly and at times unpredictably. This makes the need for accurate and timely intelligence the most critical of all five enablers. In this chapter, we define and discuss the importance of strategic intelligence, as well as the activities that produce valuable, actionable intelligence and the critical success factors that provide strategic intelligence. Key actions to developing strategic intelligence in organizations are highlighted and supported by a case study of how intelligence gathering can be used in practice.

The quote that opens this chapter, from Tom Clancy's spy novel *The Sum of All Fears*, is spit out during a heated debate in which the president of the United States is trying to find out which country has nuclear weapons capabilities outside of the well-known global actors. Despite all of the discussion among the top security team regarding the matter, it is clear the lack of information is causing significant problems in reaching a conclusion. Applied to matters of national security, this illustration seems frightening. In a sense, it is no less alarming when applied to any individual organization operating under conditions of uncertainty. Top leaders have long understood the importance of current, creditable, and actionable intelligence in any competitive setting. Yet in business situations, many managers fail to adequately take the time to collect important environmental information, analyze it, and then structure it in a way that improves decision making. Given that strategic intelligence is so vital to an organization's success, we have included it in our model as one of the critical enablers.

Strategic Intelligence is the first part of the Model Enabler portion of the PM⁴TE process (see Figure 7.1). As an enabler, strategic intelligence plays a vital role in making the Core Process function. Setting the appropriate objectives, selecting high-leverage projects, making good decisions, and taking effective action are all predicated on having the right information at the time it is needed. From our experience, most managers feel frustrated that they don't have the necessary information, despite pervasive technology and systems that allow organizations to collect and deliver more data than ever before. This is where strategic intelligence gathering comes in. To be effective today and manage through downturns and upswings,

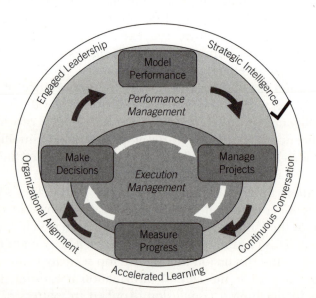

Figure 7.1   Model Enablers: Strategic Intelligence

organizations must take steps to shore up their strategic intelligence capabilities. By understanding what constitutes good intelligence and how it is gathered and analyzed, managers can turn a deficiency into a competitive advantage. Many of the tools are available already. Our observation is that few of them are used with any consistency or dexterity. Over the course of this chapter, we arm readers with the techniques and tools necessary to enhance intelligence gathering in turbulent environments. We provide more insight regarding how to share this information in Chapter 8, which covers the enabler Continuous Conversation.

Why Strategic Intelligence Is a Model Enabler

It is impossible to draw meaningful conclusions from no (or, worse, poor) information. Sadly, in our experience management teams do it all too often. The pressure associated with having to deliver consistent quarterly performance to the board of directors, the owners, or the analyst community often forces action instead of analysis. We hear comments from executives that lament the lack of time to collect good information, shortcomings in collection systems along with prohibitions in cost. We understand each of these limitations. What we do not understand is why leaders fail to make more of an effort to remove them. As highlighted in this book's title, effective performance management requires both analysis and insight. In the absence of either one, performance, let alone the management of it, will be compromised. So why is strategic intelligence such an important process enabler? There are a few simple reasons.

First, organizations—like living organisms—exist within an operating environment. That environment includes suppliers, partners, competitors, customers as well as regulators and investment institutions to name a few of the common ones. While few question the concept of food chains in the natural environment, many managers forget that the same concept applies to institutional environments. A strategic intelligence effort aimed at those most threatening features of the external environment contributes to the survival of the organization by detecting changes and actions that could be harmful.

Second, top management teams working in volatile settings must develop a rhythm to their internal functions. Teams are constantly being taxed to make decisions and take action quickly. When team members have a strong situational awareness of those factors affecting performance, they will be better able to make collective decisions. These decisions will be based on up-to-date, accurate information that requires less interpretation and discussion because it will already be known.

Finally, conditions are constantly changing and managers must work to maintain a continuous picture of performance factors that impact their organization. Knowing that the external environment is hostile is important, and having a commonly understood picture is essential, too. Updating that snapshot and turning it into more of a movie as conditions change is the most essential reason strategic intelligence is so vital to the performance management process. Rapid responses to changing conditions can literally make or break an organization's performance. Moreover, better performance accrues to those organizations that are better situated to take advantage of it. Intelligence improves that positioning.

The following example provides excellent insight into the value of strategic intelligence and, particularly in this case, competitive intelligence. The excerpt is from the article "The Power of Competitive Intelligence" by David Stauffer:

> A few years ago, in an intelligence coup that rivals any engineered by James Bond, pharmaceutical giant Merck & Company found clues to the product positioning and marketing strategy that a rival firm was likely to employ when it rolled out a potential major new drug. Merck countered the competitor's anticipated effort by repositioning one of its existing drugs to occupy the competitive space where the rival's drug was likely to be aimed. Merck's intelligence proved spot on. By repositioning the drug, Merck grabbed new market share and forced the competitor back to the drawing board, delaying the competitor's drug launch by well over a year. Merck figures the cumulative incremental sales value of this single intelligence windfall at more than $300 million.[1]

While this might seem illegal at first glance, rest assured it is not. Per the author, all information obtained in the above analysis was gleaned from open medical meetings and publicly available clinical trial data. While not every intelligence-gathering effort yields a payoff as high as Merck's, the stakes are nonetheless significant for most organizations. As such, the balance of the chapter provides some techniques and tools that managers can use to improve the quality of their strategic intelligence gathering and analysis.

Understanding Strategic Intelligence

Gathering data for purposes of informing organizational decision and action is by no means new. Ancient military strategist Sun Tzu noted the importance of intelligence gathering ages ago when he said, "If you do not know others and know yourself you will be in danger in every single battle." Clearly intelligence gathering has been ongoing for thousands of years. First taking place within military organizations, intelligence gathering has become a fixture in any organization where dynamic interaction with the external environment occurs.

Basic Concepts and Definition

Intelligence gathering and interpretation occur at virtually every organizational level. Tactical intelligence is information that pertains to ongoing activities and interactions with the organization and its environment. Observing policy makers and their discussions regarding pending legislation is an example of one type of tactical intelligence gathering. Monitoring the launch of a major competitor's new product is another example of tactical intelligence. Operational intelligence integrates and synthesizes varied tactical inputs for purposes of assessing the impact on current organizational operations. The combination of a competitor's multiple product launches along with changes in product regulation may necessitate a change in operating policy. Strategic intelligence takes operational and tactical information and uses it to help determine what the impact is on the organizations overall strategy and directions. Should the organization be moving out of a particular market and into another one? These are questions that are addressed via strategic intelligence.

In his book *Managing Strategic Intelligence*, Mark Xu and his contributing colleagues Don Marchand and Amy Hykes define strategic intelligence as follows:

> Strategic intelligence should provide a company with the information it needs about its business environment to be able to

anticipate change, design appropriate strategies that will create business value for customers and create future growth and profits for the company in new markets within or across industries.[2]

They continue to note that for a strategic intelligence process to be effective, it must become part of the company's culture. They also see valuable strategic intelligence as the by-product of an effective strategic intelligence process that consists of six steps: sensing, collecting, organizing, processing, communicating, and using intelligence information.[3] Our aim in this chapter is not to highlight how to implement a process like the one described but rather to highlight some basic frameworks almost every organization would benefit from if they implemented in a more thoughtful and rigorous way.

Strategic Intelligence Background

While intelligence gathering can be traced back thousands of years, much of what occurs in today's organizations can be linked to Francis Aguilar's seminal 1967 book, *Scanning the Business Environment*. Aguilar discusses environmental scanning activities and presents them in two overarching forms: viewing and searching.[4] *Viewing* is the simple reading of information through various published sources regarding what is occurring in the larger environment. *Searching* is deliberately looking for information pertaining to the organization. Through these activities, managers gain a good understanding of what is happening in their environments.

Over time, his approach was simplified by other researchers into what might be considered active and passive scanning. Active represents deliberate searching for specific intelligence and passive scanning existing as a general viewing of the broader environment. Today, with the high volume of information readily available on the Internet coupled with precise search technology, the challenge is less about information availability and more about information interpretation. That said, there are basic tools that organizations can and should use to improve their understanding of strategic intelligence. We discuss the most useful in the following sections.

Basic Strategic Intelligence Tools in Use Today

As mentioned at the outset of the chapter, organizations exist in dynamic and often hostile operating environments. To cope with these environments, managers employ tools that help them organize and analyze information to assess what is occurring as well as inform decisions. The two most commonly used and effective tools in practice today are the PESTEL analysis and the Five Forces Analysis. Each tool addresses one of the two major levels of the organizational environment—the macro level and the micro level.

The Macroenvironment: PESTEL Analysis All organizations, regardless of industry, are impacted by a host of what can be called *macroenvironmental factors*. Aguilar identifies four types: political, economic, social, and technological. Subsequent to his identification of the original four factors, two other factors—environmental and legal— were added by various scholars Today, the factors and the analysis itself are better known by the acronym PESTEL. Each element of the PESTEL analysis is highlighted in Table 7.1.

The PESTEL analysis enables managers to collect, synthesize and publish information pertaining to each macroenvironmental factor affecting their organization. Not all factors affect organizations equally; depending on the industry and organization, some factors have more of an effect than others. In digital photography, for example, technology would be essential, as devices such as mobile phones and pads incorporate camera technology into their features. Equally important may be social factors, as the frequency of camera use increases among consumers and camera technology is included in multiple device platforms.

Table 7.1   PESTEL Factors

Factor	Description
Political	What are the regulatory issues and forms of legislation that could affect the organization?
Economic	What major trends in the economy, such as oil prices, interest rates, reduction in income, or real spending, exist?
Social	What are major changes in tastes, preferences, and behaviors?
Technological	What significant developments on the technology frontier could impact the organization?
Environmental	What environmental concerns face the business?
Legal	What are the prevailing legal conditions and how might they affect business dealings?

The PESTEL analysis can appear laborious and slow moving. It does not have to be, however. Managers can and should assign different factors to different parts of their top teams and require that a current view of the environment be maintained. That way, scanning and searching for up-to-date information is constant and the insights are fresh. The PESTEL can also be used predictively; each factor can be forecasted ahead 3, 5, even 10 years to stimulate leaders' thinking regarding how the environment may change. Using this technique, managers can assess what their current response might be to anticipated changes in each factor.

The Microenvironment: Five Forces Model   In addition to existing within the macroenvironment, organizations jockey for advantage in the *microenvironment*. The microenvironment includes factors or forces such as suppliers, customers, and competitors.

In 1979, Harvard Business School researcher and now professor Michael Porter identified five factors or forces that drive performance within the microenvironment. These forces are bargaining power of customers, bargaining power of suppliers, threat of new entrants, availability of substitute goods and services as well as intensity of rivalry.[5] The Five Forces Model is highlighted in Figure 7.2.

Since the model's original development, a sixth influencer—*complements*—has been added. Complements help managers gauge the impact that related complementary products and services have on the industry being examined.

The power of Porter's model is its ability to determine the impact of each force on industry profitability. In environments where each of the five forces is unfavorable—such as commercial airline travel—industry profitability tends to be low, if not entirely negative. In environments where each of the five forces is favorable, industry profitability is often high, as is the case with soft drinks.

Like the PESTEL analysis, the Five Forces Analysis can seem challenging to create and not particularly dynamic. In our experience, this is untrue. The Five Forces model has proven time and again its value in helping managers understand the drivers of industry performance. It can be used like the PESTEL to help forecast what changes might occur in an environment, predict which might be the most favorable or unfavorable, and help the organization determine how best to respond.

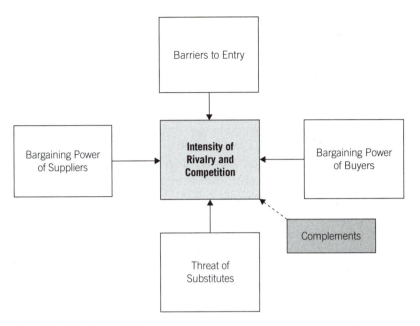

Figure 7.2 Five Forces Model

Source: Adapted from M. Porter, "The Five Competitive Forces That Shape Strategy," *Harvard Business Review* 86, no. 1 (2008): 79–93.

Both the PESTEL and Five Forces analysis are proven tools to help gather and interpret strategic intelligence—especially on a larger scale. In the next section, we discuss two more recent and focused tools.

Tools Specific to the Performance Management for Turbulence Process

Because of the economic and financial turmoil that rocked global markets and contributed to many of the largest bankruptcies in history, risk management has rushed to the forefront of the performance management process. The concept of managing key risks facing an organization is by no means new. What is new, however, is the increased emphasis on risk and the inculcation of risk management processes and activities into business processes. This is an aspect of the PM^{4}TE process as well.

Risk management can be defined as the process of identifying, assessing, and prioritizing major uncertainties facing an organization for purposes of mitigating and managing their potential impact. Part of that process—after risks have been identified—is ongoing monitoring of their status. Risks change over time, becoming more or less threatening either on their own or as a function of organization's efforts to mitigate them. Regardless, they must be monitored in an ongoing way if they are to be managed. In this sense, risk management is much like intelligence gathering. Top teams need to spend time not only identifying and assessing major strategic risks facing their organization, they must continue to collect and synthesize data necessary to understand how they are changing over time.

Strategic Issue Template   One way to do this is through the use of a strategic issue template. A strategic issue template is a simple but effective tool leaders can use to profile strategic issues—whether risks or otherwise—and then monitor their status over time.[6] An example of a Strategic Issue Template is shown in Figure 7.3.

The template provides the structure to organize information and evaluate the potential impact while simultaneously considering possible responses. Using this approach, managers can think proactively about the issues confronting their organizations and take steps to counter them before they deteriorate into an uncontrollable status. The example in Figure 7.3 shows an issue template that could have been used by an organization in the traditional music business at a time just prior to the full-scale invasion of digitized music. This organization ultimately failed (see the case in Chapter 1). The question remains, however, would they have taken different steps to counter the threat if they had more carefully monitored strategic intelligence? Given that the shift to digital music had actually begun almost 10 years earlier, maybe so.

Performance Modeling for Intelligence Purposes   One of the most significant benefits of the first phase in the Core Process model—Model Performance—is that it discloses an organization's critical performance objectives within an organizational system of performance. Using a model like the ones described in Chapter 3 helps organizations better understand what the key drivers are that cause their performance to improve. Every organization can be thought of in terms of a system of performance. What follows logically is that organizations can be analyzed using the same models we describe in Chapter 3.

Strategic Issue Name: Shift to Digitized Music	Date: 1/31/05
Current and Future Situation	
Critical Data/Information: The *New York Times* and the *Wall Street Journal* have begun publishing data from behavioral scientists that describes the shift to portable digital media. Web sites are emerging that provide file sharing and downloading. A recent trade show showcased new technologies aimed at accelerating the shift to digitized music.	Information Sources: *New York Times,* *Wall Street Journal,* Nielsen
Trends and Extrapolations: The expectation of decline in the music segment of our business could extend from low single-digit to significant double-digit decreases.	Related Objectives and Initiatives: Impact the ability to "grow revenue and improve profitability."
Impact and Response	
Potential Impact: The advent of MP3 players and alternative delivery means have provided a viable alternative to physical distribution of music. It is possible that a rapid decline in music distribution will occur over the coming years that will unfavorably impact our business and, if severe enough, could force us into bankruptcy.	Time to Impact: Starting now . . . will accelerate into 2006 and 2007.
Possible Responses: There are three responses identified at this time: 1) Continue to manage business as is. 2) Begin the development of a digital distribution organization. 3) Identify a partner to help establish relationships with emerging developers/distributors.	Chosen Response: Continue to manage the business as is.

Figure 7.3   Strategic Issues Template

Source: Adapted from E. Barrows, "Four Steps for Integrating Strategic Risk Management into Your Strategy Review Process," *Balanced Scorecard Report* 13, no. 2 (2011).

One tool that helps is a performance model analysis table. An example of one that uses the Strategy Map can be seen in Figure 7.4.[7]

This intelligence tool depicts three competitors in the low-cost segment of the commercial airline industry: AirTran, JetBlue, and Southwest. Key elements of performance, along with associated organizational objectives, are isolated and analyzed in a cross-tabular format. What this comparison enables managers to do is compare and contrast critical performance dimensions across organizations using the structure of a well-known performance model, the Strategy Map. However, the same can be done using a Success Map or a financial driver model. The power is in the practice of gathering strategic intelligence, organizing it in a comprehensible (and

	AirTran	JetBlue	Southwest
FINANCIAL PERSPECTIVE			
Return on total capital	4%	3%	5.5%
Net profit margin	1%	0.8%	4.6%
Operating margin	4.5%	11%	13%
Revenue/revenue growth	$2.3 billion/22%	$2.8 billion/20%	$9.8 billion/99%
CUSTOMER PERSPECTIVE			
Value proposition	Operational excellence/customer intimacy	Customer intimacy/innovation	Operational excellence
Segments/share	Price-sensitive business and leisure travelers (2% market share)	Value-oriented leisure and business travelers (3% market share)	No-frills business and leisure travelers (10% market share)
Service	700 flights daily to 56 destinations	550 flights daily to 53 destinations	> 3,300 flights daily to 64 destinations
Geography	Serves mostly eastern U.S. to capture dense market	Serves 21 states and Caribbean to capture largest market	Serves 32 states; largest airline by passenger
Load factor	76%	80%	72%
INTERNAL PROCESS PERSPECTIVE			
After-sales service	Rewards programs for business and student travelers	Rewards programs for business and student travelers; AMEX partnership	Rapid Rewards programs based on number of trips; VISA partnership
Marketing and sales	One-way fares, simple fee structure, walk-up rates, in-house media and PR	One-way fares, pre-assigned seats, no overbookings policy, vacation packages	One-way fares, simple fees, no assigned seating, partner credit plan

Passenger service	Affordable business class, advance seating, XM Radio	Jet Blue "Experience," DirecTV, PPV movies, XM Radio, branded snacks	Folksy customer service, limited snacks and drinks, new Business Select service
Flight operations	Hub and route service from Atlanta, baggage agreements with other air carriers (e.g., United, USAir, B.A)	Point-to-point routes from flagship (New York) or focus cities: Boston, Ft. Lauderdale, Long Beach, WDC	Point-to-point routes; short-haul, high-frequency flights serve secondary airports; fast turnarounds
Fleet planning/ procurement	Two types of aircraft (Boeing 717 and 737), 4 years old, separate business class	Two types of aircraft (Airbus 320 and Embraer 190), 3 years old, one class	One type of aircraft (Boeing 737), one class, high skill in fuel contract hedging
Infrastructure	Has own internal call center	Owns Live TV to offer in flight TV	Started "gate makeover" program
LEARNING & GROWTH PERSPECTIVE			
Human resources	8,100 FT employees, 400+ PT employees; high productivity	8,785 FT employees, 2,487 PT employees; flexible work	34,378 FT employees; 82% unionized; offers early retirement to eligible employees
Technology	Highly functional, sophisticated e-commerce platform	All electronic ticketing, most bookings through website	Limited technology investments— mostly to support key initiatives

Figure 7.4 Strategy Map Analysis Table

Source: E. Barrows and M. Frigo, "Using the Strategy Map for Competitive Analysis," *Balanced Scorecard Report* 10, no. 4 (2008).

comparative) format, and then drawing conclusions upon which managers can take action.

Strategic Intelligence and Technology

Thanks to technology, gathering strategic intelligence is much easier today than it was when the practice was originally started. More information is available on the Internet than ever before and that volume of information is growing daily. The challenge today is not so much information availability, it is getting the right, filtered information in a timely manner to facilitate analysis and interpretation. We have found a few simple sources of information that can greatly enhance the effectiveness of the intelligence gathering process.

E-mail Alerts   A very simple way to improve strategic intelligence using technology is through use of e-mail alerts. Organizations such as Google provide ongoing scanning for almost any topic or content area conceivable. When information pertaining to the topic area is published on the Web, an e-mail is sent to the person or organization requesting the alert. Google and other search engines are capable of scanning traditional news sources, blogs, video posts, even discussion groups for information pertaining to specified strategic information areas. This raw information is made readily available for anyone interested in almost any topic.

RSS Feeds   Really Simple Syndication (RSS) is a Web-feed format used to publish frequently updated information such as news, blogs, audio, and video using a standard format. Organizations that publish news and information use RSS to feed or send information to anyone who subscribes to the RSS feed. Users are given centralized information on a topic of interest across a variety of sources. Similar to alerts, RSS feeds populate information the user is looking for. Unlike an alert provided by a search engine such as Google, RSS feeds are set up by the user on a source-by-source basis. Still, they are an effective way to have information from preselected sources delivered to the user.

Blogs and Social Media   As well as relying on formal news releases, it is now possible to gather useful intelligence via social media.

Employees in organizations publish blogs, often writing about the organization's plans and activities. Customers and commentators provide updates via social media sites. Of these, LinkedIn and Twitter are useful sources of information, while TripAdvisor can be a valuable source of data for consumer insights. Scanning and searching these multiple sources of information add further information to the rich tapestry created from gathering strategic intelligence.

Text Analysis and Mining Tools   With all this information readily available, it can be time consuming to review and more difficult to interpret. Fortunately, there are software tools that facilitate both review and analysis of text. *Text analysis* and *text mining* are terms given to the process of reviewing and analyzing text for the purpose of extracting useful information. The users of this software can not only specify search terms but facilitate the development of search patterns and trends through techniques like statistical pattern learning. Information culled from published sources can be stored and analyzed in a variety of ways, improving the insights captured from the data. The applications are numerous and sophisticated and can contribute to an in-depth understanding of data from a wide variety of sources.

Critical Success Factors

Gathering and using strategic intelligence is an important enabler of the core PM^{4}TE process. But to make strategic intelligence gathering a useful practice, most organizations need to not only change their process, but reorient their entire philosophy and approach. As such, we have identified three critical success factors essential to extracting value from strategic intelligence.

Recognize the Value of Strategic Intelligence

Presented with the question of whether strategic intelligence provides value to organizations, few senior managers would respond negatively. Yet many do not seem to understand its full value. Beyond simply capturing competitor information, strategic intelligence helps managers understand how their environments are changing at the macro level, how their industry and its economics are transforming within the micro space, and the extent to which critical risks are intensifying. In turbulent environments, change is rapid and far reaching. Yet leaders often fail to prioritize strategic intelligence gathering, analysis, interpretation, and usage. This must change if managers are to ensure the success of their enterprises for today and the future.

Build the Strategic Intelligence Capability

Once the value of strategic intelligence is fully acknowledged, top teams must make building the capability to gather and use it a priority. Keep in mind that the effectiveness of the core PM^{4}TE process depends on the effectiveness of the organization in collecting and interpreting intelligence. Therefore, strategic intelligence over the long term must become an organizational capability. Necessary individual skills must be identified and developed, a process must be put in place as was highlighted at the outset of this chapter, and technology supporting the process must be adopted. As organizations find themselves increasingly buffeted by forces beyond their control, they must have in place established mechanisms to better gauge changes in their environments in real time.

Make It Part of Management Practice

Recognizing that strategic intelligence is important and having in place the capability to gather and analyze it delivers limited value if using it does not become part of how leaders manage the organization. Information flowing out of the analysis process must be communicated to managers and discussed to ensure its meaning is appropriately understood. Intelligence information must be used *prospectively*, too, meaning it must be used to forecast and hypothesize about conditions and situations that may affect the organization at some point in the future. This is where the bona fide insights reside—in the heightened understanding of the future that may impact the organization beyond the obvious challenges of the current state.

Summary

In this chapter, we discussed strategic intelligence and its role as an enabler of performance management in turbulence. Organizations must work to survive in a setting that is constantly changing. To respond quickly and with the right set and sequence of actions, managers must be able to sense and interpret what is happening. This requires the gathering, analysis, interpretation, and use of intelligence from the external environment. To do this, managers must not only collect data, but also organize it in a way that enhances their understanding. Tools like the PESTEL and Five Forces analysis have proven their effectiveness in this regard. Further, tools like the strategic issues template and performance model analysis tables can be applied with excellent effect. Most importantly however mangers must see value in strategic intelligence and build the capability within their organizations to use this specific type of environmental information to their benefit.

Case Study: Federal Bureau of Investigation

Founded in 1908, the Federal Bureau of Investigation (FBI) has historically been known as one of the world's premiere crime-fighting organizations. In 2011, the FBI—a United States Department of Justice agency—operated with a budget of just under $10 billion and a workforce of approximately 35,000 employees from its Washington, DC headquarters. A long-time subject of movie and television legend, the FBI has earned the image of a hard-nosed, no-nonsense organization committed to protecting the interests of the United States and the civil rights of its citizens.

Turbulent Situation

On the morning of September 11, 2001, the FBI's reputation was dealt a punishing blow when 19 terrorists slipped through security, hijacked four commercial airliners, and successfully carried out attacks on the World Trade Center in New York City and the Pentagon in Washington, DC. Another attack was foiled when passengers charged the terrorists flying the final plane, heading toward Washington, DC, leading to its crash in a Pennsylvania field. All told, just under 3,000 people lost their lives in a terrorist attack that shocked not only the United States but the entire world. As the events of that day and those that followed unfolded, the entire intelligence community's weaknesses were exposed, the FBI's in particular. As pointed out in the findings of the 9/11 Commission chartered expressly to examine the breakdown:

> The most serious weaknesses in agency capabilities were in the domestic arena. The FBI did not have the capability to link the collective knowledge of agents in the field to national priorities. Other domestic agencies deferred to the FBI.[8]

This conclusion, alongside a host of other findings, began a multiyear transformation effort at the FBI that made counterterrorism the number one priority for the agency.

Description of the Strategic Intelligence Process

With the dramatic shift in the threat facing the United States, the FBI quickly identified the need for an enhanced intelligence capability with improved analytical and information-sharing capacities to detect and prevent future terrorist attacks. Over the course of the next several years, the FBI began to develop an intelligence process aimed at improving its ability to detect the presence and intentions of terrorists who planned to conduct attacks in the United States.

According to unpublished FBI documents, the core intelligence functions are fourfold:

1. Collect raw intelligence.
2. Exploit and disseminate that intelligence both internally and to intelligence and law enforcement partners.
3. Analyze the intelligence.
4. Act on that intelligence, either to disrupt or dismantle a plot or network or to develop additional collection requirements.

These functions would serve as the basic foundation for the revamped intelligence process.

To be fair, the FBI has a long history of collecting intelligence for the purpose of detecting terrorist and other national security threats. But the main purpose of the intelligence historically was to drive arrests and prosecutions, not to share with the broader intelligence community domestically or abroad for purposes of detecting terrorist threats. The new approach—spearheaded by FBI Director Robert Mueller himself—would be to place intelligence at the center of the FBI's activities. The director chartered what became known as the Strategy Execution Team, a mixture of internal FBI personnel and outside advisors who over the course of two years developed a field intelligence process and aligned the organization top to bottom based upon four main activities depicted at the center of the strategy map in Figure 7.5.

Over time, the process was refined with input from Special Agents and Intelligence Analysis bolstered with documentation and technology. It was then rolled out to all 56 field offices within the United States using what are called Field Intelligence Groups. Intelligence teams were also embedded within other agencies to interface with the FBI's core process so that information would be broadly shared and understood. One of the key outputs of the intelligence process are Intelligence Information Reports or IIRs. IIRs are written assessments of raw intelligence data that help provide one piece of the larger picture of intelligence information gathered by a particular office. These reports are circulated throughout the bureau and provide the input necessary for regular analysis meetings held at the highest levels of the bureau. This level of focus ensures that leaders—including the director—maintain a full picture of terrorist, counterintelligence, cyber and criminal activities occurring throughout the United States.

Interpretations from Key Managers

The process of augmenting crime fighting with intelligence gathering was challenging at times for the FBI. Most of the workforce was steeped in the traditional case management process which was targeted toward individual criminal cases. Sharing information historically could compromise development of such work. But in the new environment, the organization had to change. "The way we were operating wasn't congruent with the requirements of the changed environment" noted Tom Harrington, associate deputy director, and 27-year veteran of the bureau. "Information has to be shared as broadly as possible and interpreted quickly if we are to maintain a lead on potential terrorist activities." Harrington personally spearheaded major elements of the transformation.

The change in the intelligence process, as well as other related management processes, has begun to transform the FBI to a more focused, more productive organization. The FBI is investing more of its energy and focus in technology and employees skilled at using it. MBAs are routinely hired and moved into key business advisory positions within the bureau, a practice that would have

FBI Strategy Map

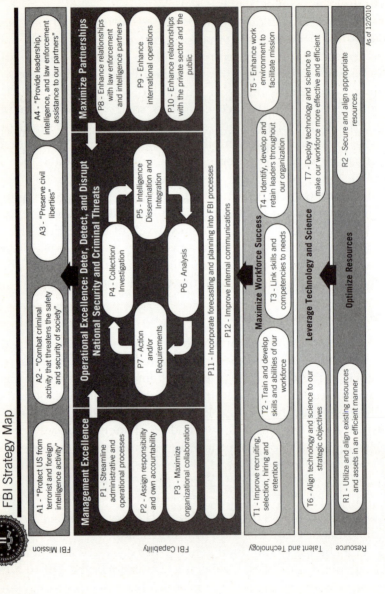

FBI Mission

A1 - "Protect US from terrorist and foreign intelligence activity"

A2 - "Combat criminal activity that threatens the safety and security of society"

A3 - "Preserve civil liberties"

A4 - "Provide leadership, intelligence, and law enforcement assistance to our partners"

FBI Capability

Management Excellence

P1 - Streamline administrative and operational processes

P2 - Assign responsibility and own accountability

P3 - Maximize organizational collaboration

Operational Excellence: Deter, Detect, and Disrupt National Security and Criminal Threats

P4 - Collection/Investigation

P5 - Intelligence Dissemination and Integration

P6 - Analysis

P7 - Action and/or Requirements

Maximize Partnerships

P8 - Enhance relationships with law enforcement and intelligence partners

P9 - Enhance international operations

P10 - Enhance relationships with the private sector and the public

P11 - Incorporate forecasting and planning into FBI processes

P12 - Improve internal communications

Talent and Technology

Maximize Workforce Success

T1 - Improve recruiting, selection, hiring and retention

T2 - Train and develop skills and abilities of our workforce

T3 - Link skills and competencies to needs

T4 - Identify, develop and retain leaders throughout our organization

T5 - Enhance work environment to facilitate mission

Leverage Technology and Science

T6 - Align technology and science to our strategic objectives

T7 - Deploy technology and science to make our workforce more effective and efficient

Resource

Optimize Resources

R1 - Utilize and align existing resources and assets in an efficient manner

R2 - Secure and align appropriate resources

As of 12/2010

Figure 7.5   FBI Strategy Map

Source: Federal Bureau of Investigation, www.fbi.gov.

been unheard of just 10 years ago. As Dave Schlendorf, assistant director for resource planning, notes, "We need to be competing with organizations like Google and GE for the best talent available." According to FBI managers, the transformation is well underway but has not yet run its full course.

Tangible Benefits and Outcomes

Since September 11, 2001, the FBI has made major changes in how it operates. The bureau has more than doubled the number of agents and analysts assigned to its national security mission. Furthermore, the FBI has an active intelligence-gathering network of personnel spread around the globe not only within its 56 field offices, but also in hundreds of resident agencies domestically and scores of international legal attaché offices. Production of intelligence reports has increased fivefold since 2004. Beyond an increase in raw intelligence reporting, the FBI has deepened a capability which enables it to develop finished analysis and a more comprehensive strategic intelligence picture of various threats. Director Mueller was recently granted an unprecedented 2-year extension beyond his 10-year maximum term, showing the high level of confidence placed in his counsel by the president. Most importantly, there has not been a major terrorist attack on U.S. soil since 9/11. This is quite obviously the most significant achievement of the intelligence process transformation.

Lessons Learned

Today, the mission of the Federal Bureau of Investigation has been expanded well beyond its crime-fighting origins:

> To protect and defend the United States against terrorist and foreign intelligence threats, to uphold and enforce the criminal laws of the United States, and to provide leadership and criminal justice services to federal, state, municipal, and international agencies and partners.

The critical enabler of this mission is the intelligence process, which is now central to how the organization operates. Most organizations, even those in turbulent settings, do not face challenges of the magnitude the FBI has dealt with. Still, there is significant value for any organization to make strategic intelligence a key element of their performance management system. The FBI provides an excellent example of the importance and benefits of doing so.

Notes

1. D. Stauffer, "The Power of Competitive Intelligence," *Harvard Business Review* (Oct. 2003).
2. M. Xu, *Managing Strategic Intelligence: Techniques and Technologies* (Hershey, PA: Information Science Reference, 2007).
3. D. Marchand and A. Hykes, "Leveraging What Your Company Really Knows: A Process View of Strategic Intelligence" in *Managing Strategic Intelligence: Techniques and Tools,* by M. Xu, (Hershey, PA: Information Science Reference, 2007).
4. F. Aguilar, *Scanning the Business Environment* (New York: Macmillan, 1967).
5. M. Porter, "The Five Competitive Forces That Shape Strategy," *Harvard Business Review* 86, no. 1 (2008): 78.
6. E. Barrows, "Four Steps for Integrating Strategic Risk Management into Your Strategy Review Process," *Balanced Scorecard Report* 13, no. 2 (2011).
7. E. Barrows and M. Frigo, "Using the Strategy Map for Competitive Analysis," *Balanced Scorecard Report* 10, no. 4 (2008).
8. T. Kean, R. Ben-Veniste, F. Fielding, J. Gorelick, S. Gorton, L. Hamilton, B. Kerrey, J. Lehman, T. Roemer, and J. Thompson. *The 9/11 Commission Report: Final Report of the National Commission on the Terrorist Attacks upon the United States* (Washington, DC: Government Printing Office, 2004).

C H A P T E R

Continuous Conversation

You only have a conversation when you don't know the outcome at the beginning.

—Hans-Georg Gadamer

The second enabler supporting the core Performance Management for Turbulent Environments process is Continuous Conversation. For organizations operating in chaotic and unpredictable environments, conditions are prone to rapid changes that begin in almost imperceptible ways. To ensure that they maintain an awareness and understanding of external changes and their potential impact on their organizations, leaders must engage in far-reaching, ongoing dialog. Continuous conversation is the means by which top managers convert strategic intelligence into awareness, collective understanding and ultimately unified action. In this chapter, we discuss the value of continuous conversation in organizations—among top management teams in particular—and describe how it promotes shared situational awareness and action. Immediate actions to improve internal communication and dialog are shown by a case study that presents ways in which continuous conversation can be enhanced in practice.

Truman Capote, the author of such classics as *Breakfast at Tiffany's* and *In Cold Blood,* said that "conversation is a dialog, not a monolog." Certainly Capote, described by Normal Mailer as "the most perfect writer of my generation," should know a few things about conversation. Yet conversation in most organizations is something that occurs outside of meetings, when managers believe information of little of value is being discussed. Standard thinking among many top teams is that effective dialog—especially during meetings—consists of leaders telling subordinates what needs to be done. In slow-moving settings, this might work, but in the high-velocity world of technology for example, where a premium is placed upon interpreting information, this is not true. Informal networks where conversations take place are active and effective mechanisms for sharing information, testing concepts, gaining understanding and generating alignment. We believe that water cooler chats and the like are important means of communication for organizations in turbulent settings. In this chapter, we explore how top leaders can set the stage for effective information communication through continuous conversation, in their organizations.

Continuous conversation, shown at the bottom right of Figure 8.1, is another essential element of the PM^{4}TE process. Continuous conversation is the primary means by which information—via the functioning of the core model or intelligence from outside the organization—is interpreted by senior leaders and ultimately translated into organizational

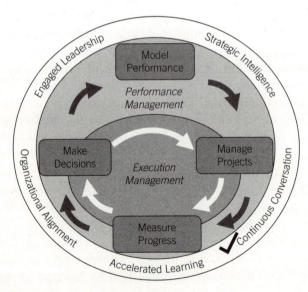

Figure 8.1   Model Enablers: Continuous Conversation

action. Unfortunately, managers in organizations are often poor at communicating with one another. There are typically a variety of inhibitors, such as a culture that promotes withholding information or an organizational structure that discourages dialog across functional boundaries. Organizations should open the door to a stream of ongoing conversations at all levels so that information is shared openly, broadly, and in an agenda-free context. Without this, the ability to know what is going on both inside and outside the organization will be limited, which will ultimately impact the effectiveness of performance management. The balance of this chapter gives readers information and techniques to enhance communication effectiveness in virtually every setting—turbulent ones in particular. We provide additional thoughts about how continuous conversation promotes learning in Chapter 9, "Accelerated Learning."

Why Continuous Conversation Is a Model Enabler

Communication in organizations is a well-studied area of management. What surveys and analyses of communication in all its forms reveal is that employees are generally not satisfied with interorganizational communication. Their satisfaction with communication from top management is usually even lower. We think some simple insights can be gained from Truman Capote's point. A major challenge is that most communication in organizations is *monological*. Managers—especially senior leaders—spend much of their time making their points of view known, influencing colleagues to adopt their ideas, and striving to get employees to accept their agendas. Less time is spent genuinely listening and questioning for the purpose of understanding what is happening in the external world. This is what organizations in turbulent settings need more of if they are to survive—open dialog regarding what is happening in the world around them along with creative thinking regarding how they can respond. Establishing continuous conversations has several important benefits for organizations in volatile settings.

To start, conversations promote active sharing of information. As mentioned in Chapter 7 on strategic intelligence, organizations are privy to more information today than ever before. Information is captured and put on the Web at an astounding pace. Technology enables managers to home in on key data more rapidly and with more precision than ever. Yet more information has not brought with it additional clarity. Information in high volumes is sometimes conflicting and its meaning is subject to a variety of interpretations. Actively sharing and openly discussing information provides a mechanism for leaders to improve their interpretation of what the data means to them and their organizations.

When conversations in organizations are continuous, heightened awareness ensues. Greater sensitivity to key issues follow. Employees at all levels avail themselves of new and different ways of thinking. With a variety of information, only a Web search away, managers can explore ideas, read articles, and find relevant statistical data, all of which collectively sensitizes the organization when done en masse. Consider an organization with thousands of employees. If each employee spent a modest amount of time daily scanning the environment for subtle developments that might impact the overall performance of his or her organization—the effect on awareness would be profound. If this were accomplished within an environment where sharing is promoted, changes in performance would likely follow.

Continuous discussion also stimulates creative thinking. Employees often feel as if they are working with only a fraction of their intellect and even less of their creativity. Structured routines and standardized policies in the main do not promote widespread creativity in organizations. In environments where information is shared and the search for new thought is encouraged, creativity will follow. Again, in workforces that house high numbers of employees, modest changes in creative thinking can yield significant results. Organizations such as 3M are known for giving workers time to explore and test new ideas. Innovation and continued relevance in the marketplace has been the persistent result.

Finally, open and frank dialog contributes to a culture of trust. In a communication study of 218 employees in large oil company, researchers found an interconnected relationship between communication and trust.[1] Specifically, the relationship between employees and senior managers is impacted by the quantity of information shared among the groups. At all levels tested in the organization, the researchers found that trust was closely tied to perceptions of organizational involvement, which also predicted employee involvement. Our opinion, which is consistent with the findings of this study, is that continuous communication is the key to effective trust and further performance in most organizations today.

Understanding Continuous Conversation

The effectiveness of the work presented in this book is predicated on the ability to communicate. But as Hans-Georg Gadamer notes in this chapter's epigraph, conversation is genuine only when the outcomes are not known or prescribed at the outset. To ensure the readers and users of this material are successful in their endeavors, we now discuss the particulars of effective conversation as well as providing tools that facilitate effective dialog within the PM^{4}TE process.

Basic Concepts and Definition

Literally everyone, every day, engages in some basic form of conversation. Whether it is discussing the lively particulars of the past weekend or communicating expectations for an upcoming project, conversation is a taken-for-granted activity in everyday life. Conversation occurs with such frequency that few people consider what a conversation is or, more specifically, what makes for an effective one. Effective conversation is a critical enabler of the PM^{4}TE process and to that end a few simple points should ensure that managers are engaging in conversation in its most effective form.

First, a *conversation* can be defined as a spoken exchange of thoughts, opinions, and experience.[2] On the surface, this definition sheds little light beyond what we already know about conversations—that they occur between two or more people and they consist of sharing ideas through spoken dialog. But it is the concept of dialog that we are most interested in. A dialog is not the same as a monolog. This is our main concern with management communication today: Most so-called conversations are really just a stream of monologs interconnected by a common topic. Managers engage in monologs for the purposes making a point, not with the intent of deepening their collective understanding of the topic being discussed. This not only represents a lost opportunity, it virtually guarantees that bona fide insights about performance are not captured. In environments of high complexity, open sharing of information for learning and accurate comprehension is essential. Constructive conversation is the conduit for learning. While effective conversation is the exception rather than the rule, there are a few rules we have found that, when applied, improve the quality of the conversation and, not surprisingly, the quality of performance management.

Principles of Effective Conversation

In our travels, we have identified a few basic requirements to effective conversation. We cannot claim ownership of these principles—we have merely identified them and supplied them here to facilitate improvement in the quality of conversations used in the PM^{4}TE process. While our focus is improved performance management, we have found that these principles contribute to the effectiveness of overall organizational performance, not just performance within the context of the PM^{4}TE process. The principles are summarized in Table 8.1.

Know the Audience   Before engaging in effective conversation, managers must make conscious efforts to understand their audience. Employees at all levels bring strong opinions, feelings, and biases to discussions. Failing to acknowledge these will contribute to a substandard dialog. Why might this be the case? Because in order to be open to influence, they must first believe that their own concerns are being heard. In most customer service failures, what the customer really wants—even more than a resolution to the particular problem—is the opportunity to have their frustrations and concerns genuinely heard and understood.

Employees are no different. They want to know their issues of greatest worry are heard and understood by leaders. Even members

Table 8.1   Principles of Effective Conversation

Principle	Description
Know the audience	Understanding the motives, concerns, and viewpoints of the conversants
Ask questions	Inquiring about performance issues and challenges for purposes of deepening understanding
Explore and challenge, don't judge and criticize	Critiquing information in a way that encourages exploring as opposed to criticizing
Above all else, just listen	Commit to learning through listening instead of talking

of top management teams want this—acknowledgment of their specific concerns. To set the stage for effective conversation, leaders must get to know their team members as individuals, learn what issues keep them up at night, and communicate with empathy that these concerns are important. Once this has been accomplished, effective two-way communication can follow. Again, in the words of Gandhi, "Seek first to understand, then be understood."

Ask Questions The French philosopher Voltaire said that a man is judged by his questions, rather than his answers. This is especially true of top teams and effective managers. The key to deepening understanding and expanding knowledge in organizations is not providing high volumes of answers, but rather asking carefully crafted, insightful questions.

Interestingly, asking good questions is not often prized as a top management skill. Managers are scripted in answering questions. What's more, managers are promoted based upon their wisdom and experience, which is to say, what they know. Asking questions gives the appearance of not knowing something. If leadership teams are to learn, they must be willing to spend time formulating important questions—the kind that, when ultimately answered, provide greater insights into organizational settings and performance than were previously known. Chapter 6, on decision making, helps senior leaders think in a way that will enhance their ability to formulate questions regardless of their current performance level.

Explore and Challenge, Don't Judge and Criticize Part of establishing an environment of trust is using conversation to explore and challenge information without being judgmental and overly critical. Unfortunately, managers will often use conversations in group settings as occasions to criticize the ideas of others for purposes of strengthening their own images. While the short-term effect may be improvement of one's own position, the long-term cost will be a dampening of the team's overall performance.

In our experience, judgment and criticism are the death knells of effective performance management. As we will see in Chapter 9, much of the PM^{4}TE Core Process is enabled by accelerated learning— learning about what is happening in the environment, what is working in the performance model. and what is the best course of action given a set of alternatives. Judgment and criticism not only cause people to refrain from sharing information, they create a sense of resentment that is difficult to overcome. These unhealthy feelings can provoke perverse actions, such as malicious compliance with critical objectives and performance measures or communication throughout the organization at cross purposes with higher-level goals. These actions serve only to undermine all the work intended to improve performance in a setting where maintaining performance is essential.

Above All Else, Just Listen   The final principle and, perhaps, the most basic is that when in conversation, above all else, just listen. It is hard to enhance understanding when the thought of making the next point is front and center in one's mind. Therefore, managers would be serving their colleagues, teams, and organizations well if they remembered to use their ears in the proportion to their mouths—two to one.

Listening to a conversation has become a lost art. We are so inundated with information today in the form of e-mail, television, radio advertising, and other electronic media that, when given the chance, most of us are bursting to share—unidirectionally—all we know. In good conversation, this temptation must be resisted. Listening is the precursor to effective conversation, not the byproduct of it. If top teams took this simple step—listened more than they talked—we believe understanding of performance and execution of it would be improved.

Conversations Clarified

Earlier, we defined a conversation as a spoken exchange of thoughts, opinions, or experiences. However, despite the array of topics that can be included in almost any conversation, we are concerned with conversations that relate to the core PM⁴TE process. We are chiefly interested in critical performance objectives, major projects, and performance measures that gauge progress, problems, and decisions the organization faces. We are bounding the conversation to areas relevant to performance management. These conversations are a chance to engage in critical thinking, not just a simple exchange of ideas. To that end, there are two basic critical reasoning approaches to reach conclusions in any conversation.

Deduction When sharing information in conversations, managers work to reach conclusions or a logical summary of the exchange of ideas in a dialog. One method of reaching a conclusion is through *deduction.*

In deduction, a series of premises or statements of fact are made initially. Using only these statements of fact, a conclusion is drawn that must logically follow if the original premises themselves are true. Deduction is much like a detective exploring a crime scene. A host of evidence (e.g., facts) is collected from which a conclusion can be drawn. If the facts are true, then the conclusion that follows must be true as well.

Applying this kind of critical thinking to a performance management problem enables us to view deduction at work. Table 8.2 shows the deductive logic applied to a situation where a company is losing market share.

In this example, it is clear to see that the conclusion drawn must be true if both of the premises are true. The company must be growing at a rate slower than the industry and that is causing the loss of market share. The point of deduction is that the conclusion necessarily follows from the initial claims.

Induction In *induction,* the conclusion drawn is likely true given the premises, but it is not necessarily the case. Again, like deduction, a series of premises or statements of fact are made. However, because of the nature of the premises themselves, a conclusion drawn from them does not have to necessarily be true. Usually, it is probably true to some degree, but it may not be. Induction is commonly used in research and in instances where inferences are broadly made about a set of facts. Table 8.3 demonstrates another market share example, in which inductive reasoning is used. Note the difference between this and the deductive thinking process in Table 8.2.

Table 8.2 Deductive Logic Example

Principle	Description
Premise 1	Industry revenues are growing at a rate of 5% per year.
Premise 2	Our revenue grew at a rate of 4% per year.
Conclusion	The industry grew at a faster rate than we did.

Table 8.3   Inductive Logic Example

Principle	Description
Premise 1	Most large competitors are growing at a rate of 5% per year.
Premise 2	Our revenue grew at a rate of 4% per year.
Conclusion	Our largest competitors grew at a faster rate than we did.

In this example, it is likely that the company is losing share to its largest competitors; but this is not necessarily the case. Here some large competitors could be losing share too—it is not certain at this point. In induction, the conclusion does not necessarily follow from the initial claims.

Why is this type of reasoning important? Simply put, most managers spend their time in conversations sharing information not only to enhance their understanding but also to reach conclusions about the world around them. Both critical thinking techniques are used by leaders, just largely in an unconscious way. What we have seen happen is that managers will reach conclusions using induction believing it is actually deduction. They draw conclusions that give the appearance of being based on sound thinking and critical reasoning when many times this is not the case. Certainty is assumed when the conclusion is probabilistic at best. In conversation, sound principles of critical thinking need to be applied, otherwise the conclusions drawn will be spurious.

The Socratic Method   Those familiar with law school or legal studies are typically trained in what is known as the Socratic method. Managers are usually less familiar with it, which we aim to change.

Named for the Greek philosopher Socrates, the Socratic method is a mode of inquiry and debate between people based on asking questions and then answering them using critical thinking throughout the process. In short, it is a form of hypothesis testing in which a question is asked, responded to, and refined through dialog that seeks to uncover beliefs and points of view about that question. In the process, the participants' thinking is challenged, as are the commonly held beliefs. The purpose of the process is to arrive at more firmly established views or, more appropriately, facts about the area of inquiry. While seemingly complex, it is a process that contributes significantly to clarity in understanding.

By engaging in a more thoughtful, deliberate conversation, the quality of performance management analysis can be enhanced in the same way. Leadership teams can improve the quality of their structured dialog and problem solving by engaging in the Socratic method. In meetings where performance is being examined, the challenges to performance, for example, can be posed as a series of questions that are addressed by the team. Opposing thoughts are encouraged as are challenges to the basic question. The conversation can be summarized by identifying what is known to be true and what is commonly accepted about the area of inquiry. Further investigation can be conducted after the conversation to deepen understanding.

Critical Success Factors

Conversations will continue in organizations whether or not managers read this chapter. That is good news. However, we believe that in applying the principles and critical thinking methods highlighted here, there is an added benefit of deepened understanding, better quality thinking, and ultimately, improved decision making and problem solving. To that end, we have identified two critical success factors tantamount to improving conversations in organization for those managers committed to doing so.

Establish a Climate of Trust

The first and most important success factor is establishing an environment of trust in the organization. As was pointed out in the research at the beginning of the chapter, communication establishes trust. We believe the reverse is also true: An environment of trust facilitates communication. It is essential that employees at all levels believe they can share information—especially unfavorable or unpopular information—in a safe setting, otherwise they will be unwilling to do so. When this is the case, vital information regarding the current situation may fail to be shared, which potentially hurts the performance of the organization.

To build a foundation of trust, leaders must commit to exploring all issues openly and honestly. Moreover, the message of trust and openness must be reinforced with action. It must be consistent and repeatedly relayed throughout the organization and it must be followed up with visible engagement in dialog. Exploring issues broadly and sharing ideas with the express purpose of establishing mutual understanding will, over time, lay the foundation for the type of internally stable conditions essential for managing external instability well.

Create a Culture of Conversation

Most managers dismiss the thought of reading academic research as a source of for new knowledge almost immediately. As the authors of such papers, we understand this thinking. Academic writing can be complex and confusing. Sometimes it is downright verbose. Yet, for those intimately involved in academic writing, it is one of the most effective forms of conversation they know. Previously published articles (i.e., dialog) are cited, new questions are raised relating to those asked before, critical thinking is applied to questions, conclusions are drawn using structured thinking and analysis, and new questions are subsequently stimulated. While we are not advocating taking pen to paper for purposes of conversing inside organizations, we do advocate sparking thoughtful conversations that are germane to the organization's central issues.

In short, if employees believe they can engage in open, honest dialog, they will start having conversations with one another. Senior leaders must be involved too, and aid in this process. Managers need to actively promote conversations in their organizations wherever they go. We believe setting up forums expressly for the purpose of conversation is a valuable use of limited resources, not a waste of them. As consultant Tony Golsby-Smith points out in a *Harvard Business Review* blog post, "The best way to energize thinking is to hold conversations rather than meetings. In our personal lives, we are used to talking openly with one another, but most organizations have failed to capitalize on the power of conversations in a business setting."[3] Managers using the PM^{4}TE process have the power to change this.

Summary

In this chapter, we examined the topic of continuous conversations. We explained that conversations are critical to the PM^{4}TE process because they promote the ongoing discussion of key issues where ideas can be exchanged, explored, and challenged in an environment of trust. There are a set of four principles and three critical thinking techniques that promote quality thinking in conversation. Teams would be wise to employ them. To be effective in establishing continuous conversation, leaders need to establish a climate of trust as well as seek occasions for creating a culture of conversation within their areas of critical performance. In that way, conversation becomes a competitive enabler instead of a barrier to effective performance. In the next chapter, we discuss how to use these conversations to promote learning within the PM^{4}TE process.

Case Study: Google

Most people who have ever done an Internet search are familiar with the search engine company Google. Google has revolutionized not only Internet searches, but the advertising industry as well. Its mission statement is as follows:

> Google is a global technology leader focused on improving the ways people connect with information. We aspire to build products that improve the lives of billions of people globally. Our mission is to organize the world's information and make it universally accessible and useful.[4]

Incorporated in 1998, the company delivers focused, cost-effective online advertising. Google's AdWords program helps advertisers of all types to promote their products and services with customized, targeted messages. Google has expanded its services over the years to include e-mail (Gmail), telephony (Google Mobile), and even television advertising (GoogleTV). The company serves billions of people around the world via its massive technology platform.

Turbulent Situation

Despite what might be considered a superdominant position, Google competes in a highly competitive and turbulent industry. The company's annual report describes its industry as "characterized by rapid change and converging, as well as new and disruptive, technologies. We face formidable competition in every aspect of our business, particularly from companies that seek to connect people with information on the web and provide them with relevant advertising." Direct competitors are listed as other search engines, both general and specialty, social networks, old media advertising (such as TV and radio), and software companies such as Microsoft and Apple. The company itself, in the span of 10 years, grew from revenues of $19 million in 2000 to over $29 billion in 2010, making it one of the fastest growing companies in history.

Description of the Continuous Conversation Process

It might seem that Google is an organization that by its very nature would foster very few conversations. First, the pace of work is rapid—innovation is a constant within the organization. Thus, there might appear to be little time for conversation in this environment. Second, traditional organizational hierarchies are limited. Within a standard organizational bureaucracy managers normally supervise up to seven or so employees that would constitute a lower-level work team. At Google, the number is more like 20 to 50, leaving managers with little time to directly supervise. Finally, the workforce is highly decentralized. Small teams often work independently for what can be weeks or months at a time. But these conditions aside, conversations are anything but limited at Google.

Google employees work long hours, longer in fact than many comparable old-line companies. To support workers spending so much time in the office, Google has put in place a variety of mechanisms to support employees, ranging from a café that provides free meals to special interest groups on topics from wine tasting to medication. Per Google's Executive Chairman Eric Schmidt:

> The goal is to strip away everything that gets in our employees' way. We provide a standard package of fringe benefits, but on top of that are first-class dining facilities, gyms, laundry rooms, massage rooms, haircuts, car washes, dry cleaning, commuting buses—just about anything a hardworking employee might want. Let's face it: programmers want to program, they don't want to do their laundry. So we make it easy for them to do both.[5]

Employees also work in small teams—sometimes as few as three. These teams operate out of huddle rooms and shared cubes; very few offices are provided for employees, resulting in constant opportunities for interaction at an almost atomic level. The company also sponsors internal educational events such as talks from management gurus like Marshall Goldsmith and other leading edge thinkers like Thomas L. Friedman, author of *The World is Flat*. Google encourages employees to take full advantage of these benefits so that they can continue to thinking creatively and constructively about concepts that affect the entire world around them, not just the technology component of it—and share their ideas with coworkers. Each week the company holds all-hands meetings where employees are encouraged to challenge everyone up to and including the senior executives.

This excerpt from the company's web site provides insight into the type of intimate communication culture that has evolved at Google:

> At lunchtime, almost everyone eats in the office café, sitting at whatever table has an opening and enjoying conversations with Googlers from different teams. Our commitment to innovation depends on everyone being comfortable sharing ideas and opinions. Every employee is a hands-on contributor, and everyone wears several hats.[6]

The conversation, however, is not restricted to the physical world. As might be expected, Google employees are encouraged to blog on personal or professional blogs on topics ranging from project progress to industry competition. Blogs that are useful and popular internally proliferate; those that are not disappear. Blogging within an organization enhances the conversation as Bernard Girard points out in his book *The Google Way*:

> The benefit of blogs to a business like Google are immediate. They translate into the following:
>
> - Time Saved: Rather than attending seemingly interminable meetings where you listen to people talk about things that don't concern you or get involved with paperwork that has no practical value, employees can turn to blogs for the information they need, when they need it.
> - Concentrated Information: The information on blogs is of high quality and depth. Information in a blog will be

focused on the needs of a limited number of subscribers who consult the blog and comment when they have time.[7]

These short anecdotes reflect some of the some simple—and not so simple—ways Google maintains its internal communities and conversation across the company. Despite the pace and scale of one of the most sophisticated companies on earth, the communication has in no way been limited.

Interpretations from Key Managers

Across the board, managers and employees alike enjoy working at Google. Aside from the free food (which is said to be outstanding), employees genuinely relish working with smart, dedicated colleagues from all walks of life who are trying to make a difference through their work. Despite scaling dramatically over the past decade, the company has been successful in maintaining its start-up company feel. The practice of keeping employees engaged on small teams and allowing them to interact both professionally and socially throughout the organization has enabled Google to keep information flowing all across the organization at a point in its life cycle when that could have easily not been the case.

Tangible Benefits and Outcomes

Google's success comes not only in the area of attracting, retaining, and developing some of the world's best talent; it has also managed to deliver eye-popping financial performance at the same time. Net income from the $29 billion in revenues in 2010 was $8.5 billion—a whopping 30 percent margin. At this writing, the stock was trading at over $500 per share. Performance like this is impressive for an organization that did not exist 20 years ago.

Lessons Learned

In the world of Internet search, it can be said that information maintains a premium value. This is also the case of information within an organization. Traditional structures such as lengthy meetings, carefully crafted e-mails, and corporate memos cannot keep pace with the speed of change inherent inside—and outside— a company like Google. Managers in the company have adopted a philosophy and promoted structures that support continuous conversation while maintaining both productivity and performance. If one of the largest and most sophisticated companies operating today can manage to keep conversations alive, so should other more conventional organizations.

Notes

1. G. Thomas, R. Zolin, and J. Hartman, "The Central Role of Communication in Developing Trust and Its Effect on Employee Involvement," *Journal of Business Communication* 46, no. 3 (2009): 287.
2. *The Merriam-Webster Dictionary* (New York: Encyclopedia Britannica, 2010).
3. T. Golsby-Smith, "Hold Conversations, Not Meetings," *HBR Blog Network,* February 15, 2011, http://blogs.hbr.org/cs/2011/02/hold_conversations_not_meeting.html.
4. Google, Inc., 2010 Form 10K.
5. Google, Inc., "Benefits," *Life at Google,* 2011, www.google.com/jobs/lifeatgoogle/benefits.html.
6. Google, Inc., "Google Culture," *Everything Google,* 2011, www.google.com/about/corporate/company/culture.html.
7. B. Girard, *The Google Way* (San Francisco: No Starch Press, Inc., 2009).

Accelerated Learning

All wish to possess knowledge, but few, comparatively speaking, are willing to pay the price.

—Juvenal

Accelerated Learning is the third enabler supporting the PM⁴TE Core Process. Information gathered from the external environment and combined with performance feedback from the application of the Core Process, must not only be analyzed and shared, it must also form the basis of learning throughout the organization. In volatile environments, the ability of the organization to collectively learn from successes and failures directly determines how skillfully the organization adapts to conditions in the marketplace. The need to adapt quickly and accurately in such environments makes the ability to gain insights from performance information a particularly critical skill. In this chapter, we discuss the value of accelerated learning, what it is, and activities that generate effective learning, and provide a summary of critical success factors that promote accelerated learning practices. Essential activities that drive learning in organizations are highlighted and supported by a case study showing how top leaders can gain more from the learning process.

Most performance management systems are predicated on the concept of control. At the start of a planning period, performance expectations or standards are set. Typically these fall into the financial arena as well as others essential to organization performance. During execution, results are compared to the preexisting standards and action is taken. While this type of performance management is essential, it reflects only one dimension of learning. Another dimension is challenging underlying assumptions and strategies used to set standards at the outset. This type of learning is what we are concerned with in this chapter; learning that asks and seeks to answer questions such as, "Are these our most important priorities?" and "Are the assumptions underlying our strategy accurate?" We also explain how organizations can improve the way they learn because learning—indeed, rapid learning—is a critical ingredient for not only keeping the pace, but setting it in turbulent settings. Senior leaders, therefore, need to become chief learning officers within their own organizations. In a sense, organizations need to learn how to learn.

The Accelerated Learning enabler is depicted at the bottom of Figure 9.1. Accelerated learning plays an essential role in making the entire PM^{4}TE system work—the Core Process as well as the full set of model enablers. Gathering performance information, interpreting it, analyzing it systematically, harvesting and sharing insights, and ultimately translating those insights into action are activities that are seldom given deliberate thought in organizations. This is unfortunate, but understandable. In fast-moving settings, a premium is placed on taking action, and organizations are loath to pay the price to learn how they acquire knowledge. Learning—especially learning quickly—is a critical skill leaders and their teams need to master if they are to enjoy long-term success in turbulent settings. Accelerated learning enables managers to rapidly assess what is working and what is not, generate new ideas, and experiment in ways that build the performance capacity in an organization. By understanding how individuals and organizations learn, the PM^{4}TE process can be transformed from a simple performance management process into an accelerated execution system, replete with insights that lead to improved individual, team, and organizational performance. Fortunately, learning how to learn is something that can be improved with a basic understanding of how organizations can incorporate learning into the PM^{4}TE process overall. In this chapter, we discuss basic learning concepts, key learning activities, and conditions for learning success, and provide simple tools that aid top teams in the development of this vital capability. We will discuss how

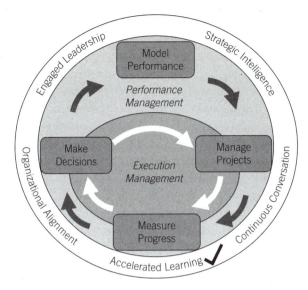

Figure 9.1   Model Enablers: Accelerated Learning

leaders share this process with their organizations in Chapter 10, "Organizational Alignment."

Why Accelerated Learning Is a Model Enabler

As this chapter's introduction points out, one of the most important skills a management team can develop is the capacity to collectively learn. Learning enables leaders to assess the effectiveness of their decisions, the consequences of their actions, the results of organizational performance, and a host of other factors vital to adapting the organization for enhanced competitiveness. If the organization's ability to learn is limited, it will persist in making choices that, over time, contribute to declines in performance.

But learning by itself is not sufficient in turbulent setting. In dynamic and rapidly changing environments, leaders must ensure that their organizations are learning and adapting quickly—ideally at a rate faster than competitors. Research suggests that organizations that learn more quickly than their competitors and are then able to translate those insights into action perform better than their competitors. There are a few straightforward reasons supporting this claim.

Volatile environments are typically fast-moving ones as well. Product life cycles can be short—as short as six months in the fashion and video game industries. Technology changes rapidly, too, as is the case in personal computers and consumer electronics. The windows of opportunity only present themselves for brief periods of time. This requires not only rapid movement but *informed* movement. Organizations that are able to act quickly to capitalize on opportunities and avoid threats are the ones that have the ability to sense and interpret what is happening quickly and accurately.

Moreover, the general business environment today is accelerating to the point where the effectiveness of traditional strategic and deliberate planning approaches is becoming limited. The era of the detailed plan that specifies goals and actions over a five-year time horizon is gone. Organizations today plan their strategy using horizons of three years or less and engage in planning annually. As planning an uncertain future becomes increasingly unrealistic, learning to adapt to multiple futures takes on a new level of importance. So too does the capability to learn.

Finally, knowledge-based organizations—which constitute most organizations today—compete based on the cumulative knowledge of their workforces. Learning and thinking are no longer the sole domains of the top management team. Knowledge-generating practices must be embedded in the fabric of the entire organization. The quality of the thinking throughout the organization impacts the performance of the enterprise. Faster learning leads to better thinking, which in turn drives improved performance.

Despite the organizations being knowledge-based, learning is not a process most organizations have the tolerance for. As David Garvin, Harvard Business School professor, writes in his book, *Learning in Action:*

> Most managers remain surprisingly ambivalent about learning. Many give lip service to its importance voicing strong public support for efforts to broaden employees' knowledge and skills. But when pressed, they usually express very different feelings. For too many managers, learning is of questionable value because it diverts employees' attention from "real work."[1]

Despite the odds of improving the focus on learning not being in our favor, the success of performance management in such environments relies on it. With that in mind, we begin with a discussion about the basics of learning today.

Understanding Accelerated Learning

We measure progress to gauge the efficiency and effectiveness of our actions. The results of those actions must be interpreted and understood in a way that leads to improved performance the next time decisions are made and actions are taken. That is the purpose of learning and it manifests itself in several key activities discussed in this section.

Basic Definition and Key Activities

To learn is to gain knowledge or comprehension, or master something through experience or study. As the core PM^{4}TE process is executed, managers must actively work to gain insights regarding the extent to which critical performance objectives are being achieved. For this to occur, a set of activities needs to take place systematically within organization. Those activities are highlighted in Table 9.1.

Gather Information   The first activity in accelerating learning is gathering information. Information can be the by-product of the PM^{4}TE Core Process, such as metric data or milestone progress on key projects. It can also come from strategic intelligence, such as scanning specific areas within the external environment. In some cases, it can be generated from inside the organization through surveys and analysis of the employee base. Regardless of the source, information starts the learning process. Often this information is in a raw

Table 9.1   Key Learning Activities

Activity	Description
Gather information	Collect information regarding key performance areas.
Analyze information	Assess information to understand critical relationships.
Interpret meaning	Identify potential implications of the information for the organization.
Share insights	Communicate and share the information with members of the organization.
Take action	Translate insights into action.

and unfiltered form and must be interpreted before it can be shared broadly.

Analyze Information   After information has been gathered, it is typically analyzed at some level. Analysis may consist of simply comparing actual performance to predetermined target performance levels. Or it may require conducting tests such as regression analysis. Highly unstructured data may first require basic organization, as was the case with the Strategic Issue Template described in Chapter 7. However, some type of analysis—especially if the data are quantitative—will need to be performed to aid in determining the actual meaning for the organization.

Interpret Meaning   Once sufficient analysis has been completed, managers can turn to determining what the data mean for the organization. Ultimately, the results of the analysis have to be converted into context-specific findings. The performance context is that of the organization itself. Are performance results significantly worse than expected? Are actions being taken ineffective? What do the results of the customer value proposition survey mean? These are the kinds of questions managers must pose when interrogating the data to determine what the data mean specifically for their organization.

Share Insights   To learn and not share what is learned is to not really have learned at all. With the meanings identified, the information should be shared with employees throughout the organization. Employees' ability to understand the performance context is essential if they are to modify their own actions in response to performance results or changes in environmental conditions. The more thoroughly people in the organization understand the meaning of the information gathered (e.g., we are losing share to our most aggressive competitor), the higher the likelihood they can address vital performance challenges head on.

Take Action   With the organization now fully aware of the interpreted information, action can be taken with the specific intent of improving performance. At this point, collective understanding is improved with regard to the data originally collected. It can now be used to alter the organization's response to changing conditions in a manner that improves future outcomes. This is the true purpose of performance management—making decisions and taking action that improves the performance outcomes of the organization.

While these activities may seem slow and static, there is no limit to how quickly they can be performed. Additionally, as the organization gathers multiple pieces of information, it can process them in parallel. This provides the organization with a "multiplier effect"; that is, the whole of the individual learning is greater than the sum of its parts.

Learning Tools for the PM⁴TE Process

The activities described thus far provide the foundation for any effective learning process regardless of organizational type or the environment within which an organization operates. There are, however, a few key concepts and tools that we have found relevant to organizations in high-velocity settings. The concepts of learning loops, performance reviews, and best-practice sharing are presented in this section.

Learning Loops In their seminal work on learning, *Organizational Learning: A Theory of Action Perspective,* researchers Chris Argyris and Don Schoen describe the concepts of single- and double-loop learning.[2] While this theory is not new, its application in performance management is fairly recent. Each concept describes the ways in which employees in organizations learn based upon expectations regarding what the performance outcomes are to begin with.

In single-loop learning, employees, managers, and organizations take action based on the variance between expected performance and actual performance. In this approach, the performance expectations and the causes of performance deviations are known. An example of single-loop learning would be a manager or controller reviewing excessive travel expenses for the reporting period. The expected outcome was understood and the cause of the deviation from the expected outcome—spending too much on travel—is well known.

In double-loop learning, employees not only examine deviations from expected performance, they use those deviations to question the assumptions and policies that contributed to the development of the performance expectations to begin with. When managers expect to gain market share but find they have lost share, they examine not only what caused the loss, but also the logic behind the expectation that they would gain share. This learning and the refinement therein contributes to the development of single-loop learning as well.

The learning loop concept is important in the PM^{4}TE process for two reasons. First, learning, in the macro sense, is likely to form an ongoing loop or process whereby the key learning activities in Table 9.1 are executed repeatedly over time. The more capably the organization cycles through the steps, the better it will become at learning. Second, due to the very nature of the performance models discussed in Chapter 3, most of the time spent in the PM^{4}TE process will be in double-loop learning. Managers will spend much of their time understanding not only performance results and variances, but also whether the performance expectations were appropriate.

Performance Planning   Much of the learning regarding organization performance occurs in and around performance review meetings, which we call *performance planning meetings*. Performance planning meetings are action oriented and future looking whereas traditional performance reviews are essentially defensive, leading to the mind-set, "If you tell me you are going to review my business unit's performance, I'll prepare my excuse for what's not going well and I'll be sure to emphasize what is going well." In essence, performance reviews become a defensive routine and defensive routines hinder learning.

Performance planning, however, is designed to provoke a much more open conversation. The question to ask is not "Why are we where we are?" in terms of performance, but instead "How are we going to get to where we want to be?" The orientation is toward the future and the focus is on what we can learn and what we should do next.

Performance planning meetings should occur regularly—weekly for vital projects and monthly for critical objectives and measures—so that a continuous snapshot of performance is maintained. There are two keys to effective performance planning. First, the meetings must be scheduled and held. Second, they must be organized using an agenda that will facilitate discussion, problem solving, and decision making. Vital project reviews are just that—standard cost and schedule project reviews. However, performance planning meetings overall, where the performance model itself is assessed, are different. An example of an effective performance planning agenda is provided in Table 9.2.

We discuss the important elements of the performance planning meeting in the following sections.

Action Item Review/Summary At the start of each performance planning meeting, action items from the previous meeting should be recapped to ensure they have been completed. Performance management improves significantly when specific actions, deliverables, due dates, and accountabilities are assigned and followed through. This basic discipline is a key driver of execution and should only take a few minutes to complete. Also, at the close of each meeting, action items from the meeting should be identified, assigned a due date, and a responsible party. Beyond the performance planning meeting, this discipline should be incorporated into every meeting.

Performance Model Overview Early in the meeting—typically after action items have been covered—the performance model should be reviewed in total. The purpose of the performance model review is to determine if the critical performance objectives are being achieved. Measurement data from each of the key measures associated

Table 9.2 Performance Planning Agenda

Timing	Meeting Activity	Purpose
15 minutes	Action item review	Review action items from the prior meeting for purposes of close out.
30 minutes	Performance model overview	Discuss the results of the performance model overall.
30 minutes	Vital project overview	High-level status review of all of the vital projects.
1 hour	Critical objective and measure discussion	Critical objectives from the performance model are selected for in-depth analysis and discussion.
1 hour	Major challenge problem solving	Data is analyzed and problem-solving techniques are applied to performance deviations for critical objectives.
30 minutes	Course of action selection	Based upon the results of problem solving and analysis, courses of action are identified and one is selected.
15 minutes	Action item summary	Action items from the current performance review are identified and assigned a due date and responsible party.

with individual objectives should be updated and coded using a red/yellow/green coding scheme to reflect the adequacy of progress toward each individual target. This overview not only gives a high-level picture of performance across the organizational system, it also focuses management attention on those areas in need of analysis.

Vital Project Overview At the top team level, vital projects should be looked at overall to determine if the portfolio of individual projects is collectively on or off track. Given that vital projects drive the progress of measures toward targets, executives must maintain a watchful eye on them—especially those few that are directly linked to the organization's performance model. Each project should also be coded with a red, yellow, or green indicator contingent upon whether it is on or off schedule. In cases where projects are falling behind, the management team may want to spend time understanding why.

Critical Objective and Measure Discussion Once the performance model and vital projects have been reviewed, the top team can then turn its attention to discussing specific performance challenges for selected critical performance objectives. Recall that the critical performance objectives reflect the key outcomes the organization is trying to achieve; these outcomes are arrayed in a set of causal relationships across the organizational system. In instances where performance is not being achieved, leaders must enact the learning double-loop process. They must understand basic deviations in expected performance, but more importantly, examine the assumptions and motivations underlying critical objectives and measures. Their discussion should work to uncover both true performance drivers and the causes of variances in performance. Once these causes have been discussed, they can then be examined in more detail.

Major Challenge Problem Solving If the performance model is truly challenging organizational performance, there will be issues associated with its critical objective achievement. Given that the top team is typically present for performance planning meetings, these serve as excellent forums to engage in issue-based problem solving pertaining to the organization's most pressing challenges. Once a major challenge has been identified (usually in advance of the meeting), the techniques highlighted in Chapter 6 can be applied in full. The top team should frame the problem, create an issue tree, examine potential drivers/root causes of deficiencies, and formulate a plan to test their analysis using data. It's important to see the performance planning meeting as a way not only to problem solve but to build top managers' skills in the process.

Course of Action Selection   If the problem-solving session provides sufficient information, and leaders have generated a set of options they are comfortable with, then they can compare these options and select a course of action. Generating realistic, competing options is the sign of an effective process versus the generation of one preferred option along with a set of unrealistic, undervalued choices. Organizing managers into smaller teams to generate options stimulates the creativity of the group as well as the effectiveness of the decision-making process in general.

Accelerated Learning Techniques Today

Accelerated learning is not simply the name for an enabler—a body of research and practice exists focused on accelerated learning theories and techniques. In PM^{4}TE-focused accelerated learning, we look for ways to accelerate the ability of top teams to understand performance and what drives it. Factors that contribute to speed in learning include engagement of the total range of intelligence—including mathematical, logical, spatial, interpersonal, and visual intelligences.

To this point, we have embedded two key techniques—modeling and group collaboration—into the PM^{4}TE process. Modeling is a way to visually depict data and relationship in a format that improves comprehension. Group collaboration is a technique used to accelerate understanding by focusing the power of a group of people (e.g., a top management team) on the challenges it faces rather than working them in isolation. Two other techniques that we use in the PM^{4}TE process—mind mapping and scenario exploration—are highlighted next.

Mind Mapping   Mind mapping is a technique in which a diagram is used to document and link ideas, activities, and any significant concepts in a way that promotes organization and analysis around a central idea or theme. The technique has been in use for well over 50 years and the modern approach is credited to British psychologist

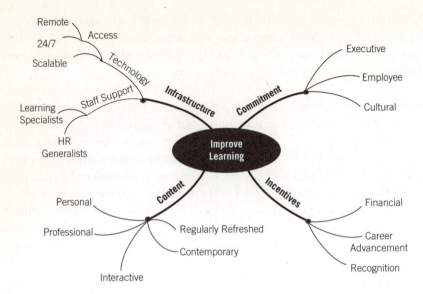

Figure 9.2   Sample Mind Map

Tony Buzan. His book, *The Mind Map Book*, is considered to be a modern-day treatise on the subject.[3]

Mind maps have a variety of uses, from the simple organization of notes to solving business problems. Using a nontraditional, network-like structure of colors, shapes, and size distinctions to present information in a more natural format, mind maps help individuals and teams share information, collaborate, and structure their thoughts in a dynamic and cogent way. An example of a mind map is provided in Figure 9.2.

Scenario Exploration   Oftentimes, managers are bound by their current situations. Because they work daily under challenging conditions and constraints, they cannot always envision realities without them. Sometimes when conditions are changing in turbulent environments, managers' marriage to the conditions of the past prevents their seeing changes that may be unfolding literally right before their eyes. To help free managers from this blindness, scenario exploration is a particularly effective tool.

Although scenario planning has been in use for decades, its development within the area of business is credited to Royal Dutch

Shell, which developed scenarios for its strategic planning process in the 1970s. Today, scenario planning is used by a multitude of organizations in both the public sector—the military, in particular—as well as the private sector.

In scenario planning, a series of key environmental variables are identified, such as growth rate, competitive intensity, buyer consolidation, and the like. Different ranges of performance are identified for each variable (e.g., high growth rate versus low growth rate). The variables are then plotted against one another and different scenarios are developed for each (e.g., high growth rate is matched with high competitive intensity). Scenarios for each set of variables are then developed, which can contain a mixture of qualitative and quantitative information. Teams use each scenario to envision a future environment that may be significantly different from the one in which they are currently operating. Not surprisingly, over the past several years scenario analysis and exploration has grown in popularity as the uncertainty level in the broader business environment has increased.

Critical Success Factors

We have not only built a case for accelerated learning in organizations today, but also described steps to achieve it. These steps, however, do not guarantee success. Several key factors should be present to ensure this enabler provides its full measure of value. Each is discussed in the following sections.

Mobilize and Employ Teams

One essential factor in accelerating learning is mobilizing and employing teams. Teams—from the top management team to work groups comprised of front-line employees—are a powerful way to build a learning capability within an organization.

In our experience, teams are leveraged insufficiently and improperly within business settings. To be sure, when there are key projects to be executed, teams are the preferred structure, but a teaming mentality is far from present in today's organizations. Most employees lament—accurately—that their managers do not fully tap the creativity and experience of their subordinates. Problems like succession planning, morale issues, and determination of plausible organizational futures, to cite a few of the more common ones, go unaddressed for literally years at a time because managers fail to take the time to educate, mobilize, and deploy teams throughout the organization. What a tremendous loss of potential! As the Chinese proverb states, "Tell me and I'll forget. Show me and I may remember. Involve me and I'll understand." Learning and understanding are increased when employees are fully mobilized and employed.

Do Not Be Afraid to Experiment

Stakes can be high and the margin for error slim in turbulent environments. Consequently, the inclination to control performance of all types is strong on the part of senior managers. But for organizations to learn they must be willing to test and adapt. Testing and adapting—as is the case with any experiment—invariably involves making mistakes.

Most people know Thomas Edison as a great inventor. Before he developed the incandescent light bulb, he developed almost 3,000 theories for electric light and only two ended up being true. In organizations, it is unlikely that more than a handful of theories of performance will be developed. Many of them will be, at least partially, incorrect. But that should not deter management teams from experimenting.

The performance models listed in Chapter 3 are, in reality, theories of performance. While some are based on more knowns than unknowns, there are occasions when performance does not meet expectations. Top teams must be comfortable with the fact that much of what they do is oriented around hypothesis testing and theory development—that is, performance theory. So too must they be comfortable with the notion that effective performance management entails a healthy dose of experimentation.

Be Positive

This undoubtedly sounds like one of the most worn-out principles known to mankind, but when it comes to learning, few factors have as much impact on performance as maintaining a positive attitude. In fact, much of the literature about accelerated learning recommends maintaining a positive attitude and open environment as key techniques to improve overall learning.

Gaining competitive advantage in any setting is challenging; in turbulent settings it can be doubly so. The demands on organizational resources and executive attention in high-velocity environments are herculean. This is why maintaining a positive attitude is so important. Being positive is essential to maintaining high morale while motivating teams that work at high speed. While there is no shortage of quotes on positive thinking, we came across one from Oscar Wilde that encapsulates particularly well the spirit of operating in turbulent environments: "The basis of optimism is sheer terror."

Summary

In this chapter, we explored the enabler of Accelerated Learning and described not only its importance, but specific activities organizations can undertake to improve their ability to learn. Assessing the effectiveness of decisions and actions requires five key activities: gathering information, analyzing it, interpreting meaning, sharing insights, and taking action. From our vantage, much of the learning pertaining to the PM^{4}TE model occurs during the performance review meeting, where a focused agenda like the one presented in Table 9.2 will set the stage for key learning activities. Additionally, techniques such as mind mapping and scenario exploration help organizations think more fluidly about their current challenges and future settings. These important tools influence performance results in the short and long term. In Chapter 10, we discuss how to ensure that accelerated learning and key insights are captured in the structure of an aligned organization.

Case Study: Progress Software

Progress Software, headquartered in Bedford, Massachusetts, is a global provider of enterprise software to help organizations achieve improved business performance by enhancing real-time operational responsiveness. A publicly traded company, Progress Software generates revenues of just over $500 million annually.

Turbulent Situation

Progress competes in one of the most intensely competitive marketplaces known today—computer software. The company identifies direct competitors as giants IBM Corporation, Microsoft Corporation, and Oracle Corporation, all of which possess significantly more resources and reach than Progress. The company identifies no fewer than 17 risks that directly affect its business, ranging from fluctuations in demand both domestically and internationally to loss of critically skilled technology employees.

From 2007 to 2010, the company experienced uneven revenue and profit performance through its business. Analysts covering the stock at the time questioned the company's ability to generate sustained growth in both areas due to what was believed to be a mature product portfolio and a "middle ground" positioning that gave Progress Software neither the coolness of a start-up company nor the strength of an industry juggernaut. The strategy of the company was unclear as well. Company management recognized this and began to take steps to understand the sources of the challenges.

Description of Accelerated Learning Process

Top managers at the company began exploring what was causing the challenges in performance. A company-wide employee survey was conducted with over 1,600 employees and reviewed in conjunction with a deep-dive internal financial performance analysis. The results were sobering. Leaders learned that employees did not understand the company's strategy as it pertained to the markets it served and the products it made. The employees questioned the effectiveness and visibility of the company's leadership team as well and expressed an overall feeling of having little or no empowerment. These factors, coupled with a host of other operational issues, culminated in a sense of organizational paralysis and the perception that the company could not be successful because too many organizational barriers stood in the way. As one manager, an anonymous survey respondent, noted, "I used to get things done very quickly, [but] now, with the lack of clarity, it is difficult to act, or determine who to talk with." In 2009, Rick Reidy, Progress's chief operating officer since 2008, was moved into the chief executive role. Shortly after he moved into the top spot, he took action by shoring up key management positions and engaging upper-middle management throughout the company. To assist in this, he authorized and participated in a multiyear senior leadership development program with a local business school aimed at skilling emerging leaders with tools they would need to address the most significant challenges the company was facing. "In order to drive the kind of performance demanded by our industry, leaders at all levels would need to help change how we did business."

Over the course of two years, scores of top managers participated in development workshops aimed at "identifying, understanding, and solving important business problems for Progress Software." Cross-functional teams worked on topics ranging from business problem solving (discussed in Chapter 6) to interpersonal communication, all designed to address key issues the survey identified. At the same time the executive committee gave them a handful of specific, critical issues they wanted the teams to address. One of those issues was innovation—asking and answering the question, "How can the company best innovate to stay competitive in the future?" The teams started working on the issues during the executive education sessions and then brought them back to their workplaces for further development and implementation.

As a result of the ongoing learning in the classroom and in the work spaces of the organization, the company made significant advancements in achieving its vision of becoming "One Progress." The company adopted a significantly more integrated product strategy and began standardizing systems internally. Emphasis was placed on becoming market driven and solution oriented, which gave Progress Software a clearer positioning with its customers as well as within its industry.

Interpretations from Key Managers

"This was a major undertaking for us" noted John Melo, vice president of human resources at Progress and senior leader in charge of the executive education sessions. "We had gotten to the point where the company was stalling. What Rick [Reidy] and the rest of the EXCOM leaders did was not only charter the program, they directed development by targeting it not only at building our next generation of leadership but by also making it focused on our most pressing challenges."

Melo formulated the program around three themes. First, the programs would incorporate an action learning approach. Skilled facilitators would work with Progress teams to ensure classroom instruction was applied in a real-time manner. Second, the focus of the programs would be on solving relevant business challenges as uncovered during the surveys and through interviews with key executives. Lastly, the program would incorporate a refresher on strategy—with specific emphasis on how strategy is executed. At the end of the sessions, not only did the executive committee have specific, actionable recommendations, it also had an organization that was beginning to rally around the One Progress vision.

Tangible Benefits and Outcomes

By 2011, the company had made significant strides within its core markets. At the end of the first quarter, revenues were up 5 percent in aggregate and 9 percent in the licensing area. Income swung from a $1 million loss to a $20 million gain. The stock moved from an 11-year low of $11.17 on March 31, 2009 to near its historic high, reaching $29.09 on March 31, 2011. As written in one analyst report:

> Management is effectively managing its total resources to generate profits for the company when compared to industry averages. The company's long and short term debt ratios are in line with industry averages reflecting a solid financial condition. Operating margins are improving and operating cash flow remains positive. Demand for the company's products and services has been strong as sales for the last quarter grew 5.24% rising to $134.24 million. Looking forward, the analyst consensus forecast for revenue and earnings for the next two quarters is expected to show improvement versus the prior quarter. Price momentum is strong and the stock has the market should recognize this strength and the stock should be an above average performer over the intermediate term.[4]

While any investment strategist would be quick to point out that past performance is no guarantee of future results, the Progress Software leadership team can identify one element as certain: The company is committed to improvement by accelerating learning throughout the organization.

Lessons Learned

The senior leadership team members at Progress Software, knowingly or not, worked themselves through the five key steps necessary to generate learning in an organization. After experiencing unfavorable performance outcomes, they gathered information from inside and outside the organization. They analyzed the information completely and then discussed the meaning and implications within their executive development sessions, where they shared and generated insights and then took action. Consistent with our belief that organizations need to deliberately learn how to learn, Progress took an innovative approach, combining executive education with problem solving focused on its most pressing challenges. While organizations may not care to engage in as formalized and far-reaching a learning process as the one Progress developed, they do need to understand that learning is an active process that must engage the entire organization.

Notes

1. D. Garvin, *Learning in Action* (Boston: Harvard Business School Publishing, 2000).
2. C. Argyris and D. Schoen. *Organizational Learning: A Theory of Action Perspective* (Reading, MA: Addison Wesley, 1978).
3. T. Buzan and B. Buzan. *The Mind Map Book* (New York: Plume, 1996).
4. Computrade Systems, Inc., "Progress Software," Market Edge Equity Research Report, 2011.

10

Organizational Alignment

A business leader has to keep their organization focused on the mission. That sounds easy, but it can be tremendously challenging in today's competitive and ever changing business environment.

—Meg Whitman, CEO, eBay

The fourth enabler supporting the core PM^{4}TE process is Organizational Alignment. Considered by many managers to be the holy grail of performance management, organizational alignment is an essential condition for successful execution throughout an organization. In today's era of global supply chains, intra-industry partnerships, and networked organizations, alignment is more important—and more challenging—than ever. Add the complexity of turbulent environments where even the loosest connections are hard to maintain and alignment for many becomes little more than a fleeting hope. Yet somehow alignment must be achieved. In this chapter, we discuss the criticality of organizational alignment, its definition, and those activities leaders can engage to better align their organization at all levels. Tools and techniques that drive alignment are presented, as are observations of how effective organizations achieve alignment. Key steps to creating alignment within an organization are highlighted and supported by a case study showing how alignment can be established in practice.

Despite its being the subject of numerous books and articles over the years, effective alignment within organizations remains elusive. Mission statements are created, as are measures and critical objectives that cascade throughout organizations. Yet misalignment still persists, especially at the front-line employee level. Organizations that operate with misaligned workforces cannot effectively compete, especially in turbulent settings. Too many uncertainties are levied on employees who, in the absence of a clear sense of direction, can veer off course. In this chapter, we discuss the concept of alignment and provide techniques and tools that help managers improve it. Although alignment is a simple concept, making it happen in a dynamic environment is where some of the most significant challenges lie, which is why we address alignment within the context of the PM⁴TE process.

Organizational Alignment's place in the overall PM⁴TE process is shown in the outer ring at the bottom left of Figure 10.1. Organizational alignment is an essential enabler because it keeps everyone focused on the mission, which is critically important. We agree with Meg Whitman's quote at the beginning of this chapter—alignment sounds like a deceptively simple task. But as any executive who has directed the efforts of even a modest-sized

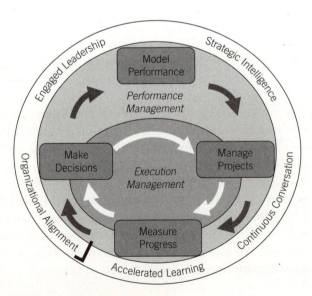

Figure 10.1   Model Enabler: Organizational Alignment

organization can attest, keeping employees focused on the mission amid the raft of day-to-day activities is a perennial challenge. This is why we've included it as a model enabler. Without alignment, the effects of the Core Process model will be modest at best.

From our observations, the challenge in achieving alignment does not stem from managers not knowing what alignment is. The problem is that managers do not know how to do it. The good news is that alignment of the many is really the same as alignment of the few. In practice senior leaders need to take deliberate steps to ensure that the priorities and actions of the many are indeed aligned with those few at the top of the organizational hierarchy. Active organizational alignment is the ultimate goal we are trying to achieve, and cascading the critical objectives, vital projects, and key measures is the means to achieve it. When an entire organization is working from the same set of priorities—ideally those articulated in the core PM^4TE process—that is when alignment occurs. By understanding what alignment looks like and, more importantly, how it is achieved through the cascading process, top managers can turn their fleeting hopes into a tangible reality. All of the main inputs needed to drive alignment have been discussed in the preceding chapters. In this chapter, we show managers how to cascade their priorities into an organization using a simple set of tools that are effective for any set of priorities. We provide more insight regarding the role leaders play in alignment in Chapter 11, which covers the Engaged Leadership enabler.

Why Organizational Alignment Is a Model Enabler

It should be readily apparent why organizational alignment is a process enabler. However, if it is not, performance management experts Robert Kaplan and David Norton in their book *Alignment: Using the Balanced Scorecard to Create Corporate Synergies* neatly summarize the challenge most organizations face today:

> Many corporations are like an uncoordinated shell. They consist of wonderful business units, each populated by highly trained, experienced and motivated executives. But the efforts of the individual business units are not coordinated. At best, the units don't interfere with each other, and the corporate performance equals the sum of the individual

business unit's performance minus the cost of the corporate headquarters. More likely, however, some of the business units' efforts create conflicts over shared customers or shared resources, or the units lose opportunities for even higher performance by failing to coordinate their actions. Their combined results fall considerably short of what they could have achieved had they worked better together.[1]

So why does better alignment improve the conditions highlighted above? We believe there are four things it accomplishes that are essential to effective performance management.

First, alignment forces the organization to clarify what the vision is as well as the plan for achieving it. Executives in organizations are like captains of ships—they must not only specify the destination well beyond the visible horizon, but also chart the course for getting the ship and crew there. Employees regularly lament that they have little idea where their leaders are taking the organization. We find this disheartening. Lack of clarity regarding destination causes confusion in the short term and leads to job dissatisfaction in the long run. When subordinates are unaware of the direction the organization is heading or the plan to get there, they have a very difficult time aligning their own goals and activities toward that future state. This is why clarifying strategy and direction are so important—without them the organization cannot achieve alignment. Organizational alignment forces a clarification of the strategy that sets the stage for improved performance.

Second, organizational alignment enables the development of a common set of priorities. In the Core Process, the organization— at whatever level—lists its critical performance objectives, vital projects, and key measures. When these are passed down through and across the organization, different units are then able to use them as the basis for setting their own priorities. The common priorities throughout the organization contribute to the kind of focus essential in high velocity environments.

Third, a clear strategy and a focused set of priorities help organizational units and employees determine what their specific contribution is. We find that in organizations units and individual employees are often unclear about their specific contribution to the organization's mission and plan. When there is no stated strategy, it is understandable why this is difficult. But even when there is a documented strategy or model of performance, many employees are still unsure how they contribute. As Peter Drucker points out in *The Essential Drucker*, "The focus on contribution is key to effectiveness: in one's own work . . . in one's relationship with others . . . and in the use of the tools of the executive such as meetings or reports . . ."[2] What alignment does is force an answer to the following question: "What is your specific contribution to the organization's top priorities and overall strategy?" Responding to this question simply and clearly promotes effective alignment.

Finally, an aligned organization understands the criteria by which results will be gauged. As critical objectives, vital projects, and key measures are cascaded into and across the organization, the narrow set of performance criteria become widely known (and, ideally, accepted) by employees. When this common picture of performance is created, employees at all levels are better able to adjust their day-to-day activities in support of those criteria. What this does is promote one common view of what's institutionally important. This increases the emphasis on key results and improves the focus on those activities that contribute to results.

In reality, there are many other reasons why organizational alignment is a process enabler; however, the four described above are the most critical. In the balance of the chapter, we describe what alignment is and how organizations can achieve alignment by using focused tools to drive priorities through the enterprise.

Understanding Organizational Alignment

Organizations today take many forms—from simple, functional structures, to complex multidivisional and matrix structures. There is no one right organizational form—all forms are contingent upon the nature of the work being performance in conjunction with the markets being served. Our purpose is not to opine on the right organizational structure—that is the work of organizational theorists—but to ensure that whatever form is chosen, the units and individual members within the structure focus on the same set of priorities.

Definition and Basic Concepts

Align means "to adjust to produce a proper relationship or condition."[3] For organizations, the proper relationship is one where each element of the organization is working on the same or a related set of priorities. Since this section focuses on *how* to align versus *why*, we must first emphasize that alignment is a noun and an outcome. Align is the verb or the active process, whereby the priorities of the organization are set collectively among members. Within an organization, alignment takes place between the major units, departments, and individuals. Alignment can include entities outside the organization such as suppliers or distributors, but our focus here will be alignment inside the traditional structure. Figure 10.2 provides a basic organizational structure with alignment requirements highlighted.

Corporate Headquarters Regardless of size, every organization has some type of corporate headquarters that consists of those senior executives charged with its overall supervision. In most organizations, the corporate officers—namely the chief executive and his staff—are responsible for setting the policies and strategy for the organization. They plan strategy, create and execute budgets, make investments, allocate resources, guide operations, and develop human capital. In this capacity, they determine overall priorities that typically include

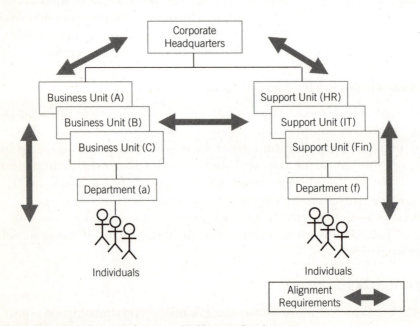

Figure 10.2 Basic Corporate Structure with Alignment Requirements

critical objectives and vital projects as previously defined. Further, they identify the measures that determine whether the organization is meeting its performance goals. Reporting inside as well as outside the entity may be done as part of this process. The process of alignment ideally begins with the clear articulation of priorities by the corporate headquarters to business units, support units, departments, and individuals.

Business Units Business units are typically externally facing units within an organization. *Externally facing* means they interface with customers in the delivery of products or services. Business units may be comprised of product or service groups, market groups, or a combination. Business units are generally considered the primary vehicle through which an organization executes its key priorities because they are the means by which value is created for the customer. Alignment occurs between business units and the corporate headquarters as well as between the business units and their counterparts, the support units.

Support Units Support units are internally facing entities. Their customers are actually the business units. Common support units in organizations are finance, human resources, and information technology. In some organizations, marketing can be a support unit as well, if it is not embedded in the business units. Support units exist not as islands to themselves, but to support execution within the business units. As such, they must be aligned with the corporate headquarters priorities as well as with those of the business units.

Departments Both business and support units consist of specialized departments or units of some form. In finance there is often a treasury function, a controller activity, and sometimes a strategic finance function. The priorities of each of these units—whether a business unit or a support unit—must be cascaded to the departments within that unit to ensure that the priorities of the unit are consistent with those of the departments.

Individuals Finally, individuals throughout the organization must have their own individual goals and development plans linked back to those of their department. Priorities must be normalized among coworkers. Groups of employees often have common or shared goals on behalf of their department or business unit. While it is challenging to create alignment down to the individual level, the individual employee is typically where the most significant opportunities for alignment exist. When individual employees in an organization—especially a large organization—have their goals aligned with the priorities of the entity overall, then alignment has been truly achieved.

Key Alignment Activities

As mentioned, each step of the PM^{4}TE model provides the necessary inputs for aligning the organization. These inputs are three-fold: (1) the performance model with critical objectives, (2) the vital projects, and (3) the key performance measures. How alignment incorporates each of these elements of the model is discussed in the following sections.

Cascade Critical Objectives   In the first phase of the Core Process, critical performance objectives are identified within the framework of a performance model. Ideally the performance model is developed at the corporate headquarters level. This may not always be the case, but for illustrative purposes, we will assume it is.

The performance model—or more specifically the objectives housed therein—should serve as the starting point for aligning the rest of the organization. Each objective within the framework becomes a candidate for cascading to the next level. Corporate staff should specify which critical objectives are passed through the corporate hierarchy and should provide guidance to the business units and support units regarding which specific objectives they must adopt. Typically, the business units are aligned to corporate priorities first, followed by support units. Given that the support units serve the business units, the business unit priorities must come first. Once objectives are aligned from corporate headquarters to the business units and from the corporate headquarters and business unit to support units, then unit leadership can begin the cascading process into departments and then individuals.

Regardless of the cascade's progression, the most important point to keep in mind as the cascading unfolds is that the corporate headquarters' priorities remain priorities throughout. If this fails to be the case, misalignment will occur.

Assign Vital Projects Starting again at the corporate level, vital project plans of actions and milestones (POA&Ms) should be created, reviewed, and passed to those parts of the organization where the projects can best be managed. In all likelihood, vital projects are already managed throughout the organizational hierarchy. Still, it is top management's job to review the entire project portfolio to determine that they are all being managed at the appropriate level in the organization. An assumption that they are will likely be incorrect, and the misalignment of projects is a problem second in severity only to misalignment of critical objectives. Visibility of project performance must be maintained through the structure by senior leaders; but effective project management must take place. Vital projects must be assigned to the right units at the right level.

Cascade Key Measures Aligning objectives and projects is important, but equally critical is the alignment of key measures. Again, each objective will have key measures and each project will have a set of milestones. The measures—alongside the critical objectives—must be passed down the organizational structure, ultimately reaching the individual level. As these measures cascade, the number that pass from one level to the next generally gets smaller. Whereas the corporate headquarters may have 20 to 30 key measures, a business or support unit may have 15 to 20, a department 8 to 10 and an individual 4 to 6. The reasoning behind this is simple: As measures cascade down the hierarchy, the hierarchy widens. Fewer measures are needed at each level—especially the individual level—to cover all the critical components of the organization's priorities. The ultimate outcome in cascading measures is to ensure that each unit and level of the organization is focused first and foremost on those measures that drive corporate progress. These measures are directly associated with critical objectives and vital projects.

Alignment Tools for the PM⁴TE Process

Aligning the organization around key activities sounds like a simple task. In practice, it is quite challenging. To aid in the alignment process, there are three tools that make the cascading effort easier. The tools are a mission statement cascading framework, the objective and measure alignment table, and the project priority table.

Mission Statement Framework   While the focus of the cascade is the three areas reflected earlier, we have found it useful to first ensure each level of the organization has its core purpose or mission defined. In his best-selling book *The Seven Habits of Highly Effective People*, Stephen Covey tells the story of how he visited various parts of a hotel chain and found cascaded mission statements from the overall hotel chain to individual hotels to the front desk and, finally, to the individuals who worked with him during his visit. Covey expressed his amazement at how well aligned the actions of every individual were with the mission of the hotel chain.[4] The key was not just the mission statements themselves, although they played an important role. It was the fact that all the employees, right down to the housekeeper, took the time to develop a mission statement aligned with the highest purpose of the organization.

We believe developing cascaded mission statements or other simple statements of purpose, help employees at all levels focus simultaneously on the purpose of the organization overall as well as the purpose of the unit or department in which they work, even in the absence of specifics such as critical objectives, vital projects, and key measures. For those who do not put much credence in mission statements, developing cascaded mission statements may seem trite. But every organization has a purpose, whether it is documented or not. Writing it down provides the opportunity to clarify the mission, share what it means with employees and other stakeholders, and ensure that the missions of various organizational units work in harmony with one another. As Roger Martin, Dean of the Rotman School of Business wrote in his *Harvard Business Review* article "The Execution Trap," executing strategy stems from cascading a series of choices throughout the organization:

> Those at the top of the company make the broader, more abstract choices involving larger, long-term investments, whereas employees at the bottom make more concrete, day-to-day decisions that directly influence customer service and satisfaction.[5]

Clarity about core purpose and the scope of activities in every unit helps what Martin refers to as the "choice cascade" process.

Mission statements can be developed and cascaded using what we call the *mission statement cascading framework*. The mission statement framework lists four areas where identity and purpose—the essentials of any mission—should be listed:

1. Who we are (within the organization)
2. What we do
3. Who our customers are
4. Why we do this

An example of a mission statement cascading framework is provided for a national hotel chain in Table 10.1. In the first column,

Table 10.1   Mission Statement Cascading Framework

Organizational Unit	Who We Are	What We Do	Who Our Customers Are	Why We Do This
Corporate	We are the Premier Stays hotel chain.	We provide value-priced, extended-stay lodging and associated services.	Business travelers on long-term projects or engagements.	To provide a home-away-from-home environment for those away from home for an extended period.
Business Group	We are the Premier Stays Eastern Regional group.	We provide value-priced, extended-stay lodging and associated services along the Eastern seaboard.	Business travelers on long-term projects or engagements from Maine to North Carolina.	To provide a home-away-from-home environment for those away from home for an extended period.
Business Unit	We are the Premier Stays Washington, DC, location.	We provide value-priced, extended-stay lodging and associated services in the Washington DC metro area.	Business travelers and federal government workers on long-term projects or engagements in the DC area.	To provide a home-away-from-home environment for those away from home for an extended period.
Department	We are the Premier Stays Washington, DC, Housekeeping Department.	We provide personalized, top-notch room servicing to guests of our chain in the Washington DC metro area.	Business travelers and federal government workers on long-term projects or engagements in our hotel.	To ensure our guests have the most pleasant stay possible while they are in our rooms for an extended period.
Team	We are the Premier Stays Washington DC First Floor Housekeeping Team.	We provide personalized, top-notch room servicing to our friends on the first floor of our DC hotel.	Business travelers, federal government workers and their families on long term projects or engagements in our hotel.	To ensure our guests—our friends—have the most pleasant stay possible while they are in our rooms for an extended period.

each unit within the organizational hierarchy is listed, starting with the top team. Each of the four areas is developed from the top down. The process can be replicated for each business activity within the organization. The cascading framework not only helps articulate the mission, it also provides a vehicle to ensure alignment with the mission of higher levels.

Objective and Measure Alignment Table   A major step toward alignment can be accomplished if mission statements are created and cascaded throughout the organization. However, the devil is in the details when it comes to alignment. Ideally, the critical objectives and key measures associated with the overall performance model should be cascaded as well.

Cascading should begin with the critical objectives and key measures of the performance model at the highest level in the organization for which the model has been created. To organize this, we use a tool called *the objective and measure alignment table*. An example is provided in Table 10.2.

As is clear from Table 10.2, objectives are cascaded from one level to the next until the point where the alignment logically stops. It can in actuality extend down to the individual level in an organization (and, frankly, it should). The paradox in most organizations is that the people who identify critical objectives and key measures—top management—have little to do with their day-to-day achievement; front-line employees do. Therefore, it is essential that these key elements of performance make their way down into the lowest levels of the organization. The objective and measure alignment table helps accomplish this.

Project Priority Table   The final area where alignment needs to take place is within the vital project area. Since projects are so essential to driving progress, they must be managed with added emphasis. While project plans and POA&Ms have been created earlier in the PM^{4}TE process, it is essential that they be cascaded to the appropriate unit within the organization and managed in aggregate by the executive team. The project priority table shown in Table 10.3 creates this project level alignment.

Table 10.3 allows managers to list—in the leftmost column—all of the vital projects ongoing in an organization and organize them by portfolio type. In this case, strategy projects have been distinguished

Table 10.2 Objective and Measure Alignment Table

	Corporate		Business Group		Business Unit		Individual	
	Critical Objective	Key Measure	Critical Objective	Key Measure	Critical Objective	Key Measure	Critical Objective	Key Measure
Stakeholder Satisfaction								
	Be involved in community	Hours of company community service	Be involved in community	Hours of group community service	Be involved in community	Hours of unit community service	Be involved in community	Hours of personal community service
	Grow revenue	Total revenue ($)	Grow revenue	Total group revenue ($)	Grow revenue	Total BU revenue ($)	Grow revenue	Total individual sales ($)
	Increase profit	Total profit ($)	Increase profit	Total group profit ($)	Increase profit	Total BU profit ($)	n/a	n/a
Primary Strategies								
	Develop customer intimacy	Net promoter score (1–10)	Develop customer intimacy	Net promoter score (1–10)	Develop customer intimacy	Net promoter score (1–10)	Promptly handle requests	Personal net promoter score (1–10)
Key Processes								
	Provide excellent service	Customer satisfaction rating for service—company	Provide excellent service	Customer satisfaction rating for service—group	Provide excellent service	Customer satisfaction rating for service—BU	Provide excellent service	Customer satisfaction rating for service—personal
Organizational Capabilities								
	Improve problem resolution time	Problem open-to-close time—company (minutes)	Improve problem resolution time	Problem open-to-close time—group (minutes)	Improve problem resolution time	Problem open-to-close time—BU (minutes)	Improve problem resolution time	Problem open-to-close time—personal (minutes)
Stakeholder Contribution								
	Improve employee retention	Company turnover (%)	Improve employee retention	Group turnover (%)	Improve employee retention	BU turnover (%)	Reduce absentee days	Sick days (#)

217

Table 10.3 Project Priority Table

	Corporate	Status	Business Group	Status	Business/Support Unit	Status	Department	Status
Vital Strategy Projects								
Implement Pricing Module					Business Unit A & B	On track		
Develop Succession Plan					All business units	Delayed		
Develop Specialized Product for New Market							R&D for consumers	Off track
Consolidate Data Centers	Corporate IT	Delayed	East Business Group	Delayed				
Vital Operational Projects								
Consolidate Manufacturing Facilities					Western Manufacturing	On track		
Lean Manufacturing in Southern Facility					Southern Manufacturing	Delayed		
Hire Short Skill Sets					Human Resources	On track		

from operational projects. Since both are critical to successful execution, both are included for management purposes. Each project is cascaded or shown in the table based upon where it is being managed in the organization. The status of each project (whether is in on track, off track or delayed) can also be indicated using standard red/yellow/green coding. Senior leaders not only can assess vital project status, they can quickly determine accountabilities and then dive into the particulars of the project. Leaders can change project priorities and accountabilities as needed to ensure the right level of focus is maintained on key projects.

Critical Success Factors

By engaging in the activities this chapter lays out, leaders can successfully align organizations of any size at any level. Alignment is not a complicated process; however, it is an involved one meaning managers must be actively engaged for it to be effective. To ensure the process works to the fullest extent possible, executives must consider the following three key factors throughout the cascading effort.

Maintain Active Executive Engagement

Leaders must be actively engaged in the entire cascading process in order for it to be effective. Ordering subordinate managers to take the objectives, projects, and measures and go forth and align themselves does not work. Not because subordinate leaders are lazy or incompetent—quite the contrary. When presented with alignment opportunities, most leaders welcome the chance to create tighter links across the organization. What we almost always find to be lacking is direct involvement of senior leaders throughout the process, making sure their highest priorities are, in fact, trickling down to the lowest levels of the organization. Imagine the effect of improving alignment of a workforce 10,000 to 20,000 strong by 5 to 10 percent. The impact on performance would be dramatic. Executives must remain engaged in alignment from top to bottom and start to finish to ensure the integrity of key priorities.

Recognize that Alignment Is Everyone's Responsibility

While top executives and senior leaders drive the cascading process, employees throughout the organization must acknowledge that alignment is their individual responsibility too. In more cases than we care to mention, we have been told by senior leaders—heads of major functions and business units—that they are unclear about what the top team's priorities are. If that is the case then the onus rests on the shoulders of these subordinate leaders to approach executives and solicit what the most important objectives, projects, and measures are in the organization. This rings true throughout the organizational structure. At every level, employees have to be sure that their intended contribution meets the needs of the next higher level up. Until everyone gets in step, the organization will remain suboptimally aligned.

Understand that Alignment Is Continuous

While it would be ideal to align an organization once and reap the benefits over and over, this is not possible. As conditions in the environment change, so too must the organization. New people will be hired, new departments created, not to mention mergers or divestitures of parts or even the entire enterprise. This means that in the future alignment will have to be reinforced, and more than once. This is a reality of organizational life and one that executives must understand up front. Alignment is a continuous process that leaders must drive continually to be effective.

Summary

We have covered a challenging topic—organizational alignment—in this chapter. As mentioned at the outset, alignment is a straightforward concept that every manager understands, but it is difficult to accomplish in practice. The actions required to put an organization's units into a proper relationship or condition require understanding missions at all levels, prioritizing critical objectives, vital projects, and key measures. Once this has been accomplished, each unit and successive level in an enterprise can be aligned to those essential performance elements. What leaders must do to make alignment happen is apply the tools provided here while ensuring they stay engaged in the process and communicate the importance of everyone's role. Moreover, leaders must realize that alignment is a constantly moving target that will come into focus only with an ongoing, sustained effort on their part.

Case Study: Altra Industrial Motion

Altra Industrial Motion, Inc., headquartered in Braintree, Massachusetts, is a global manufacturer of mechanical power transmission and motion control products. Through its 52 subsidiaries organized into six different business platforms, the company serves customers across a diverse group of industries, including energy, general industrial, material handling, mining, transportation, and turf and garden. Its product portfolio includes industrial clutches and brakes, enclosed gear drives, open gearing, belted drives, couplings, engineered bearing assemblies along with a variety of other components used in a mission-critical, high-volume manufacturing processes. The company prides itself on the reliability and accuracy of its wide range of products that help customers avoid downtime and enhance the efficiency of their manufacturing operations. For the year ending December 31, 2010, Altra Industrial Motion earned net sales of $520.2 million and net income of $24.5 million.

Turbulent Situation

Altra competes in a highly fragmented, highly competitive mechanical power transmission industry. The company faces competition from over 1,000 organizations of all sizes operating across the globe. The business is subject to high levels of cyclicality related to raw material inputs, consistently pressured by customers to improve quality while lowering costs, and constantly subject to fluctuations in currency values related to its international operations. In 2009, as manufacturing customers began to slow production, Altra's business also began to slow. In response, the company suspended retirement plan contributions, froze all nonunion salaries, and reduced work schedules. A restructuring charge was taken related to plant impairment and several facilities were also closed. The workforce was reduced at the same time. These actions—while short-term in nature—were in part intended to impact the company's long-term competitive position and eliminate the 2009 operating loss of $2.1 million.

Description of the Organizational Alignment Process

While all of these actions were taking place, Altra still had to execute its strategy throughout all six of its platforms and 52 subsidiaries. The company's strategy is encapsulated in seven critical objectives:[6]

1. Leverage the sales and distribution network.
2. Focus strategic marketing on new growth opportunities.
3. Accelerate new product and technology development.
4. Capitalize on growth and sourcing opportunities in the Asia-Pacific market.
5. Continue to improve operational and manufacturing efficiencies through Altra Business System (i.e., lean manufacturing).
6. Continue to focus on cost-reduction initiatives.
7. Selectively pursue strategic acquisitions that complement our strong platform.

To align the organization to focus on these objectives Altra executives implemented what they call the *Strategy Deployment process.*

The Strategy Deployment process was taken from Hoshin Planning, a long-standing Japanese strategic planning and deployment approach. From February to June of each year, the company formulates and deploys its strategy in order to drive alignment and action around the seven objectives listed above. According to company leaders, the process creates a chain of cause and effect by linking priorities, plans, resources, and actions together logically from top to bottom in the organization. To accomplish this deployment, Altra uses the seven-step strategy deployment process shown in Figure 10.3.

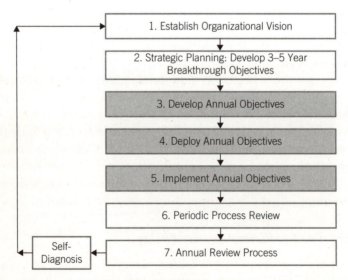

Figure 10.3   Seven-Step Strategy Deployment Process
Source: Hypothetical example.

Figure 10.4   Annual Objectives Example
Source: Hypothetical example.

For purposes of illustration, the remainder of the case will focus on steps 3 to 5, highlighted in the figure.

After the company confirms the vision, values, and mission, a handful of long-term breakthrough objectives are identified. From these objectives, senior managers begin developing annual objectives related to each of their six platforms. For each of the breakthrough objectives, a series of annual objectives is developed that will collectively drive its achievement. An example of this is shown in Figure 10.4.

In this example, the breakthrough objective of market share growth is driven by three successive, annual objectives: reduce product development, introduce new products to Asia, and convert two major European original equipment manufacturers (OEMs). Once these annual objectives have been created, they are then deployed into each of the groups and departments in each platform. An example of how this is done for the first annual objective—reduce new product development—is depicted in Figure 10.5.

Each of the subordinate departments creates cascaded objectives linked to the objectives at the higher level in the organization. In effect, each of the lower levels addresses the question, "How will we contribute to the achievement of our parent's objective?" This deployment continues until the lowest level in the organization is reached which is typically the department level. At that point, the objectives become translated into action at what the company refers to as "the point of impact." These action plans constitute the daily "to do's" that collectively drive the progress of the strategy

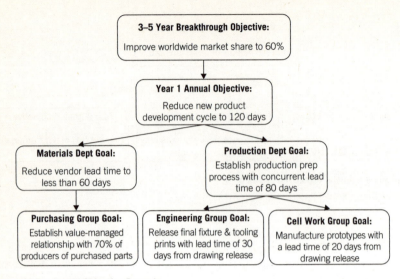

Figure 10.5   Annual Objective Example
Source: Hypothetical example.

across the organization. An example of an action plan is shown in Figure 10.6.

Once fully deployed throughout the business, the action plans and objectives are reviewed regularly to ensure that employees and managers are operationalizing the tactics necessary to fully execute the strategy. Regular reviews—weekly for the action plans and monthly for the objectives themselves—ensure that execution stays on track.

Interpretations from Key Managers

For managers throughout Altra, the strategy deployment process has become embedded in the fabric of how they run the business. "This is how we put our strategy to work," says Craig Schuele, Vice President of Marketing and Business Development and champion of the strategy deployment process. "Everyone from the top team to the shop floor understands how the process works and sees clearly how it contributes to the success of the company. Strategy deployment isn't something in addition to our day jobs, in many ways it is part of our ongoing work."

CEO Carl Christiansen notes that strategy deployment was an essential element of the company's performance in 2010. "We

POLICY DEPLOYMENT ACTION PLAN AND TRACKING

Improvement Priority/Project:	Reduce final fixture and tooling prints lead time		Date	1/1/2012
Objectives and Expectations:	Improve worldwide market share 60%		Revised	

Team Purpose/Scope:

Team Empowerment Boundaries:

Team Members:

No.	Improvement Priority	Measure	JCP	2012	JAN	FEB	MAR	APR	MAY	JUN	JUL	AUG	SEP	OCT	NOV	DEC	Target
1	Reduce final fixture and tooling prints lead time	LT from drawing release	60 days	Plan	68	58	52	50	48	46	42	38	34	32	32	30	30
				Actual													

No.	Action Plans	Owner	Timing														Target
1	Standardize tooling/fixture design rules	JH	Plan														
			Actual														
2	Streamline drafting and approval process	RS	Plan														
			Actual														
3			Plan														
			Actual														
4			Plan														
			Actual														
5			Plan														
			Actual														
6			Plan														
			Actual														
7			Plan														
			Actual														

Figure 10.6 Action Plan Template

Source: Hypothetical example.

executed well on our growth strategy in 2010, and we expect that the continued implementation of that strategy will lead to improved shareholder value for the long-term. Our strategy deployment process was a major driver of that success."

Tangible Benefits and Outcomes

At the close of 2010, Altra had experienced a resurgence in demand for its products and started to reap the benefits of the actions taken early in 2009. Gross margins grew to 29.6 percent and operating margins increased by to 10.6 percent. EPS increased by more than 200 percent to $1.02 and the company's cash position increased by 41 percent to close the period at $72.7 million. Altra now stands in a position to make several key acquisitions aligned with their last strategic objective. Between January 2009 and May 2011, the company's stock price rose from just over $2.00 per share to $26.50 per share.

Lessons Learned

The simplified strategy deployment process presented here hides a more complicated alignment process that the company commits to annually. Still, the major concepts and approach are as designed. Altra Industrial Motion places significant time, money, and human capital resources into their alignment process. While it is not perfect, it does have the intended effect of linking organizational performance from top to bottom. Organizations would be wise to consider investing the kind of time in alignment that Altra's managers do. A tenfold-plus increase in shareholder value during one of the worst economic environments in recent history forces one to consider that there must be some value to both the strategy deployment approach and organizational alignment in general.

Notes

1. R. Kaplan, and D. Norton, *Alignment: Using the Balanced Scorecard to Create Corporate Synergies* (Boston: Harvard Business School Press, 2006) 1–2.
2. P. Drucker, *The Essential Drucker: The Best of Sixty Years of Peter Drucker's Essential Writings on Management* (New York: HarperCollins, 2001).

3. *The Merriam-Webster Dictionary* (New York: Encyclopedia Britannica, 2010).

4. S. Covey, *The Seven Habits of Highly Effective People*, 2nd ed. (New York: Free Press, 2004).

5. R. Martin, "The Execution Trap," *Harvard Business Review* 88, nos. 7 and 8 (2010): 64–71.

6. Altra Holdings, Inc., 2010 Form 10K.

Engaged Leadership

Leaders aren't born, they are made. And they are made just like anything else, through hard work. And that's the price we'll have to pay to achieve that goal, or any goal.

—Vince Lombardi

The fifth and final enabler supporting the core PM⁴TE process is Engaged Leadership. Managing performance to achieve great results in turbulent environments, or any environment for that matter, is more about working hard and working smart than anything else. The tools in the PM⁴TE process will help achieve results, but not without the effort of leaders who are committed to their sustained use. In this chapter, we talk about the role leaders play in both implementing and driving the PM⁴TE process. We discuss what leaders in organizations do in a general sense and describe more specifically what leaders must do in the context of the PM⁴TE process. We highlight techniques leaders can use to set the stage for performance management success and describe the critical success factors leaders must keep in mind as they execute their priorities.

It should come as no surprise that leadership is an important element of any performance management process. As organizations plan and carry out their vital projects in support of critical objectives, challenges are bound to occur. Performance will likely fall short of expectations in some cases; in others, the assumptions underlying the performance model may prove incorrect. Engaged leadership is required to identify these issues, understand what is causing them, make decisions, and ultimately carry out actions intended to put performance plans back on track. In many respects, leading the PM^{4}TE process is as much about change management as it is performance management. Top managers, as well as employees throughout the organization, will be required to do things differently. Leadership helps them see how changes in their behavior will produce the desired results. In this chapter, we explore the activities and behaviors leaders need to commit themselves to in order to become engaged leaders.

Engaged Leadership is the final enabler in the PM^{4}TE, shown at the top left of Figure 11.1. In short, leaders get things done in organizations through their attitudes and their actions more than anything else. Effective leaders establish the vision for the organization, craft strategies to achieve it, build coalitions of employees at all levels, allocate resources to vital projects, inspire employees, and demand accountability. In short, they instill in organizations the motivation to succeed.

Few people would ever question the importance of leadership in any organizational setting. But outstanding leaders are a rarity—

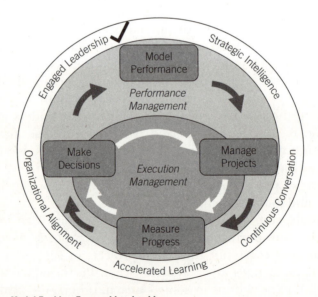

Figure 11.1   Model Enabler: Engaged Leadership

indeed, most employees complain that leadership is lacking in top management ranks. We agree—we encounter many more managers than we do leaders in our research and consulting. We subscribe to Vince Lombardi's words at the beginning of this chapter—leaders aren't born, they are made, and the way they are made is through focused effort and hard work.

Implementing the PM^{4}TE process is indeed hard work. We know because we have done it. Organizations have a natural tendency toward maintaining the status quo. There is typically little motivation to change the way work is done. But leaders, knowing that their environments are rapidly evolving, must show the organization the need for change and structuring itself for ongoing adaptation. In this chapter, we discuss who leaders are, what their work entails, differentiate leadership from management, and provide insights regarding how leaders can drive the PM^{4}TE process throughout their organizations.

Why Engaged Leadership Is a Model Enabler

The importance of good leadership in organizational life is undisputed. Nations elect leaders to guide them out of trying economic times. Military leaders are appointed to turn the tides of battle when losses are mounting and future victory is in question. In the business community, revered corporate chiefs, such as Lou Gerstner and Jack Welch, are hired for their ability to turn companies like IBM and GE around. Yet, as critical as leadership is in organizations, few people can put their finger on exactly what it is leaders are supposed to do and how that differs from day-to-day management.

In his seminal book *What Leaders Really Do*, Harvard professor John Kotter provides prescient insight into how leadership differs from management:

> Leadership, by contrast, is about coping with change. Part of the reason it has become so important in recent years is that the business world has become more competitive and more volatile . . . The net result is that doing what was done yesterday, or doing it 5% better, is no longer a formula for success. Major changes are more and more necessary to survive and compete effectively in this new environment. More change always demands more leadership.[1]

What is interesting about this quote is that it came from an article Kotter wrote in 1990—more than 20 years ago. But the challenges he highlights are as relevant today as they were when the article was written. Why? We see two reasons. First, the challenges facing organizations have grown in number and magnitude due to increased volatility. Second, high-caliber leaders seem to be fewer in number now than ever before. We aren't sure why this is the case. Both inhibitors speak—in part—to why engaged leadership is a key enabler of the PM^{4}TE process.

Initially establishing the PM^{4}TE process requires doing work that most organizations have not been exposed to. The concept of modeling performance is new for many organizations, as is designing a measurement system around critical objectives and vital projects. While problem solving and decision making in organizations are not unusual activities, structured problem-solving and decision-making processes typically are. The idea of collecting strategic intelligence and socializing it through a stream of continuous conversations at all organizational levels may be entirely unique. Regardless of newness, implementing and operating the PM^{4}TE process and key enablers will require effort beyond what is the norm in most organizations today.

To sustain the PM^{4}TE process long enough to achieve results, leaders have to be willing to confront high levels of organizational inertia. When a large organization—like a public company—is accustomed to operating using a well-entrenched set of performance protocols and norms, inertia will be great and the ability to change limited. Leaders must be able to overcome routines that will be stronger than the new PM^{4}TE activities being established. Even if managers throughout the organization know that performance management needs to be done differently, they will not likely possess the skills and desire to change en masse. Leadership is the catalyst needed to push employees out of their comfort zone and into the new operating reality.

Finally, leadership is critical in keeping the organization focused on both relevancy and results. For an organization to stay continually relevant in the marketplace, it must continuously perceive and respond to changes in the broader environment. As the organization adapts to these changes, it must still focus on results. Both the short- and long-term needs of the organization have to be balanced and the PM^{4}TE process provides the means to do so. Leaders are relied upon to ensure that both dimensions of short- and long-term performance are maintained.

Leadership is required for many reasons, but leaders are the ones who most directly impact the PM⁴TE process. In the rest of this chapter, we explain what the core activities of leadership are in any organization and explain what activities leaders drive in the PM⁴TE process. Tools and techniques to assist in the execution of these activities are highlighted as well.

Understanding Leadership Engagement

Most employees can easily recognize engaged leaders when they see them. Engaged leaders are not only interested, they are involved in virtually all aspects of organizational life to some degree. Within the boundaries of the PM⁴TE process there are three specific areas that call for leadership engagement, each of which we discuss in depth in the following section, after defining what engaged leadership is.

Definition and Basic Concepts

Leadership is a broad concept. For our purposes we define leadership as setting the strategic and organizational context for performance. As said already, leaders get things done inside organizations. But they cannot do everything, despite their broad responsibilities. So what are top leaders really responsible for? In our estimation there are really three areas that leaders—especially top management teams—need to focus their energies on: strategy, organization, and stakeholder outcomes. These areas are described in Table 11.1 and elaborated in the rest of this section.

Vision and Strategy   One responsibility that falls squarely on the shoulders of top leadership is setting the overall direction and strategy

Table 11.1   Areas of Leadership Responsibility

Area	Description
Vision and Strategy	Setting and signaling the purpose and the strategy for the organization
Organization	Structuring and aligning organizational systems to deliver on the strategy
Stakeholder Outcomes	Managing the stakeholder consequences of performance

of the organization. In Chapter 10, we discussed the importance of mission or organizational purpose. Leaders need to ensure not only that their organizations have a purpose, but that the purpose is relevant given the challenges of the environments in which they operate. In conjunction with that purpose, leaders need to set a high-level direction for their organizations. Often this is called the *vision*. Vision is the long-term destination for the organization. Whether it is a particular market share goal, an innovation target, or a specific level of stakeholder satisfaction to be reached, leaders provide the overarching direction for their organizations. But having a vision is not sufficient; leaders must oversee the development of a plan to achieve their visions. Then they must model the behaviors required to enact the plan. Whereas the vision identifies what the organization wants to achieve, the strategy explains how the organization will accomplish it. Creating vision and strategy is a responsibility of top leaders.

Organization Once vision and strategy have been established, leaders must ensure the organizational structure and business process architecture are in place to drive organizational performance. While seemingly more tactical than setting high-level goals, it is no less important and also stands as a distinct responsibility of executive management.

There are many ways to structure an organization and, as such, no one best way to organize. Organizational structure and business process architecture are functions of what the top management team is trying to accomplish in the markets. Regardless of the specific strategy choices leaders make, they must follow with an organizational form that can deliver that strategy. The organization of work and the execution of routines to deliver value to customers are also responsibility areas for top managers.

Stakeholder Outcomes Perhaps no other responsibility is more important to top leaders than delivering results and managing the impact of their actions. Leaders are put into top roles in organizations for one express purpose—to get results. Leaders who fail to deliver intended results do not usually enjoy lengthy tenures in their posts. But as important as results are, they cannot be achieved without regard for costs, financial and otherwise. Top leaders must link the importance of delivering results with that of doing so responsibly. The past several years have shown the disastrous effects of leaders not considering the impacts of their actions on virtually all stakeholder groups—customers, employees, the communities in which they operate, and in some cases even competitors. Financial irresponsibility on the part of Lehman Brothers contributed greatly to the demise of financial markets on a global scale. The collapse of Enron not only sank investors, but the community in which the company was located. The failure to fully consider risk levels by BP led to one of the worst environmental crises in history. Today the responsibility of leaders extends well beyond basic financial or mission performance.

Key Leadership Activities

The three areas just described establish the domains of leadership responsibility. Within each of these areas, however, leaders must act in ways that generate results. While effective leaders have various styles, they must accomplish a basic set of activities that are common to all leaders. Presented next are those activities we believe comprise high-functioning leadership engagement.

Set Priorities   Organizations are charged with accomplishing many important things. In turbulent settings the range of critical activities is even broader than those in more stable settings. Unfortunately, we find that in a great many organizations, the list of mission-essential tasks has grown to the point where literally everything is important. What this means is that nothing is important because no one thing takes priority over anything else.

A specific leadership activity, then, is to understand the organization's essential or critical objectives and ensure that priorities are set that push managers at all levels to focus the lion's share of their energies on those priorities. In organizations the 80/20 rule applies in most cases—about 20 percent of the activities being performed generate 80 percent of the value. With that in mind, leaders need to consciously identify that high-impact 20 percent and align efforts so that the full value of those activities is reaped.

Drive High-Leverage Action   Actions, like objectives, require prioritization—not all actions are of equal value. What is worse, in organizations actions are often taken that are of limited or negative value in that they may work at cross-purposes with other actions. Imagine a boat where everyone on board is rowing as hard as possible against one another—much energy is spent but little movement occurs. Leaders need to minimize this effect in their organization.

Leaders must take stock of the sum total of actions each group in the origination is taking and work to rationalize and prioritize them. Projects that are not adding clear value should be stopped. Activities that are one or two degrees removed from the main efforts of the organization should be reset and realigned. We find that leaders can be reluctant to get involved in the details of organizational action. They feel that managing this activity is the purview of subordinate leaders. It isn't. If actions are not being focused on the highest leverage outcomes, it is the leader's responsibility to correct this.

Make Decisions   Decision making is a specific activity that leaders engage in. We are not referring to routine decisions, which require little thought or analysis. We mean decisions that affect the three responsibility areas highlighted above. Leaders make strategy decisions, high-level organizational decisions, and decisions that impact stakeholder outcomes. These decisions are often difficult and intractable and exist in the domain where there are no right answers. There are usually, however, multiple bad answers. Leaders must work to tip the scales in favor of the better choices. This is one of their specific tasks.

Develop Subordinates   The final activity we attribute to leaders in organizations—at all levels—is the responsibility of developing their subordinates. Some experts believe the true measure of a leader is the number of their subordinates who eventually go on to assume positions of greater responsibility. General Electric during the Jack Welch era was known for its leadership development. When Welch retired from the chief executive post, there was a ready pool of candidates to succeed him. While Jeffrey Immelt was tapped for the top job—a position he still holds today—team members Jim McNerney and Bob Nardelli left to assume the CEO positions at 3M and Home Depot, respectively. Managers need to make developing those around them a priority to ensure the survivability of their organizations.

Tools and Techniques for the PM⁴TE Process

The PM⁴TE process provides an excellent context within which to promote the key activities presented thus far. There is no work more important than setting critical objectives, managing vital projects, measuring progress, and making decisions within the performance management process. It provides the setting within which each essential leadership task can be performed. To help in the execution of these activities, we have identified a series of tools and techniques, discussed next.

Vision Development   Before executives can set priorities, they must first articulate the direction in which the organization is going. As discussed already, this is the vision. A seminal work on vision development is a *Harvard Business Review* article, "Building Your Company's Vision," by Jim Collins and Jerry Porras.[2] They claim that a good vision contains two elements. The first is a high-level target, which they call a *big, hairy, audacious goal,* or BHAG. The BHAG is usually quantitative so that success can eventually be measured and it is positioned will into the future—usually 10 or more years out. Doubling company revenues within 10 years might be considered a BHAG for some organizations. The second element of vision for Collins and Porras is the *envisioned future.* Envisioned future is a description of the future state of the organization once it arrives at the BHAG. In essence it is a word picture of the future paired with the BHAG. Together, these two elements of vision give employees a target along with an idea of what the future might look like. We think this approach is effective and recognize that most corporate vision statements would be dramatically improved if they incorporated it.

Executive Project Review Meetings   We are intrigued by how little attention top management teams pay to the details of major projects going on in their organizations. The assumption in many cases is that capable middle-level managers are managing projects to the best of their abilities and that involvement by senior leaders only displays a lack of confidence in their skills coupled with a healthy dose of micromanagement. We would like to provide a different view.

Imagine executives in an organization are actually venture capitalists (VCs). VCs assemble investors for purposes of generating returns in an area in which they have a particular aptitude, such as microelectronics or biotechnology. After the team of VCs makes their initial investments in a small set of fledgling organizations, they meet regularly with the management teams of each portfolio company to monitor progress, provide advice, and, in some cases, bolster performance because—after all—the VCs are responsible to investors for generating the highest return possible. The best VCs are those who actively help their portfolio companies with experience and connections. It would seem unusual for VCs to remain hands off since success is so often linked intimately to their involvement.

With this example in mind, we ask executives to look at their portfolio of vital projects the same way VCs would look at their portfolio companies, that is, as investments that need to be nurtured and brought to fruition. Setting aside a fund to invest in the best projects—managed to completion with active executive engagement—is the best way to ensure the actions of the organization are spent on the highest-leverage investment possible.

Decision Comparison Template   Executives make decisions every day. At the top of an organization, the decisions are great in both magnitude and complexity. Choices the top team makes have far-reaching effects on the organization and its performance. Given that backdrop, it is essential that top leaders take the time to analyze their decisions and use a format that improves the likelihood of making the right decision. This is where option comparison comes in. Figure 11.2 presents an easy-to-use format we have found helpful when comparing decision options.

The decision comparison template enables top teams to organize their decisions using a standard set of fields—decision name, decision description, and main assumptions—and then evaluate them using criteria germane to the decision. In this notional example, an executive team is evaluating where they will source production of a new product line. There are three options available to them. The criteria the team uses to compare the options are listed on the bottom of the left-hand side: risk, cost, speed (to implement), and complexity. Each criterion is scored using a 1-to-5 scale. The option with the highest score—in this instance option 3—emerges as the preferred option. While this template does not in and of itself select the best decisions, what it does do is provide managers with an objective way to assess each option. The final determination of any decision will always remain a matter of executive judgment. Still, a format like this can be especially helpful for stimulating structured thinking during the process.

	Option 1	Option 2	Option 3
Decision Name			
Decision Description	*Domestic Manufacturing*	*International Manufacturing*	*Partnership*
	Expand the capacity existing within the domestic market to handle the new product line.	Establish a facility in a low-cost nation to accommodate the new product line.	Identify a partner to contract with the manufacture the new product line for us.
Main Assumptions	We can expand the existing facility in time for the product launch.	We will be able to find an appropriate site for development.	There is a partner that has the capability to produce a highly engineered product.
Selection Criteria (1 unfavorable – 5 favorable)			
Risk	4	3	5
Cost	2	3	4
Speed	4	1	5
Complexity	5	4	5
Total	15	11	19

Figure 11.2 Decision Comparison Template

239

Critical Success Factors

By understanding what leaders are responsible for in organizations and by specifically engaging in key leadership activities, top managers can hone their leadership skills and drive performance throughout the entire PM^{4}TE process. As this chapter's epigraph makes clear, leadership—like any other capability—can be developed through persistence and hard work. Setting the tone for a focused approach to performance management requires sustained leadership engagement. To ensure these activities yield results, we next review the critical success factors we know must be present during execution.

Set the Example

Albert Einstein said that "setting an example is not the main means of influencing others, it is the only means." In the day-to-day challenges of keeping an organization above water in the most turbulent of conditions, top leaders often forget that their actions and behaviors communicate more to employees than their words ever could. How leaders act and what they do is the true measure of their character. Leaders who are committed to performance demonstrate it by how hard they push to inculcate the practices we have outlined into the fabric of their organizations. Half-hearted efforts will not deliver sustained results. To be effective in performance management, leaders must be intimately involved in the PM^{4}TE process.

Balance Leadership and Management

A simple way to illustrate the difference between management and leadership is as follows: Management is about doing things right, whereas leadership is about doing the right things. It is a basic illustration of efficiency versus effectiveness. Top leaders must embody both skills—leadership and management. Driving the execution management phase of the core PM^{4}TE process is about efficiency—are projects being completed on time and are decisions being made to keep them on track? But generating results in the performance management section is about leadership—are the actions in the main delivering the performance we need? Both management and leadership are required to generate results. Top managers must balance both.

Create the Capacity to Change

At its very heart, the PM⁴TE process is more about change management than it is performance management. Sustained performance requires sustained change, especially in volatile settings. Products and services that provide the preponderance of benefits today cannot be expected to do so in the future. New products and services will be required, and new skills and capabilities will be necessary to provide them. Leaders have to be sure that they are preparing their organizations to evolve in whatever ways are needed to cope with changes in environmental conditions. As trite as it may sound, the only constant in turbulent settings is change. To survive, leaders must ensure that their organizations have the dynamic capability to do so.

Summary

In discussing the final enabler—leadership engagement—we offer simple but effective insights for what leaders need to do to be successful in implementing the PM⁴TE. Leadership is often considered to be more of an art than a science, contingent upon charisma instead of character. Time and time again, the opposite has proven to be true. Being effective as a leader is about setting direction, aligning actions, making decisions, and, more than anything else, getting results. How this is accomplished doesn't need to be a mystery known only to the chosen few who have been granted innate leadership abilities. In reality, results can be achieved through effective use of a process in which managers can execute the three main leadership activities. In the final chapter, we provide additional advice on how leaders can make the PM⁴TE model function effectively within their organizations.

Case Study: RSA Security

Company Background

RSA Security—now the security division of technology giant EMC—was founded in 1986 by the inventors of public key cryptography: Ron Rivest, Adi Shamir, and Leonard Adleman. Throughout its history, the company has focused on solving the basic technology need for identifying and authenticating user access to enterprise-wide technology platforms. Since its inception, RSA has thoughtfully expanded its products and services to offer cryptographic solutions that address the need for data privacy and integrity as well as provide various types of electronic solutions. As of the company's acquisition by EMC in 2006—the last year when RSA was a publicly traded entity—the company posted revenues of just over $300 million annually.

Turbulent Situation

RSA competes in the highly volatile world of security software. This market stands at approximately $17 billion, and consists of major competitors such as Symantec, Trend Micro, and McAfee, which collectively comprise almost one third of the industry. As RSA notes in its final 10K filing, "security technologies are under constant attack. The strength of our cryptographic and other e-security technologies is constantly being tested by computer professionals, academics and 'hackers.' Any significant advance in the techniques for attacking e-security solutions could make some or all of our products obsolete or unmarketable." In addition to attacks by malicious external parties, products and services are always being challenged by competitors working feverishly to create new and better security and authentication technologies. Few technology companies have been able to maintain their presence in an environment like this. RSA Security, however, has done so effectively for 25 years, thanks in large part to their visionary and dedicated leader Art Coviello.

Description of the Engaged Leadership Process

Few top executives are as engaged in their business and their markets as Art Coviello. Currently the Executive Chairman of RSA, Art was the COO of the company from 1996 until 2006, when RSA was acquired by EMC. During his stewardship, he lifted revenues from $25 million to almost $750 million. Beyond delivering eye-popping revenue and profitability growth, he established RSA as the de facto standard in what is known as two-factor authentication. He did so by focusing on, among other things, the main areas of leadership responsibility highlighted previously.

Good leaders establish long-term visions and then create realistic strategies and action plans to achieve them. Early in his tenure as CEO, Art set out to make RSA the standard in its form of authentication. He did so by establishing aggressive growth goals for the business and staying highly active in the marketplace. As he notes openly, "There's not a high-tech company that survives and prospers if it doesn't grow." To drive growth at the rate he did, he ensured that the company capitalized on significant opportunities in the environment such as smart-card technology and risk-based authentication while sticking carefully to its core business of one-time passcode authentication.

To ensure RSA detected and stayed ahead of market changes, he established an annual strategy process that maintained a three-year view of future performance. The process—which is still in place today—involves the entire leadership team and many of their direct reports. It starts with a careful study of selected issues agreed upon by the management team based on environmental changes they believe are driving the future of the industry. Cross-functional strategy teams are chartered to gather strategic intelligence and analyze each of the topics in depth; the findings are ultimately reported to the entire team at the start of strategy formulation. The strategy is then designed for each of the business units and is interlocked with the main functional areas that support the business in order to gain commitment and support. Major initiatives also developed for each business are then funded through the budgeting process. An operating plan is created and reviewed regularly alongside the major initiatives to gauge progress.

The insights that the strategy study teams provide to the organization help leaders maintain a dynamic picture of how the industry is evolving. This picture is used not only to drive RSA's strategy but also shape the evolution of the industry. Each year, Art and RSA host the RSA Security Conference—the premier industry event for security professionals around the globe. For four days, industry professionals convene to discuss the major issues and trends facing their organizations. Presentations are given on topics ranging from mobile application security to cyber-crime to risk mitigation. The attendees and speakers are a veritable who's who in global business and industry. Past participants include executives from leading technology companies like Microsoft and McAfee, scientists from top-tier universities, general officers from the Department of Defense, even former United States presidents. The event is kicked off by Art, who provides his thoughts on where he thinks the future of the security industry lies. In addition to managing the industry's leading event, Art maintains close contact with industry analysts as well as RSA's customers. He actively engages a broad base of stakeholders to ensure that a steady flow of information and intelligence pass through him to the organization. Of course, customers too are a top priority. In a recent open letter to RSA SecureID customers, Art explained the nature of security attacks on its systems, described what the company was doing to enhance its own security, and reassured customers of actions RSA was taking to ensure "customers remain our first priority."

Art and his leadership managed multiple acquisitions over his tenure at RSA. These acquisitions—linked to the company's strategy—reflected opportunities to help RSA access adjacent businesses closely related to their core business of token technology. These acquisitions included the purchase of Cyota, a privately held company that delivered online security and anti-fraud solutions to thousands of financial institutions around the world. This acquisition enabled RSA to access a consumer market by offering risk-based authentication—a major shift for the company at the time. At RSA, executives are both promoted from inside the company and brought on board from outside to provide not only a fresh perspective but the best thinking from around the industry.

With this type of focus on external issues—the main job of every CEO—it would be easy to conclude that Art spends little time managing the day-to-day business. Easy, but inaccurate. Art and his top team manage key technology development projects on a monthly basis and track global performance of revenue and profitability daily. When the business experiences deviations from its airtight operating plan, Art drives his team to analyze the key causes of performance variances and enables immediate action to stay on plan. Through his closeness to the market, the RSA team has been able to capitalize on market dips by shifting their sales priorities and, in some cases, purchasing competitors within compressed time frames. The constant vigilance and mediation between market and company put Art and RSA right at the crossroads of industry and company performance.

Interpretations from Key Managers

Many members of the top management team that works with Art have been working alongside him for years. They readily admit Art is indeed a visionary and that his long-term view of company and industry evolution is a genuine driver of change. They also note that he is a senior leader committed to achieving what he sees as the future of the business. He maintains a focus on results and, as Ed Maggio, vice president of global operations, noted in an interview, "Art has been central to running the company. A lot of key decisions were made by or involve Art." If decision making is the specific executive task, then observation and evidence indicate Art understands this lesson well.

Tangible Benefits and Outcomes

With all of his and his team's work, Art was able to generate steady stock price growth that ultimately led to the sale of the company to EMC for $2.1 billion in 2006, a 22 percent share premium over the trading price when the sale was announced. Some industry analysts felt that EMC overpaid for the company, which had just over $300 million in revenues at that time. But EMC CEO Joe Tucci—a visionary in his own right—didn't see it that way. He viewed RSA as an integral piece of the changing data-storage puzzle. "To grow its business, EMC needs to integrate data storage and security. That is mandatory . . . the whole name of the game is how you build continued value for the long shot." Given that RSA has since doubled its revenues since the purchase in 2006 to almost $750 million, both Art and Joe have demonstrated again the important role that engaged leaders play in driving business performance.

Lessons Learned

There are a few timeless lessons senior managers everywhere can extract from this case. First, driving performance in an organization starts at the very top. It's not enough to create and underscore the importance of vision and priorities; engaged leaders like Art Coviello drive their strategies, inside and, if warranted, outside their organizations. Second, engaged leaders take an active role in setting high-level direction and ensuring day-to-day operating performance meets critical performance objectives. Senior managers often forget that leadership is more than setting lofty goals and delivering motivating speeches—it's an active process that requires constant, detail-oriented attention. Third, effective managers recognize that engaged leadership must be the standard at all levels of the organization. Across the RSA platform, leaders from around the globe are engaged in the day-to-day delivery of business performance. Lastly, in a larger sense, turbulent environments demand engaged leadership. Conditions change too rapidly for a passive, laissez-faire management style to be effective. Companies like RSA Security, with leaders like Art Coviello, show that even-handed, engaged leaders can not only transform their organizations, they can also transform their entire industries.

Notes

1. J. Kotter, *John Kotter on What Leaders Really Do* (Boston: Harvard Business Press, 1999).
2. J. Collins and J. Porras, "Building Your Company's Vision," *Harvard Business Review* 74, no. 5 (1996): 65–77.

PART 4

MAKING THE MODEL WORK

CHAPTER 12

Making It Work

Discipline is the bridge between goals and accomplishment.

—Jim Rohn

In this final chapter, we discuss how to make the entire Performance Management for Turbulent Environments process model work. For leaders to capture the full value of the PM⁴TE process, it must be implemented in full. This is easier said than done, especially for organizations trying to cope with the challenges of day-to-day operations. While the model has nine distinct elements, it is better conceptualized in three separate components: the Performance Management cycle, the Execution Management cycle, and the Model Enablers. In this chapter, we explain what we call *cycle logic* and describe how viewing the PM⁴TE process through the lens of cycles drives improved execution. We then discuss how to implement each major component of the model and provide an assessment tool that leaders can use to determine the readiness of their organization to implement the PM⁴TE process. We end with a final thought—making the process work effectively in the long run.

All of the principles, practices, tools, and techniques in this book will ultimately prove to be of little value if action is not taken to implement them. Engaged leaders must apply the PM⁴TE model if they want to experience the results enjoyed by many, if not all, of the case study organizations in this text. In this chapter, we put in context the logic behind the PM⁴TE model and provide instruction regarding what to do to implement the approach in earnest.

We have thus far presented and discussed the entire PM⁴TE process. Based on our collective work and research with over 100 different companies and our in-depth understanding of performance management literature, we believe this model—when implemented fully—will provide organizations with the process and tools needed to successfully navigate the roiling waters of turbulent settings. We know these tools—like any—will be of little value if there is no guidance regarding how best to use them. Further, we know organizations need to implement these tools quickly if they are to migrate successfully to this new approach for managing performance. In the following sections, we describe how this can be done with little disruption to the existing performance management process. Before we begin, we present the PM⁴TE process model in full within the three separate implementation stages:

Stage 1: The Performance Management Cycle
Stage 2: The Execution Management Cycle
Stage 3: The Model Enablers

The entire model and its stages are shown in Figure 12.1.

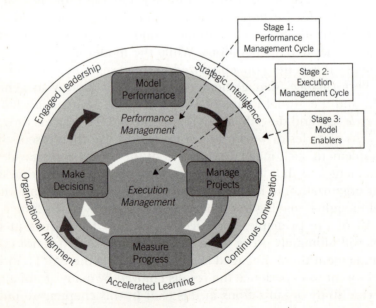

Figure 12.1   Stages of PM⁴TE Implementation

The Logic of Cycles

A cycle is a time interval in which a characteristic, regularly repeated event or sequence of events occurs. Cycles can be used to describe any set of steps or phases that repeat in a closed-loop system over time. Celestial bodies, such as the moon and planets, cycle around the earth or sun and pass through a series of phases that repeat over time (sometimes a very long time). Washing machines, too, incorporate stages—soak, wash, rinse, spin—in a cycle that can be repeated until the right level of cleanliness has been reached. The cycles we refer to in this book represent a repeating series of management activities that, when completed, drive management performance. Two other illustrations lend insights into the thinking underlying the PM^{4}TE process.

Control Theory

Virtually all performance management systems today represent manifestations of control theory. Control theory posits that an organization, and all the systems in the organization, require some form of control at all levels to ensure that the actions of the systems are congruent with the aims of the organization itself. These control mechanisms can take a variety of forms, such as the organizational structure, behavioral controls like values and norms within organizational groups, or measurement devices inside a performance management process. Performance management as a means of control reflects a basic cybernetic model in which the output of a system is evaluated for consistency with a preestablished set of criteria and any deviation from those criteria is adjusted by a controller to the system. A basic cybernetic model is depicted in Figure 12.2.

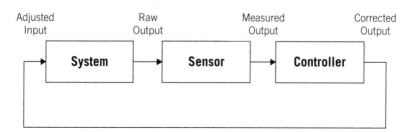

Figure 12.2   A Basic Cybernetic Model

The PM[4]TE process reflects this structure, but does so in a way that enables the managers of the organization to not only control performance, but also accelerate key aspects (e.g., projects) while testing the relationships among other elements (e.g., critical objectives). Our model rests on the belief that the faster and better an organization can execute and control performance, the better it can cope with changes in its external environment. Therefore, time is a central part of the model as well.

The Boyd Loop

One of the more interesting applications of control theory and the basic cybernetic model in a dynamic setting is the *Boyd* or *OODA* (pronounced oo-dah) *loop* shown in Figure 12.3.

The OODA loop was developed by U.S. Air Force Colonel and military strategist John Boyd, a fighter jet pilot during the 1950s and '60s. In dogfights, Boyd believed that the advantage shifts to those pilots who observe their enemy, orient to his actions, decide what to do, and then act, in a cycle faster than that of the opponent. The concept, distilled, is to cycle through the OODA loop more rapidly than the enemy can. The faster the cycle is repeated, the more quickly actions are executed and adjusted, until the enemy cannot cope and is ultimately defeated.

While not quite as dire as dog fighting, organizations are, indeed, fighting for their survival in volatile environments full of combatants and rife with changing factors. While the risks may not be readily observable as air-to-air combat, they are unquestionably present, and managers must remain vigilant to conditions that affect their organizations. They would also be advised to use the PM[4]TE to help in accelerating their own responses.

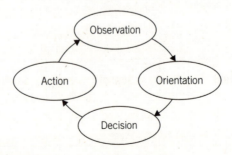

Figure 12.3   The Boyd or OODA Loop

Stage 1: Performance Management Cycle

Turning our full attention to the implementation of the PM⁴TE process, we recommend that managers begin implementation with the PM⁴TE Core Process, or what we call Stage 1, the Performance Management cycle. The Performance Management cycle is shown in Figure 12.4. The basic purpose of the Performance Management cycle is *effectiveness*—determining the organization's value creation model, its most important prioritized objectives, its most vital projects, and its critical gauges of progress. This effort sets up the performance system for rapid execution in the rest of the PM⁴TE process.

What to Do

The Performance Management cycle is the basic starting point for the PM⁴TE process. Recall from Part Two of the book that the Performance Management cycle contains the first four phases of the PM⁴TE Core Process—Model Performance, Manage Projects, Measure Progress, and Make Decisions. The first two phases— Model Performance and Manage Projects—can be dovetailed into strategic planning at the overall business, business-unit, or

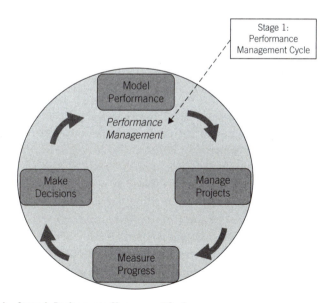

Figure 12.4   Stage 1: Performance Management Cycle

support-unit level. The organization should select a model of value creation such as a success map or a financial driver model to begin the process. The specific model is not important as long as managers buy into the approach and feel the model reflects the critical performance objectives of their unit.

Once selected, leaders should take time to educate themselves on the particulars of how the model works. One or two managers should take the lead on creating education materials and preparing workbooks necessary to facilitate sessions that develop the model. Ample information exists regarding how to build a Strategy Map, basic driver model, or any other model of value creation.

Building the model usually requires input from prior strategic planning activities, financial performance data, current strategy formulation work (see Chapter 7, "Strategic Intelligence") or business process improvement efforts. These can serve as key informants to the process. This information can be augmented with manager interviews that solicit their input about what the organization's objectives and goals should be.

After the development of the performance model, vital projects should be collected, documented, and then aligned to the critical performance objectives within the framework of the performance model. Chapters 3 and 4 on modeling performance and managing projects describe how to accomplish both activities in detail; the first two steps are complete when there is a complete, agreed-on model of performance with a small set of vital projects aligned to it.

Next, each of the objectives in the performance model should be assigned a measure from which performance can be assessed—the third phase in the model, Measure Progress. Ideally, there would be only one measure for each objective, and for each measure there should be a *baseline*, which shows current state performance, and a *target*, which expresses the desired future state. The full set of measures and targets serves as a scorecard for the performance model. Once this set of objective performance measures is developed, high-level project plans with measureable milestones should be created for each vital project that links to the performance model. The vital projects should drive progress of the organization as gauged by measures moving from the baseline to the target. In cases where there is no vital project to accomplish an objective, one should be created.

Once the performance model has been developed, the vital projects are organized into portfolios of high-level project plans and a scorecard of measures (each with a baseline and target) is created for the full set of critical objectives. At this point, the performance management system has essentially been established. What the leadership team must do now is collect baseline data to determine where the organization currently stands with respect to the accomplishment of each performance objective. The first set of decisions is the fourth phase of the process—Make Decisions—the point associated with making sure the objectives, measures, and targets are set appropriately and the means to collect the first round of performance data are in place.

The first iteration of the Performance Management cycle is accomplished with the express intent of setting up the cycle for on-going management. Once the cycle is established and the data informs the cycle itself, then a focus on driving execution can be developed.

How to Do It

To build the tools and templates in the Performance Management cycle, each unit leadership team needs to set aside time—a few full-day sessions are not uncommon—to create all the templates. Normally, several full days will be needed to develop and refine the performance model. The same time span will be needed to collect and document the vital projects. The process also requires a few days to select the measures, establish the baselines, and set the targets. Approximate time frames are provided in Table 12.1.

It is essential that the team work together at this time to develop a shared understanding of unit performance. These first few meetings can be challenging and reflect a development process that will require several iterations. But keep in mind that significant value comes from completing each step in the cycle as a team. This approach not only facilitates initial learning, it also develops a sense of shared ownership for the process and more importantly, for the performance objectives within the process.

Stage 2: Execution Management Cycle

Once the Performance Management cycle has been constructed, leaders should transition immediately into execution. Execution occurs almost entirely within Stage 2, the Execution Management

Table 12.1   Activities to Create the Performance Management Cycle

Activity	Purpose	Participants	Duration
Develop the performance model	Understand the performance model, identify the critical objectives, and construct the key linkages within the model.	Entire unit leadership team	1–2 days total time
Collect and align vital projects	Document vital projects and align them with the performance model.	Entire unit leadership team	1–2 days total time
Build measures for each objective and vital project	Create high-level project plans for each vital project and individual measures, baselines, and targets for critical performance objectives.	Entire unit leadership team	2–3 days total time
Make decisions regarding model, objectives, and projects, and measure efficacy	Collect the first round of data and assess the goodness of the entire set of performance management information (e.g., performance model, portfolio of vital projects, and scorecard).	Entire unit leadership team	2–3 days total time

cycle. Unlike the Performance Management cycle, which is about *effectiveness*, the Execution Management cycle is focused on *efficiency*. The Execution Management cycle is depicted in Figure 12.5.

At first glance, it is tempting to conclude that the Execution Management cycle is simply a derivative or subset of the Performance Management cycle. In fact, it is a nesting of the first

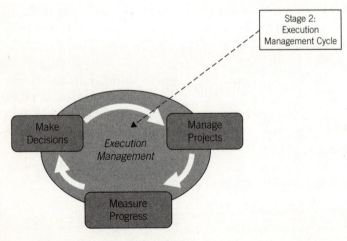

Figure 12.5   Stage 2: Execution Management Cycle

three phases of the Performance Management cycle. But in this cycle the power of the PM^{4}TE process is brought to light, in keeping with our initial exposition on control theory and the OODA loop. To accelerate execution and build the organizational capability to manage effectively in turbulent settings, leaders must establish a relentless focus on those activities (the vital projects) that drive results in the core model.

What to Do

The first step in the Execution Management cycle is Manage Projects. Unlike in the Performance Management cycle, where the purpose of this phase is to collect, document, and align vital projects, the purpose now is to aggressively manage those projects to completion. We know from our work and research that those areas where top executives are most personally involved signal to the rest of the organization a higher level of importance. Given that vital projects represent *the most important* activities in an organization, they should be focused on and managed very carefully. This will accelerate their completion and, in turn, accelerate execution. The more leaders drive toward milestone completion and the more frequently they gauge project progress, the faster execution will occur. When this happens, critical objectives within the context of the performance model are accomplished more quickly. We believe the OODA loop logic prevails at this juncture—by focusing relentlessly on Execution Management and speeding the rate at which the cycle is completed managers enable their organizations to build change capacity and ultimately generate ongoing change at a rate faster than competitors can cope with and environmental conditions can dictate. Execution Management within the context of a well-constructed Performance Management cycle, we know, delivers results in even the most turbulent settings.

How to Do It

Establishing the tools and templates within the Performance Management cycle can take considerable time to accomplish. While this may seem at cross purposes with the book's overall theme, we think leadership teams should take whatever time is necessary when completing the initial cycle. However, this is absolutely not the case when moving into the Execution Management cycle. At this point a relentless—we might even say exclusive—focus on project completion and problem solving should prevail.

If executives are serious about building capabilities, then the approach to managing the organization must change. Time must be set aside to focus solely on vital project execution and problem solving within the Execution Management cycle. Mechanisms must be put in place to accomplish this. We advocate holding both weekly vital project reviews and problem-solving meetings for the express purpose of building organizational skills. Based on our observations, project management and problem solving are two of the most underdeveloped capabilities in organizational management today—and they are, perhaps, the most essential to successful execution. To correct this deficiency, we recommend adding time to the governance calendar to expressly focus work on these two areas. Table 12.2 shows the basic activity information.

Why set time aside to work only on these two areas? There are several reasons. First, both of these are individual skills, the sum total of which reflects organizational capabilities. Focusing on problem solving and project management can develop them. There is no better way to improve each than by working on them in the context of real organizational projects and challenges. Second, both are areas in which executives need to be involved. If the only type of leadership that works is setting an example, then top managers need to set the example by being involved in the activities. Lastly, no organization has a shortage of either projects or problems. Setting specific time aside to address them is simply good management.

Table 12.2   Activities to Create the Execution Management Cycle

Activity	Purpose	Participants	Duration
Vital project management meetings	Measure project progress, shift resources where needed, remove short-term obstacles, maintain focus and management attention.	Entire unit leadership team	1–2 hours per week
Problem-solving sessions	Identify challenges with project progress and objective achievement.	Entire unit leadership team	1–2 hours per week
		Working groups	4–8 hours per week

With the Performance Management and Execution Management cycles in place, leaders should start fully building the Model Enablers necessary to sustain their success.

Stage 3: Model Enablers

The effectiveness and efficiency of the PM^{4}TE Core Process (i.e., the Performance and Execution Management cycles) rests on the Model Enablers, comprising the five individual enablers identified in Figure 12.6. In Stage 3, each of these is developed within the organization.

What to Do

Chapters 7 through 11 discuss each of the individual Model Enablers, so we will not review them here. After the Core Process has been established and both cycles put in place, executives should assess and then improve their organizations' capabilities with respect to each individual enabler. Organizations are not expected to have fully developed capabilities in each of these areas. More likely there are areas that do not formally exist, even in more sophisticated entities. Our recommendation is that depending on the results of their initial assessment, leaders work to implement

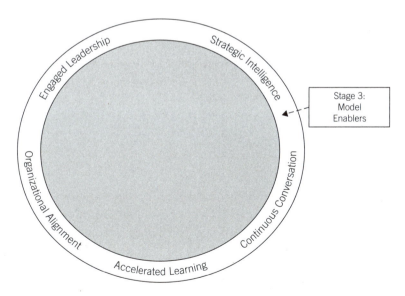

Figure 12.6   Stage 3: Model Enablers

the tools and techniques discussed in each chapter to more fully establish the foundation necessary for sustained success in the core PM^{4}TE process.

How to Do It

It is tempting to sequence the development of each enabler in a way that mirrors the way each was presented in this book. The challenge is that they are all equally important; the success of the model rests upon the collective set, not any one by itself. That said, we know that without engaged, committed leadership, the PM^{4}TE process will not get moving at all. Managers at a given level can put in place the infrastructure and the phases of the core model, but until the appropriate level of leadership becomes involved there will be little opportunity to reap the rewards the process can deliver. With engaged leadership, each of the other enablers—as well as the Core Process itself—will fall into place.

The Performance Management in Turbulent Environments Assessment: Determining the Current State of the Model

To guide managers in the development of the PM^{4}TE model, we have created an assessment that provides the direction necessary to focus implementation activities. Again, based on our work with hundreds of organizations, the assessment provides a set of self-perception measures within two areas: (1) major components of the model themselves and (2) behaviors of managers where the model is intended to operate. This assessment is free to anyone and can be accessed at our companion website, www.pm4te.com. Many of the tools and templates presented in this book are available there for free as well.

Summary

This final chapter provided both background and direction needed to successfully implement the PM^{4}TE process. The model itself is based on sound principles from both control theory and cybernetics—two of the main theoretical backgrounds on which many of the modern-day performance management processes are developed. Additionally, we have blended this thinking with another closed-loop process— the Boyd or OODA loop—which adds the dimension of time to the model. The element of time and its acceleration will ultimately prove to be one of the main determinants of how successful organizations will be in environments of turbulence. The three major components of the PM^{4}TE process model can be implemented in three separate stages. In Stage 1, the Performance Management cycle is established. In Stage 2, the Execution Management cycle is created and then accelerated. Finally, in Stage 3, the Model Enablers are fully developed. The Core Process is housed in Stages 1 and 2. The process of performance management for turbulence starts here. The Model Enablers can be built over time. Regardless of the starting point, engaged leadership will be required to not only install, but sustain the process into the future.

Appendix: Deloitte Enterprise Value Map Excerpt

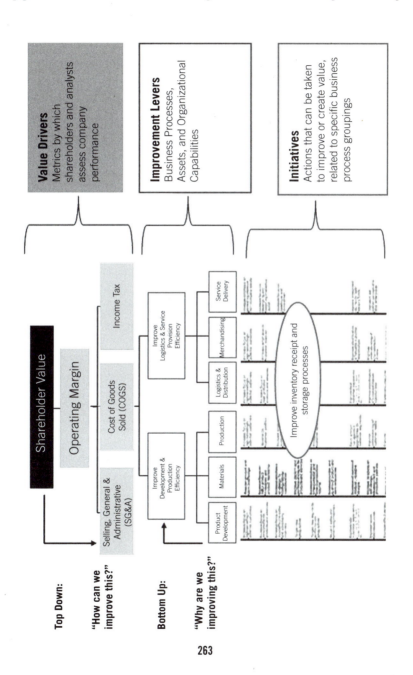

About the Authors

Ed Barrows is an expert in the area of strategic planning, strategy execution, and strategic decision making. As a management researcher and consultant, he specializes in helping top leadership teams improve their strategic management capability. He has two decades of hands-on experience and has held professional services positions with Deloitte, GE Capital, PricewaterhouseCoopers, and most recently, with the Palladium Group, where he was a vice president. While at Palladium, four of his clients were inducted into Palladium's Balanced Scorecard Hall of Fame for strategy execution.

Ed lectures at Babson College and Boston College, where he teaches both Operations and Strategic Management. He is a DBA candidate at Cranfield School of Management and is a Certified Public Accountant in Virginia. He can be reached via e-mail at ed@cambridgeperformancepartners.com.

Professor Andy Neely is widely recognized as one of the world's leading authorities on organizational performance measurement and management. He has authored over 100 books and articles, including *Measuring Business Performance: Why, What and How,* a title in the Economist Book series, and *The Performance Prism: The Scorecard for Measuring and Managing Business Success,* published by the Financial Times Press. He has won numerous awards for his research and chairs the Performance Measurement Association, an international network for those interested in the performance measurement and management.

Andy currently holds joint appointments at Cambridge University and Cranfield School of Management. He is also deputy director of the Advanced Instituted of Management Research, the United Kingdom's Management Research Initiative. Previously he has held appointments at London Business School; Cambridge University, where he was a Fellow of Churchill College; Nottingham University, where he completed his PhD; and British Aerospace. He was elected a Fellow of the Sunningdale Institute in 2005, a Fellow of the British Academy of Management in 2007, and an Academician of the Academy of Social Sciences in 2008. His e-mail address is andy@cambridgeperformancepartners.com.

Index